250

70

ARTICULATING WEST

WEST

essays on purpose and form
in modern Canadian literature

W H New

new press
Toronto
1972

Copyright © 1972 W. H. New

ISBN   0-88770-704-1   cloth
ISBN   0-88770-705-X   paper

First printing
123456   77   76   75   74   73   72

new press

Order Department
553 Richmond Street West,
Toronto 133, Ontario

Design: Pamela Patrick
Typeset by Compose
Printed by The Hunter Rose Company, Toronto
Manufactured in Canada

contents

For Peggy

acknowledgements

Many of the essays collected in this volume first appeared in earlier form in the following journals:

Canadian Literature: "A Life and Four Landscapes"; "Carol Coates Cassidy"; "A Feeling of Completion"; "Sinclair Ross's Ambivalent World"; "The Apprenticeship of Discovery"; "Winter and the Night-People"; "The Disappointed Decade"; "A Fiction Chronicle"; "Lowry, the Cabbala and Charles Jones";

Critique: "The Irony of Order";

Journal of Canadian Studies: "The Genius of Place and Time"; part of "Equatorial Zones and Polar Opposites"; under the title "Africanadiana";

Journal of Commonwealth Literature: part of "Equatorial Zones and Polar Opposites";

Literary Half-Yearly: "The Identity of Articulation"; "Gabriola";

Poetry Aurtralia: "Six Poets";

Queens Quarterly: "The Storm and After";

Twentieth Century Literature: "The Mind's Eyes (I's) (Ice)."

The author is grateful to the following for permission to reprint copyright material:

McClelland and Stewart Limited, Toronto, for "Life and Time," which first appeared as the introduction to the New Canadian Library edition of Margaret Laurence's *The Stone Angel*.

For Margaret Avison's poems quoted in "The Mind's Eyes (I's) (Ice)": the author for "Gatineau" and "Tennis"; W.W. Norton & Co. Inc., New York, for "In Eporphyrial Harness" which was first published in *The Dumbfounding* (1966).

introduction

Canada's regional identities have always fairly readily reduced to two: 'East' and 'West'—and these two have always engaged in rather heady opposition. The trouble with the terms is that they're only loosely tied to geography and hence alter their meaning from place to place. For denizens of the Pacific Coast, 'East' variously begins in the Orient, at the Lakehead, and at the Alberta border. For denizens of Toronto, 'West' begins at Hamilton. For Maritimers, the whole continent is a Western hinterland. And that a major 'Eastern' Canadian university is known through the country simply as 'Western' demonstrates the idiosyncrasy of the usage with concrete pungency.

That the terms continue to be so widely used suggests that they do have meaning, however, meaning of a less palpable sort that underlies their simple directional geography and somehow enunciates the inchoate basic assumptions of a way of life. The physical realities represented by 'East' and 'West' shift as the *ideas* of 'East' and 'West' alter, and the interaction between knowledge and imagination that affects this process of change also characterizes the method by which a writer wrestles life into an artistic form. To speak the language of 'West' is not to be merely regional in bias, therefore, but to articulate the tension between order and disorder, myth and reality, that underlies Canadian writing.

As Canadian writers have attempted to identify their culture by solving what Northrop Frye has called the problem of locating "where *here* is," they have inevitably responded to the physical landscape. Often, in fact, critics have suggested that the land becomes a stronger presence than the human figures in Canadian fiction, a character in its own right, an actor as well as an activating power in the psychological and metaphysical dramas being unveiled. One can point, for example, to E.J. Pratt transforming the Canadian Shield into a giant lizard in *Towards the Last Spike*, or to Sinclair Ross, W.O. Mitchell, Martha Ostenso, Henry Kreisel and Frederick Philip Grove all animating the prairie, or to MacLennan's Alan Ainslie in *Return of the Sphinx*, half-consciously observing:

> Images of the land: the long wash of the decisive ocean against the granite; sunlight spangling the mist over the estuary the old navigator had mistaken for the North-west Passage leading to the indispensable dream . . . .

What these writers are also doing is creating a rhetoric of landscape. As A.J.M. Smith observed directly in "To Hold in a Poem", words could be "as crisp and as white / As our snow"; verse could be "as austere / As the spirit of prairie and river." And as F.R. Scott more obliquely wrote of the "Laurentian Shield":

> This land stares at the sun in a huge silence
> Endlessly repeating something we cannot hear.

It is:

> Inarticulate, arctic,
> Not written on by history, empty as paper . . . .

To 'sentence' that identity, to find words to articulate it, is paradoxically at once to create and to limit it. In the act of articulation, the endlessness of possibility is circumscribed, for an actual identity is announced. But that identity is promptly absorbed by the existing one. As Margaret Atwood puts it somewhat despondently in "Migration: C.P.R.":

> Escaping from allegories
> in the misty east, where inherited events
> barnacle on the mind . . .
>
> and language is the law

we ran west

wanting
a place of absolute
unformed beginning . . .

[but] even the mountains
at the approach, were
conical, iconic
again . . .
There are more secondhand
stores here than we expected:
though we brought nothing with us
(we thought)
we have begun to unpack.

The real *known* must then come again into tension with the impalpable *unknown*, for both of them prove necessary to the human imagination. So when part of the unknown is explored and made known, often for the sake of survival in an inhospitable land—it is the dilemma of the Tennysonian Ulysses—a new horizon will beckon, a new myth condense, and a new idea of 'West' form in the mind of man. What the rhetoric in a sense displays, therefore, is the elusiveness of its subject and the ambivalence necessary to convey such Protean vitality.

For the central characters of Frances Brooke's eighteenth century novel *The History of Emily Montague*, Canada was merely an idea, a *balance* to the idea of English order that helped outline a coherent ideal system; only those who were sensitive to what they actually saw in the wilderness settlements could perceive reality, but they were then forced to alter their imaginative expectations. Similarly, Susanna Moodie, in *Roughing It in the Bush*, observing Grosse Ile to be paradisal "at a distance," is forced to acknowledge disease and hardship when she actually lands. And, as Victor Hopwood points out in the *Literary History of Canada*, the British response to the explorers' travels bore only romantic relationship to the rough realities of the actual ventures; a reviewer of Alexander Mackenzie's *Voyages* wrote in *The Edinburgh Review* of 1802:

There is something in the idea of traversing a vast and unknown continent, that gives an agreeable expansion to our conceptions, and the imagination is insensibly engaged and inflamed by the spirit of adventure, and the perils and the novelities that are implied in a voyage of discovery.

It was to appeal to just such agreeable inflammation that so many of the romantic adventures of Gilbert Parker and Ralph Connor were written, for just because a new 'West' is always dreamed, the old 'West' is never necessarily abandoned. When A.J.M. Smith writes in "Far West" of the cowboys who "rode their skin-tight stallions / over the barbarous hills of California" to satisfy the stereotyped expectations of an on-looker, he notes ironically how an old myth is preserved as a comfortable attitude by a society that has expanded its own periphery and ordering influence, no matter how far the new frontier may have moved on.

Implicit here is an equation of 'East' with a settled order which may be imaginatively static. By pandering to such stasis, however, the 'West' denies both its real distinctiveness and its mythic potential. No one knows these distinctions better than the inhabitants of a new frontier, for their realities and the imaginative designs of outsiders are constantly at variance. But the urge to clarify their realities leads them, too, into 'sentencing' their landscape. By ordering their world, they 'Easternize' it, and the dilemma is compounded when they realize that not ordering it at all would leave their identity articulated only by outsiders' preconceptions. It was to differentiate between preconception and actuality that Frederick Philip Grove, for example, wrote *A Search for America* in 1939, and it was part of the irony of his success that the novel was accepted as an autobiography for thirty years. Like his contemporary and fellow émigré Frederick Niven, who more willingly exploited the frontier stereotype, he observed his landscapes closely and accurately. In so doing he had to break from romanticizing literary forms and develop—like Mackenzie or David Thompson

charting unknown topography, or Mrs. Moodie giving the details of life in the Bush—a 'scientific' diction that would intensify the force of his landscape imagery and convey the
substance of factual experience. At the same time he had to
allow his fictional world precedence, for in it—rather than in
fact—lay the essence of the truth he was trying to distil.

The simple contrast that first informed Frances Brooke's
work located Protestant ordered real civilization in England,
and pagan (Indian, French Catholic) wilderness in Canada;
East referred to England, West to the New World. It was an
inexact view in several ways, and as *Roughing It in the Bush*
later reminds us, it had force not as fact but as myth; it was
an idea of wilderness apparently needed by England. If it
could not last in Canada itself, its demise was partly due to
the fact that settled Canada—no longer total wilderness or
pagan or unknown or mythic, but plainly genteel and real—
required a frontier myth of its own. It became, in other
words, an 'East' in its own right, locating another 'West'
further into the continent. As *The Edinburgh Review* com-
ment on Mackenzie's journal indicates, western expansion
simply reinforced in England the romantic stereotypes. In
Canada, it represented the imaginative dreams which Protestant order always kept under control. Susanna Moodie's
open challenge to the English myth of Canada and her dis-
tress at the specific realities of her life in the backwoods,
still resolve themselves in an affirmation of settled order, of
life 'in the clearings'. But as the inventive fictions of nineteenth-century writers like John Richardson, William Kirby,
and James De Mille reveal, no settlement could satisfactorily
deny the continuing existence of the adjacent wilderness,
however much it affirmed its immediate civility. The result
is the tension that draws a line between East and West while
recognizing their continuity and even their congruence. Each
new East was an old West after all and held concurrently the
knowledge of both mythic and real identities. In *Contexts
of Canadian Criticism*, Eli Mandel infers as much when he
speaks of the Canadian "identification of the academic and

the primitive". In her commentary on *The Journals of Susanna Moodie,* Margaret Atwood pursues the idea further, locating in her (fabricated/real) title character what she calls a 'cultural schizophrenia'. The simultaneous praise and blame of a beautiful and destructive landscape, the brisk commitment to material progress and concomitant elegy for the passing of wilderness, the dual sense of patriotism and detached objectivity—all these attitudes permeate the culture and character of Susanna that Atwood draws. She writes:

> We are all immigrants to this place even if we were born here: the country is too big for anyone to inhabit completely, and in the parts unknown to us we move in fear, exiles and invaders. This country is something that must be chosen . . . and if we do choose it we are still choosing a violent duality.

The conflict/entente between French and English Canada gives that sensibility an urgent political and psychological outlet. Though Quebec writers have for some time invoked the theme, some of the most stylistically textured and impressive works have appeared in the last ten years: Hubert Aquin's *Prochain Épisode* and *Trou de Mémoire,* Réjean Ducharme's *L'avalée des avalés,* Claude Jasmin's *Ethel et le terroriste,* Roch Carrier's *La Guerre, Yes Sir!* and Marie-Claire Blais's *Une saison dans la vie d'Emmanuel.* They have their English-language political counterparts in works by David Lewis Stein, David Helwig, and others, but they also bear a kind of metaphysical kinship to the mental and visionary explorations one finds in Malcolm Lowry, Leonard Cohen, and Dave Godfrey. The divided landscape is within, as much as without, and one loses oneself in it, drowns in it, in order to reappear whole. Such an image provides many Quebec poets, too, with a setting: the labyrinth of Anne Hébert's "Le tombeau des rois," for example, or the landscape of André Major's "Verte ma parole":

> le paysage m'habite cruel
> et verte verte ma parole
> —blessure donnée à mon pays—

or "La malemer" in which Rina Lasnier's persona seeks discovery and release:

> malemer—rature mon visage et noie cette larme
> où se refont des clartés,
>
> que j'oublie en toi les frontières ambiguës de mon
> propre jour—et la lucide distance du soleil.

Such a process of self-discovery is not without dangers. Saint-Denys-Garneau wrote in "Poids et mesures" that

> en regardant cela la tête à l'envers
> On aperçoit des évocations d'autres mondes
> On aperçoit des cassures dans notre monde
> qui font des trous

but adds:

> Mais un trou dans notre monde c'est déjà quelque chose . . .

To utter a route out of 'this world'—whether one sees this as a political or a spiritual activity, or both—is the writer's constant task. In "Le jeu," Saint-Denys-Garneau uses a metaphor of a child to express it, a child who knows

> que sous les mots il déplace toutes choses
> Et qu'il en agit avec les montagnes
> Comme s'il les possédait en propre.
> Il met la chambre à l'envers et vraiment l'on ne
> s'y reconnaît plus . . . .

And it is exactly that word-play, inventive and provocative and serious, that informs the spiritual and temporal quests of Margaret Avison's poetry and Aquin's *Trou de Mémoire*, and the recognition of absolute liberty that in *Manifeste Infra* Claude Péloquin calls "le réel reversible."

In *The Long Journey*, a study of attitudes to the idea of 'North'—*les pays d'en haut*—in French language Canadian literature, Jack Warwick comments specifically on the recurrent quest motif, associating it with the search for vital freedom (religious, moral, sexual, artistic, political) that surfaces so often in Quebec writing. Independence is tied to a "vision of natural man as the possessor of wholeness," which, however illusory in itself, exerts a genuine impact on the imagination.

Whether one sees *les pays d'en haut* as Gabrielle Roy's *La montagne secrète*, as the tundra and taiga of Yves Thériault's *Agaguk* and *Ashini*, as the rivers of the voyageurs, or whatever, they exemplify "a state of mind into which the boldest spirits can run to seek their self-completion."

The search for imaginative identity is not limited to Quebec; but whereas the liberating impulse epitomized by the bush journey there is curiously wedded to a Jansenist conception of man's role on earth, the same impulse in 'English' Canada is tied to Calvinist commitments to duty and work. The non-rational elements of the imaginative flight were thus overlaid by a stern rational will to possess the continent. In E.J. Pratt's *Towards the Last Spike*, Atwood's "cultural schizophrenia" thus finds yet another voice and form. When his character Macdonald tries to convince the public to support explicitly a plan to build a transcontinental railroad and implicitly an intangible dream of nationhood, Pratt admits the radically different but apparently reconcilable compulsion of 'pagan' rhetoric and logical argument. The latter convinces the Protestant purse; the former unconsciously inflames the imagination; between them, dreams are acted upon without being openly admitted. Such an eloquent evasion of declaring the nature of the national dream creates a genuine technical challenge for any writer evoking the distinctiveness of Canadian culture.

The dilemma of articulating a myth is thus re-invoked. To order it is to contain it, yet if myth speaks a truth at all, it speaks indirectly, so that what Leacock calls the "truth larger than reality" may be glimpsed rather than photographed, and uttered in images, riddles, allegories, visions, and fables of identity. Thus Sinclair Ross's imagery in *As For Me and My House* argues the ambivalence of perceptible reality; W.O. Mitchell's *Who Has Seen the Wind* poses in a concrete and comic fashion a serious metaphysical question about the relationship between natural realities and eternal verities; Ethel Wilson's careful interweaving of personal and historic time collapses any easy distinctions between fact and fancy; and Hugh MacLennan's allegorical explorations of Canadian identity give voice at their most evocative moments to a process of discovery rather than an explicit creed. Beyond the geographical landscape that each regards and uses as a setting lies another one, to which their respective literary techniques somehow allude. It is not Utopia, for perfect order seems alien to the Canadian imagination, steeped in the ambivalences of reality and the limitations of art. But it does have the substance of dream, which the visionary imagination at once grasps and fears.

Dreams, whatever their ambivalence, still articulate some kind of order. The myth of disordered wilderness, that is, is not itself disordered; implicitly it has an ordering function, making 'civilization' out of the place where the myth-maker is. Journeying westward thus invokes the East, and the search for a Northwest Passage to Cathay, the naming of Lachine, and the paradox of having the Orient off the *West* Coast give the process some tangible Canadian referents. And mythic quests have Canadian fictional counterparts—often ironic ones—in narratives by Pratt, Roy, Ringuet, Aquin and MacLennan, in Rudy Wiebe's *The Blue Mountains of China*, in Dave Godfrey's "The Hard-Headed Collector" (a reverse West-East journey showing the disintegration of the vitality of art as it gets collected and controlled), and in Robert Kroetsch's *The Studhorse Man*, which uses the formal apparatus of Classical myth to celebrate and debunk the various myths of Western identity held by Easterners and by Westerners themselves. In these and other works—the novels of Patricia Blondal and Sheila Watson, Audrey Thomas's *Munchmeyer*, Margaret Laurence's *The Fire-Dwellers*, Bill Bissett's Occidental *mantras*, and Malcolm Lowry's *October Ferry to Gabriola* with its Neoplatonic systems, for example— the West is half-mad in its visions, but attractive as well. As P.K. Page puts it in her 1946 short story "West Coast":

> Extraordinary place. To them, of course, it is home and usual as everyday or your own face in the morning mirror. But extraordinary, none the less to me. Another

week here and I fear the whole place would shift and
be viewed by that unseeing area of the eye. Contagion.

And that strange contagious madness epitomizes the wilderness myth of a folk culture; people like Page's narrator, who
belong to the sophisticated and artificial order that governs
society, are simultaneously threatened by the otherworld and
drawn to it.

The Orient and the Near East have exactly this same
mystery to the Anglo-Saxon mind; at once they represent
the stability of ancient civilizations and the disordering threat
of unfamiliar belief. Such exotic foreign settings, therefore,
also become part of the Canadian landscape and attach themselves to the myth of wilderness. The quality of order they
represent is most clearly exemplified by the Japanese art
forms that attracted Carol Cassidy and Earle Birney, the
unfamiliarity by the image of Africa that long influenced
'Western'—European and North American—thought. In the
works of Margaret Laurence, Audrey Thomas, and Dave
Godfrey, the unpredictable upsets of African experience become political and psychological images as well, describing a
process of dislocation, therefore of discovery and growth and
possible balance. As in Malcolm Lowry's or Robertson
Davies's Jungian explorations of the divisions of the mind,
wilderness is internalized, made a necessary part of each individual identity. (The progress of Lowry's character Sigbjørn
Wilderness in *Hear Us O Lord From Heaven Thy Dwelling-
Place* provides a clear instance.) In Godfrey's *The New Ancestors,* the end of the visionary African search is a generative
commitment to a social identity, too. As in Hubert Aquin's
Trou de Mémoire, where an Ivory Coast druggist becomes a
correspondent (both 'letter-writer' and 'balance') with a Montreal revolutionary, the commitment to political activism in
African and Canadian settings at once motivates the central
experience of mental turmoil and indicates the route out of
it. In such a book, as in Cohen's *Beautiful Losers*, identities
quarrel, hallucinate, do violence to each other, and merge;
they scarcely exist as empirical realities, for what is central

is an idea rather than a person, and the art form acquires a consciously artificial structure. By means of it, the writer expresses his awareness that an idea at once *is* and *transcends* its form, that the vision which generates dreams is both articulated and limited by the medium that gives it voice. The end of that awareness, however, lies in the stimulation of an unrealized imaginative identity, which will give the writer's society both life and self-respect.

An awakened sensitivity to the significance of the *indigenous* Canadian cultures would obviously parallel such a 'foreign' discovery and contribute to any genuine national folk consciousness. It would explain, to some degree, the force of Thériault's *Agaguk*, *Ashini*, and *N'Tsuk*, with their Eskimo and Indian characters. The radical difference in cultures, however—and in modes of structuring points of view—creates often insurmountable problems. Although the difficulties of interpreting such 'mysteries', which often impede the process, are shown clearly in Rudy Wiebe's "Where is the Voice Coming From? ", the discovery (in these lines from John Newlove's "The Pride") is shown to be insistently and unconsciously possible:

> the indians
> are not composed of
> the romantic stories
> about them, or of the stories
> they tell only, but
> still ride the soil . . .
> in our bodies entire, in our minds, until at
> last we become them

But any overt exploration of the mystical, irrational and metaphysical creates further problems for an artist trying to communicate with a culture that is rooted in empirical realism. To integrate the idea and the language of West therefore becomes even more technically challenging.

In *Towards the Last Spike*, exploring the nature of the truths that fire men's minds, Pratt compounds 'myth' and 'fact' by making his metaphor examine the function of the artist as well as the development of a national dream. The sweeping Protestant generalization that made all things visionary 'pagan' made the very role of the creative artist suspect at the same time, an identification that Canadian writers have constantly had to contend with. The expedient pragmatism of Pratt's Macdonald, quoting economics and the Authorized Bible while dreaming arcane dreams, shows one way of making an imaginative vision publicly acceptable. The prefaces and poems of Irving Layton, asserting Judaic rather than Anglo-Saxon roots and influences, show another:

> Appearance I both love and distrust and think of as an enchanting mistress, fertile in invention, endlessly playful. But it's Reality I'm wedded to—to Truth.
>
> *(The Swinging Flesh)*

> In a world . . . where men have forgotten that their sole reason for being is to magnify the Lord and enjoy him forever, I prefer to be known as a post-Christian pagan detesting all uniforms, the massive solemnities of religion and politics.
>
> *(Collected Poems)*

Layton's *personae* celebrate the poet's freedom from the world of everyday conventions while they insist on his commitment to physical fact. 'Reality' is thus at once flesh and spirit, fact and invention, the language of poetry and the continuously vital poem. Conventions, by contrast—old orders, moribund without knowing it—admit of no vitality, no living myth that might awake them. Hence in "The Cold Green Element":

> A great squall in the Pacific blew a dead poet
> out of the water,
> who now hangs from the city's gates.
> Crowds depart daily to see it, and return
> with grimaces and incomprehension . . . .

For Layton's poet-narrator, however, immersion in the life-giving green element is still possible, and if that suggests constant recognition of inexperience, it also augurs constant discovery.

The implicit process of dislocation is in essence the same as that experienced by Moodie, Atwood's Moodie, and Lowry's Sigbjørn Wilderness. Growth can only happen when they give up a comfortable (if unrealistic) 'paradise', when they are shocked into realizing their own identifying limitations and vital potential. In "The Cold Green Element" the life-giving myth that will challenge settled ideas, provoke moral reassessments, and refreshen/refashion the known world thus turns explicitly into poetry itself. Elsewhere Layton writes, "Whatever else, poetry is freedom," and the imaginative image of 'West' is tied to language once more.

A work like bp nichol's *The Martyrology* makes even clearer this association. The narrator, in one of his transcontinental trips, reaches Vancouver Island, discovers Phyllis Webb's poetry and understands "the importance of questions":

> focus in   language 'is' not 'was'
> words that particular form the sky is
> grey and restless

Words for him are at once holy and hellish—the 'saints' of his 'martyrology' and the rigidity or torment implied by their disjunctured names: St. And, St. Orm, St. Ranglehold, and so on. To utter "i grasp the edge of vision and am frightened" is to admit the 'presence' that at once impels and impedes creation—the will to speak language and the concurrent fear of distorting experience:

> is it the poem makes us dance?
> or simply writing, the act of ordering
> the other mind
>   blinding us
> to the greater vision

What by *standing* he cannot accomplish, however, he must dare to move towards:

> another world   vaguely seen
>
>   the bear
> (caged) cannot cross . . .
>
> the hills turn red

if you ever cross over

The experience of seeing and creating that new world is poetry; the poem itself is history's artifact, already behind the poet, who has moved on.

The Martyrology sharpens a distinction between 'realism' and other literary conventions in modern Canadian writing. It had been one of the tasks of the writers of the first half of the twentieth century—Pratt, Smith, Leacock, Scott, Grove, Ross, Wilson, MacLennan—to develop an artistic language out of the real landscapes through which they moved; for the writers who developed or were recognized in the subsequent twenty years—Birney, Avison, Lowry, Reaney, Godfrey, Layton, Watson, Klein—a major task was to explore the landscape that is language itself, for the purpose of freeing the imagination from representational strictures and affirming the compatibility of spiritual (visionary) and political (empirical) goals. The geographic frontier was not simply pushed further away—though in many ways the Arctic is now seen as a new Canadian 'West'. It was, instead, metamorphosed. Writers, fortified by the iconoclasm of admitting their 'pagan' attraction to a life force rather than a 'Protestant' adherence to social conventions, overtly transformed the frontier from a physical to a metaphysical 'place'. In the process—with antecedents in Lampman and the Transcendentalists—language became more consciously contrived, for 'reality' lay not in represented scenes and events but in the very act of representation.

That exploration of artifice has created some of the most tightly ordered and enclosed worlds of Canadian literature. The brilliant parodies of Chris Scott's *Bartleby*, for example, or the rich theatre of Gwendolyn MacEwen's *King of Egypt King of Dreams*, or the concrete designs and sound patterns of Earle Birney, Claude Péloquin, Judith Copithorne and Raoul Douguay all celebrate a process of invention that is freed from the demand to represent the ordinary sequence of empirical events. Yet their authors kindle such freedom only by rigorously controlling their artistic conventions. In that they do not differ from artists of any time or place, and they face the same dilemma: if once they take art form rather than vital art as the centre of their world, they run the danger of indulging in conventions as artificial and empty as the social ones that Layton, for example, decries.

What Stephen Leacock says at the end of *Sunshine Sketches of a Little Town*, therefore, still carries about it a kind of luminous message:

> at every crossway we can hear the long muffled roar of the whistle, dying to a melancholy wail that echoes into the woods; . . . the track plunges here and there into great stretches of bush . . . with a tangled undergrowth of brush that has defied for two generations all attempts to clear it into the form of fields.

All attempts to tame the Canadian wilderness or, that is, to structure and codify the 'Canadian imagination', ultimately fail, for implicitly they contradict the nature of what they purport to define. But if form cannot be the sole criterion by which we judge life or art, it is equally inexact to suggest that formless wilderness satisfactorily describes either the Canadian identity or the essence of artistic experience. Instead, whatever is vital about both of them is expressed when order somehow interacts with generation, east with west, Calvinist-Jansenist reality with visionary 'pagan' myth. And the points where the 'Eastern' forces of civilized restraint and the 'Western' ones of free growth meet are the moments when artist and reader alike tune in to the tension at the heart of the Canadian experience they are trying to render and realize. For Margaret Avison, as for Stephen Leacock, that moment is represented by the image of the crossway; Avison has it that

> Sparrows in the curbs
> and ditch-litter at the
> service-station crossroads
> alike instruct, distract.

The everyday reality we live in and notice has its attractions, in other words, sharpening senses and developing capacities of reason. But it also draws attention away from the intangible dreams that urge and command men's minds in another way. To be aware of that duality engenders an attitude towards literary subjects and technique; at the same time, to be conscious of the tension between subject and technique sheds light on the difficulties writers have experienced trying to articulate their cultural apprehensions.

The problem has not simply been one of distinguishing between appearance and reality, or between life and form, but also one of explaining the compulsions of a wilderness myth without either defining it or surrendering to it. To locate such a 'West' within Canada, or to make it out of Canada as a whole, or to fabricate it beyond Canada's physical borders all have their attractions and their limitations; in the relation between that often visionary subject and an often indirect literary process is the domain which Canadian writers have attempted increasingly consciously to occupy. In so doing they have discovered some of the anxious and paralysing dangers of adhering to social and literary forms for the sake of their historical merits, and some of the virtues of a society where East and West are not rigidly fixed—a society, in other words, that accepts change as part of its fabric and so countenances the possibility of constant regeneration. To devise an art flexible enough to speak this ambivalence has been the challenge they have tried to meet, one which only an imaginative grasp of the mind's and the land's various realities could satisfactorily approach.

developing
a language
of myth

A LIFE
AND FOUR
LANDSCAPES:
FREDERICK
JOHN NIVEN

Frederick John Niven is today almost unknown. That fact alone would warrant a critical investigation of him, but a study thus motivated could easily end by being merely an arid exercise. Fortunately, in Niven's case, the justifications for reappraisal are many. He warrants it because he was unusual in Canadian letters. He lived by his writing without being a hack; he was a conscious prose stylist at a time when stylists were few; he was concerned with problems which affected his time, not (for all his apparently 'regional' settings) with merely local issues; he was a man with wit, humanity, intelligence, and a willingness to exercise all three—and if this caused him to rebel quietly against orthodox social codes, to emigrate from the London literary world of the 1910's to the hinterland of British Columbia, and to dare to write honestly about the life that he knew existed, then so much the better for his fiction. He was also the friend of such diverse literary figures as Hugh Walpole, Christopher Morley, and I.A. Richards; the recipient (until he emigrated) of regular and favourable reviews both in the *T.L.S.* and from such critics as Rebecca West; and the colleague of John Murray Gibbon and John Buchan. For all this, the man is a paradox, and difficult to assess. It is probably inevitable that thirty-three books of fiction, two of verse, and a vast array of non-fiction should vary in quality; sometimes his characters were nothing more than stereotypes, and sometimes, too, he found difficulty in reconciling the fiction he was writing with the facts in which his work found its base.

This last item brings us to one of the most interesting features of Niven's work. Available criticism amply points out the difficulties in using historical data which the author faced in writing his trilogy—*The Flying Years* (1935), *Mine Inheritance* (1940), and *The Transplanted* (1944)—about the opening of the Canadian West. Comments by Desmond Pacey (*Creative Writing in Canada*) and Edward McCourt (*The Canadian West in Fiction*) show that Niven's contact with the Canadian environment allowed him to create realistic scenes and moods in these novels, and that his characters, lifted from history books or else pared to meet the demands of the factual events, tend to be wooden. Western Canada was not the only environment he knew at first hand, however, nor was it the only occasion upon which he drew from his own experience for some of the material in his books. My communications with Mrs. Pauline Niven, the author's widow, have substantiated what his autobiography, *Coloured Spectacles* (1938), suggests: that many of the characters other than the historical ones were basically pictures of his own family. In the most successful books there was some metamorphosis; the characters come alive in their own right, and the four landscapes Niven knew well—South America, Scotland, southern England, and western Canada—he sensitively recreated as fictional settings. To examine only the works set in Canada would be to limit our assessment of Niven's ability and our appreciation of what he accomplished. To trace the events of his life and the forms those events took in his work not only reveals some of the character of the man, but also suggests the scope of his literary aims.

South America appears most rarely as a setting, and always in combination with some other place. One of his best books, *Triumph* (1934), uses it well. It traces the life of a would-be musician frustrated by home and family, re-creates the social levels of an English society—consular, but not always diplomatic—in Latin America, and reveals how the man's children in various ways succeed him. The country does not correspond with any specific real one; instead, it lives separately, created on the page. The distant Andes are there and the heat and the shimmer of colour, and together they contribute palpably to the novel's success. Landscape is one of the characters in a sense, but in this book at least it does not replace the people as the focus or the reality. Works such as the pirate story, *The Island Providence* (1910), set partly in the Caribbean, or the western, *Hands Up!* (1913), which mentions a brother who dies in Panama, are more credible for their scenery than for their characters, and as works of art are better ignored. But they do raise the question of source of detail, which even a cursory investigation of Niven's life quite clearly answers.

The brother who died has a prototype in Niven's own brother, who died in Panama when Niven was still quite young. The family in *Triumph* is clearly but not exactly parallel to Niven's family, which was connected with the British consular service in Valparaiso when Niven was born there on March 31, 1878. The youngest of three children (his sister outlived him by several years), Niven did not leave Chile until he was almost six, when his family sent him to school in their native Scotland. Later they returned to Scotland themselves. His father was a manufacturer of sewed muslin there, and a lenient man; his mother was a devout, rigorous, and rigidly orthodox Calvinist.[1] Understandably, the home they supplied in Chile is only dimly remembered in Niven's work; that which they gave their son in Scotland—different in surroundings but probably not very different in kind—was one he remembered with much more detail: with wit, nostalgia, some affection, and no little asperity. In time, the two homes were to lead to substantially different environments in the fiction. *Triumph* is a later work than many of Niven's 'Scots' novels, a feature which contributes to its difference from them in thought and in direction indicated by the fictional resolution. By 1934 Niven had emigrated to Canada, and his renewed contact with the worlds of the western hemisphere caused him, in his fiction, to seek within his environment rather than outside it for the solution to the problems he raised.

Early protagonists, like Martin Moir in *Justice of the Peace* (1914), cannot succeed because they cannot escape their environment; Heriot, the musician in *Triumph*, fails because he does not exercise his ability in spite of his environment, and his artistic son can only truly know success when he can perform equally well in his father's old world or away in any other. Niven comes to this implied change in attitude partly because of personal experience. Ultimately, with his wife, he determined on one place to settle. But to do this he had to leave a beloved Scotland and an active London behind him, and he had also to escape a particular kind of home.

One suspects, without much clear basis for doing so, that Heriot is partly a picture of Niven's father. *Coloured Spectacles* mentions in passing the manufacturer's voracious appetite for literature and his linguistic facility, but nowhere is there an explanation of what Niven merely calls the man's 'restlessness'. There are in the fiction, however, some sympathetic portraits of softgoods manufacturers—Ebenezer Moir in *Justice of the Peace*, Walter Maitland in *The Story of their Days* (1939), and John Simson in *The Staff at Simson's* (1937)—which amplify our picture of his father's business and perhaps of the man himself. Certainly the other members of Niven's family appear as characters—the brother in *Hands Up!* , an unsympathetic sister in *Dead Men's Bells* (1912), and his mother almost everywhere, which makes a consideration of the factual mother-son relationship and of that in the novels a convenient and central introduction to the significance of the Scottish settings in Niven's total work.

Rachel Moir is the fictional extreme. Rebuking and then completely disowning her son Martin, she almost prevents artistry from being developed in him and she certainly goes a long way towards destroying him. Mrs. Niven, similarly, reacted strongly against Frederick's creative talent, but she was not exactly like Rachel, for she also possessed many finer qualities, According to Mrs. Pauline Niven, for example, the fortitude of the title figure in *Mrs. Barry* (1933) and the illnesses and sensitivities of the son, were the result of Niven's consciously drawing upon memory of his mother and of isolated incidents from his own childhood. But the lady's less admirable qualities and the somewhat more ambivalent ones were also to appear in the fiction. Mrs. Niven opposed any venture that was not demonstrably practical and which was not sanctioned by the dour doctrines of Calvinism, and so her vocational ambitions for her son, after he left Hutcheson's Grammar School, were bent towards stern theology or worldly practicality. They were entirely opposed to Niven's own inclinations. In his autobiography, he (typically) understates the case:

> I wanted to be a painter; I wanted—we had no Great War then—to be a war-correspondent. . . . My folks, sensibly enough, pointed out to me the extremely precarious existence of a painter—even of a war-correspondent—and compromised: How about an applied art? Or how would it be if, to begin with, I went to the Glasgow School of Art in the evenings, on trial, to see if I had the stuff in me, and was apprenticed to the manufacturing business? Designers were required in that business. I recalled that Alexander Smith had been a pattern-designer—which helped to make me amenable to parental reason, and dutiful. But my mother, I believed, regretted that I had not followed in the footsteps of her folk, alumni of the old Glasgow College, never entered its university. I broke a tradition of her family then—when we humoured each other. That's life.

'Regret' was often open antagonism and it contributed to the break that occurred between the two.

In *Dead Men's Bells*, Niven depicts a comparable break over a philosophical-religious question between Robert Lindsay, the hero, and his mother. The conflict comes to a head when Rob discontinues his ministerial training because "there is too much of the old necromancy in the theologians"— which was heresy in the mother's eyes. Later, detecting her son in a lie he felt compelled to use in order to avoid further conflict, she laments:

"Your second cousin. . . wrote at that very time, as if
the Lord wad try my soul, as was Job tried of auld,
speiring if you was thinking of the future . . . He . . .
said he could put ye in the way of a captaincy. But no—
no' after a lee. . . . Ye will see the justice o' this. Believe
me, your mither, that every sin has its punishment."
  "I ken it," said I grimly.

The Scotland of this family, like that of the Murrays in *Two
Generations* (1916), is "that land where Calvin once gloom-
ed," and the heroes, like Lindsay or Ted Murray (or like
Niven himself), find this incompatible with their own nature.
'Heretical' Rob argues with his uncle Tom about this:

"I am like the lad in an auld twelfth-century French
ballad. . . —I had rather be in the company of the happy
than wi' the constitutionally gloomy."
  "I do not ken the auld irreleegious ballads of France
. . . Life is stern and sober, and shunnor or later you will
find that it is so, and that you have a soul to save or
damn for all eternity. . . ."
  His advice given me then, as the first cobbles of the
street of Eaglesham rang under our tread, made me
think that God must laugh, which struck me as a great
thought. . . .

But this was "a night of many stars, and the Milky Way was
like a plume of feathers, and you can talk little Calvin to a
young man in the open and under stars." To Rob, then,
nature offers solace, and to nature he escapes for the adventure that occupies the major portion of the book.
  Other heroes cannot escape in this way when they discover, as in *Ellen Adair* (1913), that over their family hangs

the curse of Calvin and a misconceived Christ. . . .The
children of such families, if they love beauty, either love
it very tenderly, with a minor key in their voices, or are
carried off their feet, and are as moths round a candle.

The choice for freedom, or submission, or destruction, belongs to the individual, and as a child in such a house, Niven
himself had to choose. Aiming for freedom, he found he
could indulge a vivid imagination in solitary play. Remem-

bering this after some years, in the significantly-titled *Colour-ed Spectacles*, he sees the humour, the humanity, and the loneliness involved in such a situation:

> When I was a boy and could travel only on the atlas, Deadwood Dick took me up winding roads between scattered bull-pines into quick-rising hills. The trees were very tall. The forest glades were very quiet. I some-times wish I had a complete set of the stories in my library now to turn to occasionally from some of the discoveries of the coteries which are thrust at us with an intolerance worse than that which accompanied the advocacy of *Ministering Children*. . . . His flights into the hills were tremendous. They atoned a hundredfold for the egg-like weals upon our wrists delivered by a soulless mathematics master for deficiencies in trigon-ometry. . . . I followed Dick through the solitudes of tall timber awash with the scent of balsam, on into the thickest forest, on into the canyon. . . .
>
> Up this canyon, then (the stairs up to, and the cor-ridor of the top flat, leading to my bedroom, used to be the canyon), Deadwood Dick guided me. He went over a 'divide' (at the top of the stairs), and came down into a 'pocket' in the hills, a grassy little valley (where the passage widened), and there, having unsaddled, he left his horse free to graze. . . .
>
> Deadwood Dick strode to some bushes and breasted into their midst. I strode to my bedroom door and breasted against it, having first turned the handle. The bushes whipped back into place and right ahead was a precipice and a cave—for Dick. I presume he kept his treasure trove in the cave but I have forgotten the de-tails of his loot. What he gave me, to last for ever, was a horse, big timber, and silent mountain paths.

Such exploits were only for childhood, and not for Niven's youth, at which time conflict with his parents became most acute. But he began to enjoy solitude, and in spite of the deli-cate physical constitution which had plagued him since his removal from Chile, he loosed his immense reserve of energy by walking from Glasgow out into the countryside. Walks that Martin Moir could take in *Justice of the Peace*, or Robert Barclay in *The Three Marys* (1930) or Bliss Henry in *A Wilderness of Monkeys* (1911), draw upon these excursions for the observed details that make them come alive. A move of his parents from Glasgow to Edinburgh gave Niven new vistas, for

> instead of the Mearns Moor I had the Pentland Hills and soon, extending my tramps, I had the nearer Borders, Tweedside from Symington to Broughton. . . and on to Peebles.

It gave him new material to draw on later, too, for Peebles was to become the setting for important scenes in *Ellen Adair*.

Although the 'art question' had been curtailed for a time when it was discovered that Niven had a degree of colour blindness (regarded by his parents and sister, Mrs. Pauline Niven says, as a 'disease'), he still had no interest in the business to which he was apprenticed. In *Coloured Spectacles*, he notes his feelings:

> Tremendously though manufacturers interested me, and warehousemen, and packers, and weavers, I was not enthusiastic about manufacturing. The intention was for me to pass through the various departments and *learn the business*. I began with winceys and it was Charlie Maclean, head of the wincey department, who informed me, gazing at me solemnly one day, "Freddy, the plain fact is that ye dinna gie a spittle for your work."

Like the hero of *Justice of the Peace*, Niven attended night classes at the Glasgow School of Art, studying under Francis Newberry; after a while, like Ted Murray in *Two Generations*, he quit the warehouse to work in a library: "The only trouble was that sometimes I would be lost in a book when I ought to have been attending to a subscriber." To assist in the payment of his art school fees, Niven also worked part-time in a jewellery store, and this experience was to appear first in *Ellen Adair* and *Justice of the Peace*, and then as the background for a full novel, *Old Soldier* (1936). But the question of becoming *either* a painter *or* something practical stalemated when doctors recommended that Niven move to a drier climate. He was therefore sent in his late teens to the home of some missionary friends of his mother's in the Okanagan Valley of British Columbia, and the move, which cured his ailments for a time, was markedly to affect both his work and his life.

The move was not, this trip, a permanent one, but it did give him a number of experiences which were to lead to his becoming an author at all. For one thing, it introduced him to new settings and to another response to life, but for him the contact with North America was more important than this at first indicates. In fact he was to spend the next two decades moving back and forth from Canada to England, trying to settle down and trying to reconcile his attachments to several worlds. In his fiction, during this same period, he continually returns to two equally thorny and obviously related situations. The person in his books who rebels against Calvinism and yet remains within the Calvinist world dooms himself to attritive conflict, and the person who flees to the wild west runs the danger of being 'diseased' by an aimless and therefore crippling wanderlust. Ultimately Niven could find a satisfactory solution within both Scots and Canadian settings, but this was in works which were written well after he at last decided to emigrate. In the early Old World settings, characters like Rob Lindsay had to flee from their restricting environment in order to be successful; such characters as Harold Grey in *A Tale that is Told* (1920) are merely worn away by their environment when they remain within it. In the later New World settings, contrastingly, flight is an irresponsible act, not a constructive one. Robert Wallace in *The Transplanted* (1944) would be a failure if he left the small B.C. town in which he lived, for he would then be deserting a society to which he should and can contribute. Reflexively this solution begins to work in the later Old World settings as well, and so John Maitland in *The Story of their Days* (1939) discovers a niche—controllable, but still alive, unlike that of Harold Grey—within a larger world with which he cannot entirely agree. The difficulty here, of course, is in reconciling a responsibility to society with an equally nebulous responsibility to self.

In Canada on his first trip, Niven travelled as much as possible and worked at whatever job presented itself—on the railroad in the dry Thompson Valley near Savona, in a lumber camp near Shuswap Lake, in ditch-digging crews in Vancouver. He rode rods and walked ties with acquaintances whom in *Above Your Heads* (1911) and *Wild Honey* (1927) (published in Great Britain as *Queer Fellows*) he named Hank Slim, Billy, and Foureyes, and in *Wild Honey* he recounts in detail two of these trips: from Savona once to Vancouver and once through the Camp McKinney gold fields to the Kettle River Country. Writing later for *Saturday Night* (July 5, 1941), he remembers his first jobs in Vancouver:

> after a spell of ditch digging I had change of manual labor in shovelling macadamised rock off scows that were brought by tugboats and moored sometimes near where the Yacht Club boats lie now, sometimes at False Creek. In those days Indians used to watch us at our shovelling—with commiseration in their dark eyes I used to think. Yet what a miserable youth I was when owing to a strained muscle in my back I had to forsake manual labor and take a job indoors.

His heart and lung trouble, however, seemed in the meantime to have disappeared.

Homesickness of a kind drove him back to Scotland again, and it was after his return (aboard a cattle boat from Montreal, as described in *The S.S. Glory* [1915]), that he first took up journalism. "Three Men in a Shack" appeared as sketches of Western Life in the *Glasgow Herald,* and success led him to editorial work on various Scottish and English papers. In 1908, he was discovered in the London literary world by Mrs. Isobel Thorne, the fiction editor for Shurey's Publications. Mrs. Pauline Niven writes:

My mother. . . began to write for various magazines and ended up editing one of them published by the firm of Shurey's. As the firm grew and expanded my mother's position grew. . . . She was also responsible for Frederick's first book *The Lost Cabin Mine.* He offered it to her but she urged him to try the English publisher, John Lane, who published it and the one that followed it [*The Island Providence*] which he wrote in Devon on the advice of John Lane who was, I believe, a Devon man. I can't remember how long Frederick was in Devon, under a year, I think. I was still at school but he sent his Mss to me and I typed it in the evening.[2]

These were active years. His first novels appeared, strongly influenced by the work of Stevenson and by the Deadwood Dick stories; he was publishing also in such periodicals as the *Pall Mall Gazette* and the *Morning Leader*; and in 1911 he married Mary Pauline Thorne-Quelch, then eighteen years old and fifteen years his junior.

He spent several months of 1912 and 1913 travelling and freelance writing in Canada—four novels appearing during these two years. He had returned to London before the war broke out in 1914, but, his heart trouble recurring again in England, authorities rejected his application for military service. He served in other capacities, therefore—as Assistant Food Controller in the Ministry of Food attending to the distribution of rationed goods; and finally in the War Office under John Buchan as Associate Editor of Articles for Allied and Neutral Powers. Five more novels, a book of verse, and a collection of short stories that were written about 1912 appeared before the end of the war, and two more novels, including *A Tale that is Told*, which won the enthusiastic admiration of Rebecca West, soon followed. Quality, critical reception, and popular approval fluctuated greatly, for several works were frankly money-making pot-boilers. But even these have a place in the development of Niven's thought; they demonstrate along with the more serious works the division between Old World and New World settings which Niven consistently used.

May 1920 is a significant date for observing any change in his
work, for it was at that time that Mr. and Mrs. Niven came to
Canada together and stayed to settle. Initially it was to be
only a three-month visit, on a commission from John Murray
Gibbon of *The World's Work*, to gather material for more
articles on Canada. Several visits back to the Old Country,
however, only confirmed their choice of a home at Willow
Point, on the beach of Kootenay Lake a few miles from
Nelson, B.C. In many ways this mountainous area is like
parts of Europe, but Niven notes a difference when he speaks
of what called him back to the West:

> The Alps are in a pocket of Europe, and seem almost
> a kind of sleeping partner of Messrs. Cook; but the
> Rockies run the length of the continent, and are in
> league with Eternity. . . . What is the lure? It is a sense
> of freedom. It is the pines mounting up the steep hills,
> and the smell of the pines and the quiet under them. . .
> It is the rank tea, tasting like nectar after working in the
> woods. It is the wagon-roads, the two deep ruts, going
> down through the sands of the Okanagan, or up into the
> Cariboo, or twining through the pine-needle floors of
> the tall timber tracts in the Selkirks, the Cascades, or
> the Pallisers. It is the trails leading off from these, with
> the gashes blazed on the trees, blaze by blaze showing
> the way, as lighthouses con ships through sea channels.
> It is, as in Murray Gibbon's song, "the lakes of melted
> jade," these lakes that the winds play with, as a hand
> ruffling and smoothing velvet. It is the lonely call of
> loons in the hush before twilight, when the grasshoppers
> all suddenly cease to chirp. It is the mosquito-hawk
> that zig-zags overhead, with a flight somewhat like bat
> or swallow, in the drizzle of a reflected sunset. It is the
> clear air that lets the eyes roam over great spaces. It is
> the moon rising to silhouette a ridge of firs and light
> their tips all down the slope—and the wonder of it all
> getting into one's blood.

Significantly the details of his life now begin to appear in his
nonfiction writings, largely in periodical essays and related to
his contact with natural environment. The wilderness was
what inspired him to write (and writing was by this time his

sole source of income); at times, as *Coloured Spectacles* showed, it also reminded him of the Scotland he still loved:

> There is a season of the year. . . when. . . Scotland comes to me. . . . The creeks, tom-tomming in the gulches, clutching wanly at protruding rocks, delaying in trembling amber pools become, in fancy, Highland burns in their glens. Kootenay Lake is changed to a Scots loch. A stipple of rain is on the polished water; the hazed slopes, seen through that *smoor*, might be of heather, with a birchwood yellowing here and there. Nothing is asked of imagination save to turn the odour of weed-smoke to that of peat—and the trick is done. All Scotland is mine then, from forsaken St. Kilda and the roar of the Atlantic on its cliffs to the piping of a piper, on a Saturday night, by the Broomielaw.

But the separation from the old world still existed.

Living in Canada had its drawbacks, one of which was the tendency for his reputation in England to suffer. Niven sets forth his friends' advice and his own reply in one of his verses in *A Lover of the Land* (1925), which is noteworthy only for its biographical fact:

> "Come you back from hill and beach,
> Come and let men know your name,
> Here in London seek your fame,"
> But I cannot seek her there,
> In the heavy thrice-breathed air. . . .
> No, I live the life I write,
> Writing little for delight
> In the living with such things
> As that great hawk's patterned wings.

The natural world sets up a different kind of isolation, and it caused Niven to find in his many friendships with such persons as Mr. George Gooderham, Dr. W.O. Rose, and Dr. I.A. Richards, a reaffirmation of the necessity for human contact.

Innumerable climbs in the mountains of the Nelson and Windermere areas, trips to Calgary where he learned sign-language in order to communicate with the Blackfoot peoples,[3] occasional travel throughout B.C., to the Yukon, and to Hawaii, together with his vast memory of lands he had previously known led to a number of non-fiction articles and books: *Canada West* (1930), *Colour in the Canadian Rockies* (1937),[4] and *Coloured Spectacles* (1938)—which, except for *Mrs. Barry* (1933), was the first of Niven's books since 1920 to be given a *T.L.S.* review. More fiction had also appeared since he emigrated; *The Wolfer* and *Treasure Trail* came out in 1923 (like many of the Westerns, first written serially for New York papers), followed by a second collection of poems, and fourteen more novels to be selected as Book Society choices.

There is a development of thought in the later novels that culminates in the posthumously-published *The Transplanted* (1944), but this work is technically much weaker than many of his other novels. Always conscious of word choice (*Mine Inheritance* was completely rewritten from third to first person, for example[5]), though never what one could justifiably call a stylistic innovator, he died before revising *The Transplanted* into a final form. The heart and lung weakness which had dogged him during his life caught up with him again. In a letter to Christopher Morley in 1929, he had written:

> A long talk I fancy this may be. I have the time for it!
> I am laid up. I seem to have overdone it on my last High
> Country expeditions and have enlarged my heart. It
> feels enlarged in more senses than one. I lie here with
> a very full heart indeed, thinking, thinking—and remem-
> bering, remembering. Sometimes I feel it might burst.
> Extreme athlete's heart the doctor calls it. You know I
> am crazy about the High Country—away up above tim-
> ber. . . .

He recovered; he continued to live, to climb, to enjoy life, to write, to acquire what Jay MacPherson, in the *Literary History of Canada,* calls his "human and literary maturity," but repeated heart attacks at last caused a move from Willow Point to Nelson, and in 1943 to Vancouver, where he died in St. Paul's Hospital on January 10, 1944.

Niven's 'maturity' is most evident in an ability to evoke atmosphere. He recorded dialect well, but this was just one part of his clear perception of the world around him. His sense for the human and the natural landscape, for the world of his youth and the world of his adult life, was accurate and strong. It led to the immediacy of his descriptions of nature and to the artistic success of many of his character sketches both in fiction and non-fiction. His contact with Canada not only introduced him to a new environment and a new set of characters, it also started him writing; it heightened his sensitivity to the nature of landscape and to its influence upon people; and, in time, it altered the way in which he chose to resolve his characters' conflict. He himself absorbed the landscape in which he lived, and in his two best and most productive periods, 1913-1920, and 1930-1939, he demonstrated an appreciation of the power and beauty of descriptive language.

The problems he recounted in his work were very largely ones he had himself met and tried to solve. This does not mean that the events of his fiction are wholly autobiographical, for they are not, but they do bear a distinct relationship to the particularly itinerant life that he himself led. If matters ended there, the fiction would be exceedingly limited in scope. In many ways, however, Niven's life, and the problems he met, were typical of his age; his works have interest as Edwardian and post-Edwardian social documents, therefore, and (more importantly) the questions they concern themselves with are still significant today. One of the problems his heroes, like Rob Lindsay and Martin Moir, face, for example, involves their reaction against a code of values they find stultifying. This to some extent is an objectification of Niven's own conflict with Calvinism, but it also serves as a microcosm for his society, which was at this time reacting in different ways to moral codes that were much more overtly liberal than those current during the nineteenth century. Life was altering rapidly, and in some quarters this was equivalent to chaos. For Niven himself it meant disorder—but it also allowed another order to come into existence. The restlessness that led him part-way round the world he could ultimately control in the 'sanctuary' of a peaceful home in Canada. For his character John Maitland, 'disorder' was an unhappy marriage and a world at war, both of which seemed to negate the values which he felt he knew through art. Yet for him, too, a reachievement of order is possible: "Broad Sanctuary," which is Maitland's resting-spot in London, is, though a retreat, no escape from the world, and it becomes an image of another stability that can emerge from change.

As Niven also found out, the determination of a way of life lies in large part within the power of the individual, but a person often finds that in a complex environment he must choose not between right and wrong but only between two wrongs. This problem, too, Niven's fiction explores. Robert Wallace in *The Transplanted*, for example, is forced at the last to choose between friendship and truth; he cannot have both, and a denial of either one is contrary to the dictates of his conscience. He cannot remain neutral about the question either, for this would leave him in limbo; in order to find happiness—a third intangible—he must and ultimately does make the necessary choice. Again we can see Niven's personal reaction against one system of belief lying behind this, but like the other conflicts he presents in his fiction, it is not at the last completely personal or local. Instead, the problems his characters face are those that arise anywhere when an individual and a social conscience are at war within a solitary man. As a novelist Niven did not always present these with artistic skill; sometimes he did not even escape triteness and flatness of characterization. But his work still is worthy of attention, for at its best it transcends the doubtful fictional virtues of documentary and apologia. His imagination at those times goes beyond the facts he remembers and allows him to create out of his several landscapes an arresting and credible world.

1967

NOTES

1. Conversation with Mrs. Pauline Niven, May 28, 1962.

2. Letter to the writer, July 7, 1962. *The Lost Cabin Mine* was first published in 1908, antedating by one year the date listed in Watters.

3. One of the tribes accepted him as a member and gave him the name

Apasto (= "Talking by Signs"). See "Amerindian," *Dalhousie Review*, XIX, no. 2, (July 1939), 145.

4. Not listed in Watters. Reprinted in 1962, this is the only one of Niven's works at present in print. McClelland & Stewart proposes to reissue *The Flying Years* in 1974.

5. MSS are in the U.B.C. Library. *Mine Inheritance* was also made into a radio play for broadcast over the C.B.C. in three parts: January 8 and 14, 1959. Part III is undated.

CAROL COATES
CASSIDY AND
THE FORM DISPUTE

No-one who now reads the early issues of the *Canadian Poetry Magazine* can be insensible to the apparent 1930's proliferation of redoubtable poems by ladies with three names. Writers like Anna Letitia Wales, Maisie Nelson Devitt, and Jessie Playfair Bickford sprinkled the journal's pages with sincerity, piety, and (when World War II demanded it) a rather conventional-sounding patriotism. It is work like theirs that had inspired the anonymous Scott-like "God Bless the C.A.A.! " in *The Canadian Mercury* in 1929:

> Rosie wrote some little rhymes
> For the *Birdseye Centre Times*:
> Gushing friends did then exclaim:
> "This will surely bring you fame!
> You must join the C.A.A."

By September 1945 their pseudo-Romanticism gave the *C.P. M.* a reputation for having a "Keats-Shelley complex," a charge which the new editor, Watson Kirkconnell, attempts at once to refute. O.W. Macdonald, who had started the attack (in *Canadian Author and Bookman*), wanted another Kipling or Service after all, and by implication Kirkconnell dismisses their work as "doggerel." The *C.P.M.*, he adds, has printed some *experimental* verse, and (quoting Croce) insists that "Art is form and nothing but form."

Neither the charge nor the defence was particularly novel. In the December 1928 issue of *Canadian Mercury*, for example, Leo Kennedy had quoted S.I. Hayakawa's barbed classification of Canadian poetry as "Victorian, Neo-Victorian,

Quasi-Victorian, and Pseudo-Victorian" and himself called for "a Canadian Whitman, . . .a man of his genius and spiritual breadth" to "correctly interpret the whole Canadian consciousness." Just as Kirkconnell's statement prickles with thorny problems involving the difference between the form of art and the form of doggerel, so Kennedy's raises some question as to how to define 'correct'. But in talking of 'spirit' and the 'whole consciousness' of a people, he allows art to be made up of more than simple external structure. Which could take us back to sincerity and patriotism again, although—if injected with the genius of a Whitman—probably of an unconventional kind.

A.J.M. Smith's rallying cry in the unused preface he wrote for *New Provinces* in 1936 to some extent bridges the gap between Kennedy and Kirkconnell. Speaking for Pratt, Scott and Klein as well as for Kennedy and himself, he characterizes their purpose as one of "attempting to get rid of the facile word, the stereotyped phrase and the mechanical rhythm," and of "seeking, as the poet today must, to combine colloquialism with rhetoric." Spirit and structure are to come closer, in other words, to being united and indivisible. In the particular form of a given poem will be embodied the sensibility it attempts to convey, and thus, antedating McLuhanism, the rhetorical medium becomes at least part of its colloquial message. But if the method is mechanical and the home truth trite, or if the rhetoric is shallow and it still characterizes both technique and idea, then no correspondence between medium and message will salvage a poem from the junkpile. Archness and artificiality do sometimes afflict poems by Smith and Scott, but it is the other disease of being possessed by stereotypes that makes the work of Anna Wales, Vesta Pickel, and Jessie Bickford so much less artistically adept.

That both camps should find in the *C.P.M.* an outlet for their work is paradoxical itself; that E.J. Pratt should as editor allow it even more so, for as his own writing testifies, he respected his craft. In the second issue of the journal (April

1936), he enunciates his editorial policy: for "tolerant consideration of genuine poetic effort and against identity with any form of aesthetic whether old or new." He was against only 'fatuous sentiment', in fact, and the July 1936 issue elaborates:

> Rhyme and metre do not make a poem; they produce nothing but doggerel. The real flesh and blood of poetry lies in turns of phrases, vivid images, new and unusual thoughts and manners of expressing them. A good poem is good because it is an unusual, imaginative, arresting way of writing English. We do not speak in poetry, except at rare moments; and if a poet writes so simply as to give the effect of spoken language, that effect is all the more startling and novel.

In the 1960's such an assertion sounds slightly weary, and perhaps even in 1936 the schoolmasterish tone reflects Pratt's tiredness with the excess of two hundred manuscripts he read every week. What it also does, however, is indicate one of the reasons for the apparent gentleness with which Pratt exercised his acceptance policy; what interested him about a work was not its intellectual toughness or its stanzaic structure but its lines, its imagery, and its individual phrases. A single striking epithet was taken as the promise of a poetic talent, and thus redefined, 'form'—whether intentional or accidental, germane to the poet's ideas or unrelated to them— proved a touchstone to merit once again.

To see Carol Coates Cassidy's name in print is at once to suspect her of the same poetic sins as all the other tripartite ladies, and to read Pratt's May 1940 review of her Ryerson chapbook *Fancy Free* (1939)—in which he finds her "free of cliché"—is to suspect him of his accustomed generosity. But such a judgment here would be a distortion. Though never a polished writer, Carol Cassidy did possess a talent for poetry, and Pratt was quite justified when he accepted her work for its occasionally arresting line and its frequent ease with imagery.

Her career, however, was short-lived, beginning with undergraduate verse she distributed among friends in Vancouver about 1930, and lasting into the 1940's. Since then she has effectively disappeared (into English progressive-educational circles), and is not even mentioned in the recent *Oxford Companion to Canadian History and Literature.* The omission is a genuine oversight, for particularly during the first decade in which she published, her work represented a definite experimental departure in verse form in Canadian poetry. From 1925 on, F.R. Scott and A.J.M. Smith had attempted to free Canada of poetic lushness; Raymond Knister and (later) Dorothy Livesay had discovered ways of uniting the lyric voice with a social conscience. But in Carol Cassidy's work there operates an exotic imagism that came in part, no doubt, from the American movements of the 1910's and 1920's which intellectually influenced Smith and W.W.E. Ross as well. It emerged also from her emotional sensitivity to the exactness, spareness, and diminutiveness of symbol that characterized the art of her native Japan. "Form in poetry . . . is moulded by content—also by the environment of the poet," she states in her foreword to *Fancy Free*, and the culture that prompted her best poems was Oriental.

Born Alice Caroline Coates, in Tokyo, the daughter of an authority on Japanese Buddhism, she returned there in 1930, with her photographer husband Eugene Haanel Cassidy, and stayed in the country till 1937. *Fancy Free* illustrates the influence of Eastern "poetry, painting, flower arrangement," and again the Foreword expresses the author's intention and expectation:

> Eastern art excels in suggesting what it does not say. Therefore a ruthless selection of significant detail is of paramount importance. A poem may consist of less than a dozen expressions, yet the imagination and the technique which inspired their choice and execution are calculated to create an illusion of the whole through an illumination of the part—an illusion extending far beyond the confines of the actual presentation.

The function of the reader, therefore, is an active one—

to become a creator, to compose, so to speak, the sestet to the sonnet the artist has started for him. This is done by reflecting with more than usual care upon the tonal and rhythmic qualities of every word, savoring to the full each literal and emotional connotation.

Her aim is overt in "Gift," where she expresses the desire to bring to the reader "only a poem, / exempt from the bonds of time and space, / infinite and everlasting," and the effect is uninspiringly flat. The platitudinous abstraction encourages only a weary reaction, and the timeless, spaceless illusion for which she strives eludes both her and her readers.

Curiously, it is those poems more specifically founded in the immediate that transcend space and time. Influenced by the haiku, they work with precisely observed details which, perceived as images, communicate more than their literal meaning. The imagery of "Japanese April", for example, is quite conventional:

> April Earth
> a spring bride,
> with cherry petal confetti
> to congratulate.

Yet tightly controlled, as here, it reaches out beyond the stereotype to express a sense of delicately recurring beauty. The control lies in the form. Letting the image stand unexplained is one part of the poet's method; maintaining tone through internal vowel harmonies—here, in the *a's, e's,* and *i's,* circling at the end to the same sound with which the poem begins and so aurally reinforcing the idea of recurrence—is another. "Korean Dancer," though longer, uses a similar assonant technique. Beginning "A white miracle of motionless satin," it closes this way:

> dips and streams,
> flirts, exults, despairs,
> till suddenly fluttering, abandoned falls
> a symbol of coquetry completed.
>
> An ominous gong crashes the clapping
> across a stage searching for light.

The psychological and political implications of the final two lines give the poem a depth and humanity that phrases like "white miracle" do not at first lead us to expect. The personification of the scarf in the catalogue of verbs also might seem a little stale—yet it is that kind of animation which allows the last two lines to work symbolically as well as pictorially. It is a human situation, not an inert one, that the poem is about.

Political situations motivated the writing of quite a number of Carol Cassidy's poems, but abstractions generally take over from images in them, to their detriment. Excerpts from "Four Poems: Bushido, 1937" will illustrate. The second part of the sequence, entitled "Troop Train," opens with an intentional tonal flatness that admirably conveys the poet's horror at the blind power of a war machine:

> On the day of the tiger,
> twenty-six cars packed with khaki bodies
> ride out into the rain-soaked night
> to be shot.

> The bodies cheer,
> wave paper flags and sing—
> sing on their way to be shot.

The repetition later gets too easy, however, and Part III adds, cloyingly, "But I must still the protest in my throat". Part IV, echoing the initial rhythms of Masefield's "Cargoes", returns briefly and effectively to the theme of the war industry:

> Fifty-four bluejackets
> in neat white boxes,
> shipped home from Shanghai
> ready for burial.

But when the poem, striving for climax, proclaims "what heaviness they hold," we are removed again from the illusion of the image and thrust uncomfortably back into the world of the stock response.

During World War II itself, Mrs. Cassidy's publications

were privately printed—*The Tale of the Celestial Tea Pot* (1943), and the brief mimeographed excursion into fanciful drama called *The Jade Heart* (copyrighted by the Junior· Leagues of America Inc. in New York in 1946) for instance. Rather like "The Emperor's New Clothes" in tone, combining a sense of comedy and a verbal rhythm, its social moral is less pointed and less clear. An emperor banishes a poet; the emperor's daughter grows up and falls in love with the poet, who (magically) is connected with the return of a jade earring that her brother had tried to steal from her years before and had lost; the self-exiled brother returns as a prisoner; and the playlet ends happily when the emperor recognizes his prodigal son and allows his daughter to choose her own husband. The jade earrings and a migrating wild goose are recurrent images to argue the necessity for the poet's vision in the modern world, but neither the method nor the message is particularly fresh, and the Orientalism is by now an encumbrance rather than an ornament to her style.

When she turns directly to the war, her poems are even less successful. Like so many Canadian writers, she was committed to the cause and aghast at the destruction of lives, and her poems split in two directions—to the hyper-patriotic ("Open wide the airways of the world") and the maudlin ("Is that Human Lives Limited? / May I speak to God, please? / . . . yesterday I lost my son. . . . / I must have another.") Objectivity was hard to achieve, and the controlled distance that imagism demands is lost even from the following excerpt from "May 1941":

> . . . in the brain,
> guns thunder the minutes down
> and marching feet
> trample the ecstasy of May.

All these verses are contained in a handsome hand-printed volume (reviewed favourably both by Pratt in the *C.P.M.* and by E.K. Brown in *U.T.Q's* "Letters in Canada 1941") published by the Caronell Press in Toronto and variously titled *Poems* and *The Return and Selected Poems*. Besides the new works, it reprints pieces that had appeared in journals like *Chatelaine* and *Canadian Forum* as well as the *C.P.M.* Several were to be printed again in *Invitation to Mood* (1949), and except for a few privately distributed volumes and whatever verse Mrs. Cassidy may have written since, this constitutes her complete canon. The best works among them remain those that capture images, and in individual lines she again reveals her craftsmanlike commitment to the beautiful in Japanese culture:

> the fingers of a flower master
> coaxing a chrysanthemum
> to lift its tired head—
> (The Return)

> Stare straight up through the incredible blue
> to see the oblique wings of a bird
> slicing the sky
> (Summer Reverie)

> . . . against the ice-stencil of a window,
> one leaf, a green flame,
> leaping from a dry and brittle stick.
> (The Flame)

> The day, brittle with ice,
> snaps underfoot
> (First Flight)

But her rationalizing defence of such a commitment still intrudes into her work; poems that could stop with an image go on to explain it, and the initial effect is undermined. Though the poet affirmed that the reader should also be creator, rarely is the promise fulfilled. Possibly because the journals in which she published so demanded, her poems generally end up insisting on a particular response in an unsubtle fashion.

The problem can be approached in another way by looking again at the critical pronouncements of the *Canadian Poetry Magazine.* Pratt's eclectic policy is reaffirmed in March 1943 when W.E. Collin translates Guy Sylvestre's article on Saint-Denys-Garneau:

> Poetry is the art of signifying, by means of words, bearers of rhythm and image, what things say to our faculties of knowledge and love taken in their totality. That which makes poetry art is essentially the creation of a beautiful intelligible form; what distinguishes it from the other arts is its own peculiar means of expression: the human word animated by its essential rhythm and delivering fancies conceived in the mind and heart.

But running counter to it, though apparently not in direct conflict or open dispute, were two other critical attitudes. The first is that represented by Clara Bernhardt's statement in December 1939 concerning the poet's function: to make a reader *see*, like the blind man in John's gospel—the good poem will have "an idea or thought", "emotion", "music", and be "sincere." (It is this concern for sincerity which seems to have guided the naming of the 'prize' poems in the journal each year. The sentiment expressed seems to have been more important than the quality of the line.)

The other attitude is couched in Watson Kirkconnell's assertion in September 1944 that the magazine "will now carry articles on form and poetic law." The word 'law' is the troublesome one, for by June 1945, under the guise of continuing Pratt's policy, Kirkconnell turns to attacking Spender and Eliot for "lawless originality," "novelty without clear significance." As a result, with the rules thus effectively decided in advance, experimentalism fades; sentiment again takes over from verse quality; and (for all the resurgence of fresh talent that appeared while Earle Birney was editor from September 1945 to June 1948) the future character of the journal was set. Vanity presses started to advertise in it, and with their vacuum seal of approval, the *C.P.M.* ceased to be a significant voice.

The exact direct effect of such a dispute on a writer like Carol Cassidy is impossible to gauge, yet it is obvious that her own writing falters because of just this internal conflict. The cause of form is espoused, while the poet gives birth in the same breath to the "preaching," the "stuff of prose," that during Birney's editorship, Charles Bruce's "Remarks on

Verse" vehemently decried. When Ryerson brought out *Invitation to Mood* in 1949, nothing much had changed. The occasional sociological poem like "Black Reverie," about Paul Robeson and race prejudice, is interesting for its concern, but even that expresses a conventional 'white liberal' position, and the poem (like many others in the book, 'inviting' a particular 'mood') seems in retrospect a little high-flown.

Repeated here, too, are several pieces from her 1941 volume which indicate an attempt to arouse jocularity, but their mood is one less of humour than of unfulfilment. "Humour" is "the Alchemist" in "Parting", for example, but the love poems are wry. "Meeting," similarly, begins equally enough:

> The other side of argument we shall meet again,
> I know,
> after the silence.

> With what speech shall I greet you then?
> a laughing quip, perhaps,
> or a level maxim to formulate the spirit's unity?

But it goes on to plan the other person's glacier-like response before it happens and—therefore—to formulate an equally glacial reply. Hence there is no real humour and no release.

"Greeting Card" expresses most directly the poet's wish:

> Upon the chaste scroll of the New Year,
> I would inscribe for you
> with bold and flowing strokes,
> the Good Luck symbol,
> and with full brush delineate,
> the ideograph of Laughter.

In the light of other poems, that "*would* inscribe" takes on the tone of powerless desire rather than firm intention; contentment seems beyond reach, and in the last poems of the book, all of which seek transcendent revelation and use phrases like "the path to peace," "the karmic toll," and "the Cosmic Will," the poet's need for a "symbol of the Infinite" within which to walk *embraced, aware,* and *circum-*

scribed, is palpable. In a poem like "Museum Piece" lies her only apparent answer:

> On the ancient fresco from the monastery
> > of the Joyful Conversion,
> are schoolboy names, scribbled with surreptitious brush,
> upon the sacred folds of Buddha's robe.

> Brought now to the World of the Western Sun
> > from far Shensi,
> how curious that the mischievous
> > have achieved immortality
> beside the sublime!

Here the poet still wavers, however, between a relaxed acceptance of the fact and an almost Calvinist upset that it should be so. The poem itself gains from such ellipsis, but as an eschatalogical answer it would obviously prove within this frame of reference uncircumscribing and so unsatisfactory.

Quiet and deceptively atonal, the poem is one of the best of her later works, but during the 1940's when the poetic climate in Canada changed so radically, she ceased being an innovator and her position among Canadian writers considerably waned. The qualities for which A.J.M. Smith included her "First Flight" in his first *Book of Canadian Poetry* (1943) were not developed, and from subsequent editions she has been excluded. For all her commitment to imagism, she was never really able to reconcile language and perception in any consistent way. Her doctrine of poetic form did not in her own writing withstand the pressures of conventional techniques, and so—like the journal that discovered her—she was capable of uncritically publishing some amazingly flaccid lines. Other times she pared her words down till only illusive images remained; by bringing them together she could illuminate the world she saw, and suggest in a few details the larger issues that she accepted as infinite and human truths. "Today I am a god," she wrote in *Fancy Free*, "for I have made a universe with flowers." On rare occasions it was so, as when in *Invitation to Mood* she asks "Would you with boundaries bind the subtle spaces of affection? " and answers:

Sooner count sand,
crack stars,
or garner moonbeams in a sieve.

At those times, however uneasily, she became the poet she had the talent to be.

1971

THE IDENTITY
OF ARTICULATION:
PRATT'S
TOWARDS THE
LAST SPIKE

Pratt's *Towards the Last Spike* (1952) was the last major poem of his career, the last of his scholarly, folksy narrative adventures that documents his culture's history while at the same time it grandly celebrates the indomitable spirit of mankind. The dual tone and purpose was typical of the way he approached his art. Satisfactorily blending factual data with the stir of romance and the deeper maze of truth was a way of transcending discord. As another late poem "Myth and Fact" puts the problem of living in an unstable world:

> The make-believe had furnished to the mind
> Asylum in the foliage.
>
> Draw down the blinds and lock the doors tonight:
> We would be safe from that which hovers
> Above the eaves.

In the implicit conflict between the "would be" and the "is," Pratt found his topics. If dream drew men on, daily events harried them—but such an opposition was too neat, too simple. Various kinds of inversion also proved true. If systems protected men's conscious perspective, systems also endangered their subconscious selves; if imaginative foresight promoted development, only moment-by-moment time could bring a dream to fruition. In a curious way the "antagonists" of fact and dream thus become one, and in the ironic *unity* of "opposites" the poet finds not a stalemate but a measure of man's private torment and potential.

In his earlier *Brébeuf and his Brethren* (1940), for example, savage pagan ritual and militant Christianity oppose each other into a mutual strength of faith. For the missionaries from France, discovering in Canada the "Cathay Passage" of their childhood, the "*myth* at last resolved into the *fact*! " And for the poet, viewing the struggle from a three-hundred-year vantage point, the facts dissolve once more into myth. Pratt's modern Canadian society is founded in such tension, in the pull between expediency and passionate local pride, between survival and dream, and of all his poems *Towards the Last Spike* most clearly enunciates its national character-istics: "Romance and realism, double dose." In turn lyrical, rhetorical, jubilant, and wry, the poem tells of the forging of the transcontinental railway that bound the ends of Canada together in the late nineteenth century, helping to tie re-gional identities into a national one. (The point-of-view may be arguable, the sociological accuracy in doubt, despite the merits of the poetic image.) But if it ended there, its interest would be largely as a political parable. Fortunately it makes intelligent and artistic use of the tension and of the ambiva-lent relationship between man and land.

Pratt's aim (as politically aware, still, as it was in a Spanish War poem like "The Prize Cat") is much more selfconsciously literary. *Towards the Last Spike* is a poem about language, about poetry, as well as about nation-building; and as such it becomes a kind of counterpart to Wallace Stevens's "Notes toward a Supreme Fiction." For Pratt, the nation and the poem are at once artifact and idea, sounded and yet still waiting to be sounded, a complete tradition and a life waiting to be fashioned anew. Such literary concern ought not to be unexpected, considering the group of poets with whom Pratt was associated as early as the 1930's: Leo Kennedy, Frank Scott, A.J.M. Smith, Abraham Klein. Together they tried to remake and thus refreshen the art form in which they work-ed. Scott's satires pricked at empty literary pretensions, and in the battle against floridity were matched by Smith's suc-cinct attempts to "take words / As crisp and as white as our snow . . . / To hold in a verse as austere / As the spirit of prairie . . . / The North . . . ." Pratt's grand expansive style seems at first more unlike than like their writing, yet the intent is the same: to examine not only the culture that has fostered them but also the language that allows them to celebrate it. Scott's "Laurentian Shield" (which he calls "inarticulate, arctic, / . . . empty as paper") in fact employs the same image Pratt does to express that dual aim:

> This waiting is wanting.
> It will choose its language
> When it has chosen its technic. . . .
>
> Now there are pre-words,
> Cabin syllables,
> Nouns of settlement
> Slowly forming, with steel syntax,
> The long sentence of its exploitation.

And in those words Scott states his own ambivalent relationship with the process and the result. The unbounded landscape is perfectly free, with open potential; cabined, sentenced, exploited, it discovers an identity with limits, for which its makers are responsible. It becomes what it is by the way it is made. The mythic past turns almost inevitably into the factual present; to make the present live its myth is at once the poet's social and literary task and his 'guilt'. For Pratt, as for Scott, to mark the movement towards national consciousness, towards 'the last spike', is to mark a poetic quest for linguistic method (and thus meaning), which again forces the visionary imagination and expediency to collide.

The tension is dramatized in *Towards the Last Spike* in four related ways: in the parliamentary conflict between the Prime Minister (Sir John A. Macdonald) and the Opposition spokesman (Edward Blake), in the rivalry between Canada and the United States for the territory of British Columbia, in the struggle between the engineer Van Horne and the landscape through which he was carving the railroad, and in the temperamental difference between youth and age. The last of these—broaching as it does the theme that makes Scott's poem so ambivalent: the difference between Innocence's

tabula rasa and Experience's exploitation—underlies the celebration of identity and marks its special character. Throughout the poem we are made conscious of the age of the
country in terms of the ages of man. Canada and the United
States are (rather archly) personified into rivals for the hand
of the lady British Columbia, for example (with loyalty and
the railroad being Canada's pragmatic bait in the guise of
honorable intention), and the thirteen-year 'courtship', while
the railroad-building is stalled, turns one party grim and the
other into a harridan. Time works a comparable effect on individuals within the country as well. Macdonald increasingly
requires alcoholic fortification to "translate age to youth";
Van Horne, committing himself more and more to his project, grows silent into himself. And yet *translation*—out of
age into youth, out of silence into voice—is possible. Macdonald takes hold of his plan firmly enough to bring it into
effect; similarly, news of the financing that will allow the
final rail link to be built can change Van Horne into a boy
again, as "Some thirty years erased like blackboard chalk."
The *sense* of the blank slate remains embedded within them,
to be called forth by the challenge (but not the direct antagonism) to the "passive corporal bulk" of the landscape to
which they increasingly belong.

Just as the temporally-governed men are capable of re-
leasing in age their free childhood vision, moreover, the
geologically dateable land is infused with a time-free spirit,
which animates and affects the substance against which the
men prove themselves. The passage that describes the Laurentian Shield is the most quoted of the poem:

> On the North Shore a reptile lay asleep—
> A hybrid that the myths might have conceived,
> But not delivered . . . .
> 　　　　　　　　In continental reach
> The neck went past the Great Bear Lake until
> Its head was hidden in the Arctic Seas.
> This folded reptile was asleep or dead:
> So motionless she seemed stone dead—just seemed:
> She was too old for death, too old for life . . . .

And later:

> A warning, that was all for now. 'Twas sleep
> She wanted, sleep, for drowsing was her pastime
> And waiting through eternities of seasons.
> As for intruders bred for skeletons—
> Some day perhaps when ice began to move,
> Or some convulsion ran fires through her tombs,
> She might stir in her sleep and far below
> The reach of steel and blast of dynamite,
> She'd claim their bones as her possessive right
> And wrap them cold in her pre-Cambrian folds.

Belonging to the ages rather than to the age, the Shield and the "sea" of Cordilleran Mountains are "mothers of the myths"; and myth resolves into fact again when men build their way into them:

> This was a range
> That looked like some strange dread outside a door
> Which gave its name but would not show its features,
> Leaving them to the mind to guess at.

The mind, however, expresses itself in words, shouts in "alien tongues," invokes sacred texts, writes histories, pens names on maps, grasps at myths in song and story, reads like Magellan "The barbarous language of [the] Strait by calling / For echoes from the rocky hieroglyphs . . . ." To distinguish between shout and echo, to blend myth and fact satisfactorily in present time, remains a problem.

Suffering the pressures of limited time, Van Horne and Macdonald urge their project onwards—to be interrupted by an election, by Macdonald's defeat and the new Prime Minister Mackenzie's unventuresome "economy," his phlegmatic attempt to find accord with God's "plodding, patient, planetary time"; and it is only allowed to ignite when 1878 sees Macdonald's return to power. Pratt writes of this moment:

> the huge task announced
> Ten years before had now to start afresh—
> The moulding of men's minds was harder far
> Than moulding of the steel and prior to it.
> It was the battle of ideas and words

> And kindred images called by the same name . . . .
>   Canyons and cliffs
> Were precipices down which men were hurled,
> Or something to be bridged and sheared and scaled.
> Likewise the Pass had its ambiguous meaning.
> The leaders of the factions in the House
> And through the country spelled the word the same:
> The way they got their tongue around the word
> Was different, for some could make it hiss
> With sound of blizzards screaming over ramparts:
> The Pass—the Yellowhead, the Kicking Horse—
> Or jam it with *coureur-de-bois* romance,
> Or join it to the empyrean.

The political quarrels, that is, debate the railroad-building in a rhetoric that is about language as much as it is language, probing the identity that articulation invokes as much as the idea being articulated. Blake and Macdonald are both skilled orators, but the difference between them—Blake attracted by marshalled facts and the *idea* of truth, and Macdonald by the response of his audience and a *vision* of mythic dimension—spells out their degree of political control.

Blake's "appetite, edged by a moral hone, / Could surfeit only on the Verities." Leading the House

>   from facts
> Like telegrams and stolen private letters,
> He soared into the realm of principles
> To find his scourge . . . .
>
> Each word, each phrase, each clause went to position,
> Each sentence regimented like a lockstep.

But "The only thing that would not pace was time"; Blake's argumentative, unimpassioned rhetoric proves ultimately soporific, and all that Macdonald really fears from him are his almost accidental stumbles into a mind-arresting phrase:

> He did not mind the close
> Mosaic of the words—too intricate,
> Too massive in design. Men might admire
> The speech and talk about it, then forget it.
> But few possessed the patience or the mind

> To tread the mazes of the labyrinth.

Pratt's language is chosen from myth deliberately. Conscious of the mind's divided workings, he applies Macdonald's linguistic knowledge to the difference between convention (which hides human fears by finding a respectable outlet for them, as "Myth and Fact" suggests) and the irrational (which, recognized, admitted, may overpower a tenuous social stability).

> The waking sound was not—"*It can't be done*"
> That was a dogma, anyone might say it.
> It was the following burning corollary:
> "*To build a Road over that sea of mountains.*"
> This carried more than argument. It was
> A flash of fire which might with proper kindling
> Consume its way into the public mind.

Macdonald gives *his* mythic vision a socially acceptable size by finding an authorized religious phrase in which to couch it; for the new national motto he suggests the geographically applicable *A mari usque ad mare,* from *Psalm* 72 (echoed in *Zechariah*): "He shall have dominion from sea to sea, and from the river unto the ends of the earth." At the same time, he recognizes that the brooding underside of the mind, once linguistically aroused, will overpower an insecure foundation in conventional respectability—hence his wariness of Blake: "Sir John's '*from sea to sea*' was Biblical; / It had the stamp of reverent approval / But Blake's was pagan, frightening, congealing." The tension for Macdonald lies in his knowledge that he possesses this dual attachment to myth and fact within himself and that it governs his political act. It is he who must finance the project and keep it *appearing* respectable; it is he, too, who knows the greater (yet somehow internal) dimensions of the identity his imagination has seized upon and sought to arouse.

If the brooding lizard landscape is animated to impede the westward flow of men, therefore, paralleling the unconscious mind's arousal, it still only forms half of Pratt's poetic equation. Man is landscape as well. The Dutch-American Van

Horne performs one half of the activity:

> Nothing less
> Than geologic space his field of work,
> He had in Illinois explored the creeks
> And valleys, brooded on the rocks and quarries.
> Using slate fragments, he became a draughtsman,
> Bringing to life a landscape or a cloud,
> Turning a tree into a beard, a cliff
> Into a jaw, a creek into a mouth
> With banks for lips. He loved to work on shadows.

The oatmeal-fed Scots-Canadians perform the rest:

> Foreheads grew into cliffs, jaws into juts:
> The meal, so changed, engaged the follicles:
> Eyebrows came out as gorse, the beards as thistles,
> And the chest-hair the fell of Grampian rams . . . .
> The food released its fearsome racial products:—
> The power to strike a bargain like a foe,
> To win an argument upon a burr,
> Invest the language with a Bannockburn . . . .

> The logic in the sound, escaping print,
> Would seep through channels and befog the cortex.

The landscape-mind is as much 'mother of the myths' as the animated mountains are; the 'nation' is within, waiting to be pronounced, waiting for its illogical logic to be recognized and built when imaginative vision and physical sight combine.

Van Horne, like Macdonald, knows the unity of the two: "his bugles knew / Only one call—the summons to advance / Against two fortresses: the mind, the rock." The temptation is to differentiate too radically between them, to see the inner eye and the compass and transit as ocular approaches to separable realities. Thus the landscape would become unpassable:

> Terror and beauty like twin signal flags
> Flew on the peaks for men to keep their distance . . . .
> They needed miles to render up their beauty,
> As if the gods in high aesthetic moments,
> Resenting the profanity of touch,
> Chiselled this sculpture for the eye alone.

But Pratt's *"as if"* denies such separation, as Van Horne realizes and Blake does not:

> The farther off, as by a paradox
> Of magnets, was the golden lure the stronger:
> Two thousand miles away, imagined peaks
> Had the vacation pull of mountaineering,
> But with the closer vision would the legs
> Follow the mind? 'Twas Blake who raised the question
> And answered it. Though with his natural eyes
> Up to this time he had not sighted mountains,
> He was an expert with the telescope.

During Prime Minister Mackenzie's interlude, indeed, public attitude accepts Blake's division:

> Measured and rationed was the language
> Directed to the stringency of pockets.
> The eye must be convinced before the *vision.*
> *"But one step at a time,"* exclaimed the feet.

But as Pratt makes clear from the very beginning, the focus of his poem is on the vitality of language to effect an identity between vision and eye.

His conservative South African contemporary, Roy Campbell, observed at one point in his autobiography, *Light on a Dark Horse* (1951), that "the eye is far more important than the pince-nez, the telescope, or the microscope." But thus Pratt:

> It was the same world then as now—the same,
> Except for little differences of speed
> And power, and means to treat myopia
> To show an axe-blade infinitely sharp
> Splitting things infinitely small, or else
> Provide the telescopic sight to roam
> Through curved dominions never found in fables.
> The same, but for new particles of speech—
> Those algebraic substitutes for nouns
> That sky cartographers would hang like signboards
> Along the trespass of our thoughts to stop
> The stutters of our tongues with their equations.

The new science does not inhibit speech, that is, nor deny myth; it is speech, and thus evokes new 'seas' for 'dominion' to be held over and new fables to spur the mind to imaginative sight. The task is to make its myth and methods fruitful: "To smite the rock and bring forth living water . . . . / Why not? No more a myth than pelts should be / . . . fabricated into bricks of gold." Yet Pratt reaches not towards golden Eden but towards the inhabitable Canada, rugged and imperfect, a myth of men rather than of gods. When it comes time to hammer the last spike, therefore, the nail bends, has to be replaced, and in any event is unadorned:

> Silver or gold? Van Horne had rumbled "*Iron*."
> No flags or bands announced this ceremony,
> No Morse in circulation through the world . . . .
>   The air was taut
> With silences as rigid as the spruces
> Forming the background in November mist.

But if silence typifies the new identity as little as alchemical gold does, the problem then is to find the *right* language for celebration, how to (in F.R. Scott's phrase) "turn this rock into children." For Pratt there are, typically, two kinds of speech necessary, made of ironic exaggerations and affirmative understatements, and the controlled tension between them characterizes not only the rhetoric that structures his poem but also the creative poetic voice that most aptly utters his nation's identity. The "massed continental chorus" of hurrahs that applauds the last spike is

> ended when Van Horne spat out some phlegm
> To ratify the tumult with "*Well Done*"
> Tied in a knot of monosyllables.

But the process is more important than the event, for it absorbs the event in its continuity. The centre of things lies not in the spike, in final answers, but in the movement *towards* it, in the "monosyllabic" momentary knots of psychological tension that tie together the various regions that the mind inhabits and knows. Admitting one's mental landscape, and finding a poetry to articulate it, thus happen simultaneously and over a course of time:

> on the morrow
> The last blow on the spike would stir the mould
> Under the drumming of the prairie wheels . . . .
> Like a gavel it would close
> Debate, making Macdonald's *"sea to sea"*
> Pour through two oceanic megaphones . . .
> And somewhere in the middle of the line
> Of steel, even the lizard heard . . . .
> To drown
> The traffic chorus, she must blend the sound
> With those inaugural, narcotic notes
> Of storm and thunder which would send her back
> Deeper than ever in Laurentian sleep.

The roots are not dead, but living absorbed by the conscious mind; the debate is closed only because the eye and telescope could at one point fasten on the same view; the inaugural sounds of nationality and poetry are then uttered together, for the poet in search of a language and the country in search of its image and voice. The poem blends Pratt's high delight in the absurd with his passionate sense of spiritual strength; it seethes with dark and lyrical romance and coruscates with precisely turned social detail; it rumbles in rumination, hovers in catalogues, anecdotes, and deliberate digressions, and flings itself towards its end, accumulating the ideological stands of the poet's career in a triumphant commitment to his society and his art.

1972

problems
of ordering
reality

A FEELING
OF COMPLETION:
ASPECTS OF
W.O. MITCHELL

When I became a man," wrote Saint Paul to the Corinthians, "I put away childish things." In context, this exchange of childish for mature behaviour is related specifically to man's perception of God, but the question of human growth and development, of man's relationship with time during his mortal existence, is one that varies with each society's estimation of what constitutes appropriate reaction and behaviour in childhood and in maturity. The transition itself is many-sided, and when it is recorded in written literature or in folk traditions, it takes on different forms and emphasizes various concepts. In his two novels, *The Kite* and *Who Has Seen the Wind,* W.O. Mitchell makes use of this transition as a means to consider man's awareness of time and perception of reality during his life's span on earth. The two novels explore these questions, however, from different points of view. Though one is an artistic success while the other falls short of this, part of their interest lies in the extent to which they complement each other, and an examination of the intent, method, and accomplishment of the two works leads to a clearer understanding of the questions that Mitchell asks about life and of the answers that he postulates.

Mitchell's first novel, *Who Has Seen the Wind,* is the success. It is a study of the development involved in a boy's increasing conscious awareness of abstraction, a study of Brian O'Connal's transition from the perfection of sensitive childhood, through conflict, to a balance that is achieved in early maturity. In *The Kite*, which fails largely because of technical difficulties, Keith Maclean is parallel to Brian in many respects, but the author is concerned less with the growth of a child than with the effect of continuing awareness of time on an old man, Daddy Sherry, and the late awareness of the truth of emotional abstractions that comes to the apparently mature David Lang.

Brian O'Connal's growth begins in perfection. He is a child, complete in his own environment, when *Who Has Seen the Wind* opens; he meets existence from an awareness of self and by sense perception of the material things around him. For the actual growth to take place, however, this state of harmonious innocence must be disrupted, and it is, by the conflict that is aroused in Brian as he is brought into contact with death. An examination of each of the six death scenes in the novel will demonstrate Brian's changing reactions—his growth—and the extent to which he transcends age in developing to maturity.

Before he encounters death for the first time, Brian is given a dog for a pet, to serve as a diversion from the incipient jealousy he feels towards his younger brother Bobbie and to counteract the fantasy world of R.W. God which he invents to escape the imagined tyranny of his grandmother. When the dog is taken from him because it annoyed the grandmother, Brian seeks another pet in a baby pigeon and inadvertently kills it in his attempt to love. Because death deprived him of the pet he wanted, he cries; and drying tears stain his face when he seeks explanatory knowledge from his father, asking " 'Why does it happen to things? ' " (cf. Keith Maclean: " 'Why does stuff have to die? ' ") But not till the bird's body ("just like dirt, he thought, like prairie dirt that wasn't alive at all") was placed in the prairie was Brian "aware of a sudden relief"; not till then was "the sadness . . . lifted from him." Immediately following this first contact with death, however, he is reunited with the dog, and he then experiences a "soft explosion of feeling. It was one of completion and of culmination." The sought-after knowledge concerning the abstract is forgotten in the immediacy of the child's egocentric world. "The boy was aware that the yard was not still. Every grass blade and leaf and flower seemed to be breathing, or perhaps, whispering—something *to him*—something *for him*." (Italics mine.) His world is complete; the truth he knows begins and ends in himself, in sense perception. It is only disturbed when emotion is kindled in him by contact with the implied complements of life and death, with the abstracts that youth does not and cannot comprehend.

The feeling of completion alters in character as Brian grows older, however, for with growth and experience comes an intimation that beyond the private world is a social world and beyond that another, a universal world, wherein Absolute Truth and Basic Reality can be known. But certainty still eludes him.

> The barest breath of a wind stirred at his face, and its caress was part of the strange enchantment too. Within him something was opening, releasing shyly as the petals of a flower open, with such gradualness that he was hardly aware of it . . . He was filled with breathlessness and expectancy, as though he were going to be given something, as though he were about to find something.

But though the feeling is intermittent, it carries, by the time Brian encounters the second death, a tremendous impact. Brian, Art, Fat, and Bobbie at this time go to the prairie to drown gophers, but when Art begins to torture an animal by pulling its tail off, Brian

> realized with a start that an excitement, akin to the feeling that had moved him so often, was beginning to tremble within him. His knees felt weak with it; the Young Ben could cause it too. The Young Ben was part of it.

Indeed, the very old Young Ben, who was "born growed up," springs into action at this moment, killing the gopher with "one merciful squeeze" and clawing Art in a violent retributive attack.

Uninhibited and primitive, the Young Ben is a personified eternal in the novel; one with the prairie, he is a sort of incarnate life-urge that in microcosm and in physical terms demonstrates in his attack on Art the potent retributive violence that knowledge of not having acted justly can wreak upon the spirit and mind—the conscience, or the childhood memory of perfect order—of man. Art, who repeated tearfully " 'I didn't do anything to *him*,' " did realize that he was "doing something" to Life: which, however, amounts to the same thing. Bobbie's reaction in this situation is the child's reaction of crying, but Brian's, characteristically, is introspection.

> The feeling was in Brian now, fierce—uncontrollably so, with wild and unbidden power, with a new, frightening quality. . . . Prairie's awful, thought Brian, and in his mind there loomed vaguely fearful images of a still and brooding spirit, a quiescent power unsmiling from everlasting to everlasting. . . . The Young Ben was part of all this.

In introducing characters such as the Young Ben or Saint Sammy, who are in some ways the most vividly drawn of all the people in the book, Mitchell runs the danger of letting his focus shift from the central development. Such a shift occurs in *The Kite* and weakens that book, but in *Who Has Seen the Wind* the focus is fortunately sustained, and because of this, the author achieves a remarkable insight into the operation of his central character's mind. Though much of this novel deals with characters other than Brian O'Connal, Brian's growth to responsibility always remains central, and the various successful and unsuccessful adaptations that the minor characters make in their respective situations of conflict, reflect upon this central growth. Svarich, for example, fails to accept his Ukrainian identity; Hislop fails to accept the existence of opposition in his church and merely resigns. Sean, Digby, and Miss Thompson, however, come to take responsible positions in their own spheres; they act positively to solve the conflict in which they find themselves, and yet they are able at the same time to accept what they cannot control. Brian, therefore, has both examples before him. Also before him are the vividly-drawn Saint Sammy and Young Ben with their strange adaptive abilities, but even they remain minor figures, because they, too, serve to contribute to an understanding of the emotional sensitivity of Brian himself.

After Brian has encountered death for the second time, this sensitivity brings him to a vague awareness of a difference between death inevitable and death avoidable and of the bond of life that joins all mortal creatures. He must then come to a realization that in life there is deformity, but that this can be lived with and even loved. His first reaction to such deformity is one of shock. "The feeling," when he looks at a dead two-headed calf, for example, "was fierce in Brian as he stared down . . . ; he felt as though he were on a tightrope high in the air. . . . It was wrong!" His judgment is based on the still vivid recollection of completion—of perfect order—but the very recognition of deformity leads to a movement away from the complete awareness of this perfection, and the feeling "lacked the sharper quality of the other times." The knowledge of perfection decreases, therefore, to the extent that the knowledge of departure from perfection (deformity) increases.

Later in the novel Brian becomes aware that the deformities men recognize are those that differentiate physical realities from earthly norms, but that some deviations from those norms do not necessitate correction in order that human love can be expressed toward them. On Sean's farm he looks down at a pet runt pig and considers:

> It would always be a runt, he decided, a shivery runt. It had no twist to its tail; it never would have. The world was a funny place. He loved his runt pig that wasn't good for anything. Ab was fussy about Noreen, the snuffiest cow in the herd, with her wheezing and sneezing and coughing. Before Annie's eyes had been straightened he had . . . [loved her too].
> Brian knew then.

But by loving what exists on earth, man moves imperceptibly further and further from instinctive love of antecedent perfection. By consciously becoming aware of love *per se*, as of death, he is becoming increasingly aware of conceptual and emotional abstractions which sensory perception cannot explain.

To the deaths which he has heretofore encountered, Brian has been largely able to maintain an objective attitude. Even towards the baby pigeon, the love expressed was in infancy as well as the child who loved. With growth and with acquaintance with the love object, however, comes a more fully developed emotion, and when that is disturbed, as in the case of the fourth death when Brian's dog Jappy is killed under the wheels of a dray, the boy's reaction is as profound as it is subjective. Though he "looked as though he were going to cry," he does not. Though filled with memories of the dog's life, he also "remembers the stiffness of the body, the turned head, the filmed eyes. He knew that a lifeless thing was under the earth. *His* dog was dead." (Italics mine.) With this personal deprivation comes also a knowledge of personal mortality, and the feeling of completion, once so strong, is lost.

> Somewhere within Brian something was gone; ever since the accident it had been leaving him as the sand of an hourglass threads away grain by tiny grain. Now there was an emptiness that wasn't to be believed.

It is at this stage that *The Kite* can be again considered, for the reader knows of David Lang's childhood completeness only by inference from his loss of it. As a boy, David had anticipated a day of kite-flying with Lon Burke, only to be disappointed by lack of space, by bad weather, and finally by Lon's heart attack, at which time David loses the kite:

> as he walked towards home, the late guilt he felt could not overcome his sense of irreparable loss, mortal loss too great for tears. It would never soar for him . . . . While he had been fruitlessly searching for his kite, Lon had died.

David tries to fill the void he has now encountered by taking "explosion-pills," by experiencing as it were "explosions of feeling," and knowledge of the pills "soothed and reminded him of when he used to suck his thumb, though he hadn't done that for years." But this is an unsatisfactory solution, for it is in effect an attempt to regress to a stage of childhood that he had already left behind, and so after the pills are used up, the emptiness returns, partly because David has been using another's remedy, partly because in attempting to achieve a reversal of time, he is attempting that which is impossible.

The "other sort of legacy from Lon," however, was the encyclopaedia, and by immersing himself in knowledge, David can grow intellectually and after some time accept adult occupations in journalism and in the television industry. But these do not complete him; "In a way it was as though he were being requested to die—as himself." What he lacks he lost when he never flew the kite: the elasticity, the acrobatics, that would allow him emotional maturity, that would give him an awareness of life whereby he could realize that social participation does not necessarily mean concomitant death of individuality. His visit to Daddy Sherry is the growth of this awareness.

David does not know what he is looking for when he first heads to Shelby; nor does he understand Mr. Dalgliesh when the latter says, " 'I suppose all of us at one time or another have had something to do with Daddy that's—well especially between ourselves and—and Daddy.' " Like the Young Ben, Daddy Sherry is more in the novel than an individual character; like the Young Ben, too, he is a sort of incarnation of a life urge. " 'He *is* excitement'," says Harry Richardson; " 'The life force sparkles more through him,' the minister suggested"; and after some time in Shelby, David himself realizes that Daddy "had been too immersed in living to build historical significance out of his days." He too has to have an individual contact with Daddy, with life; he too must find, in living, the completeness that has only been known before in his childhood lack of awareness of anything that might disturb the apparent immortality of the immediately perceived world. David is of course attempting to write and complete a story, but the completion he needs and of which he becomes aware in the old man, is bound with the other need for completion at an emotional level; "the crosswilled old human had completely won him, and somehow—if Daddy were to die now, their relationship would have failed to complete itself."

David's contact with Daddy is the central relationship in *The Kite*, and the growth that occurs through this relationship is David's, not Daddy's. The danger of shift of focus, however, that had been circumvented in the case of the Young Ben and Saint Sammy in *Who Has Seen the Wind*, recurs here with results that weaken this novel. Structurally and thematically, Daddy Sherry is a minor figure, but the vividness with which he is drawn and the frequency with which he appears in the novel combine to draw attention away from David Lang. Neither character is sufficiently created to take a central position therefore, and the novel suffers from the resultant lack of an insight into human behaviour comparable to that achieved in the depiction of Brian O'Connal.

To achieve in *The Kite* the focus he desires, Mitchell has set up reflector patterns in the subplots comparable to those in *Who Has Seen the Wind*; he depicts a series of relationships with Daddy on the part of the Shelby townspeople that should act as reflectors or commentaries on the central interaction. Unfortunately this device fails in operation. Because Daddy figures prominently in each case, and because David himself remains relatively passive during the recounted anecdotes, the focus shifts to Daddy, and David's centrality is concomitantly diminished. Daddy, however, remains a constant throughout the book, albeit a constant vitality; he does not change. It is David who suffers the development and who discovers the 'answer', achieving completion, at the end of the book and at the end of his stay in Shelby.

Like David Lang, Brian O'Connal, too, must move from

childhood completion through emptiness to a new completion. The "explosions of feeling" which he has felt before his "emptiness" do momentarily return after Jappy's death and before his own final glimpse of the nature of reality. A visit to Saint Sammy on the prairie, who mystically in age can know (to his own satisfaction) the "majesty of His glory" and "the greatness His work" stirs up the feeling once more, but this time "coloured with sickening guilt." In his development, Brian, again like David, has been acquiring knowledge, but when that knowledge deals grossly with the physical facts of birth and life and death, it 'spoils' the inherent knowledge of immortality. Brian is in conflict with experience, and more often than not,

harshness of life.

> it was as though he listened to the drearing wind and in the spread darkness of the prairie night was being drained of his very self. He was trying to hold together something within himself, that the wind demanded and was relentlessly leaching from him.

At this stage in Brian's development, his father succumbs to hepatitis and dies, and Brian is forced again on a highly personal level to recognize the inevitability of death—this, however, the death of a human being. Moving as he has been from childish reaction in emotional situations (the tears of deprivation) towards more verbal response, Brian "did not feel like crying" at the death of his father. Tears of relief come only when he realizes responsibility for others and a direction to take during his own life: his mother "needed him now." Aware of death, he is maturing; aware of some inevitabilities, he begins to accept what he cannot control; and some years later his grandmother MacMurray's expected death "did not come with the shocking impact."

Brian's "growing sense of responsibility" accompanies the growth of this awareness; expressed towards all around him, it is a manifestation of his increasingly competent and humanistic attempts to rectify the unjust and the improperly controlled in that part of his environment over which he has influence. But as the growth takes place, the feeling disappears, and Brian would wonder "with regret, that he never had a return of the old excitement since he had heard the meadow lark sing to him the day of his father's funeral." The egocentric world becomes a sociocentric one with Brian outward-oriented, a transition which culminates in his desire to be a "dirt doctor," in his laying plans for his own future in terms of living in the physical and the social world.

Still seeking certainty in his new role, Brian meets Digby and Palmer in the harness shop and puzzles at the adult difficulties of Berkeleyan philosophy. Digby's first impression that Brian was "not old enough" to understand, that his approach to understanding would be through the child's sense perception of material things, is changed when Brian abruptly tells him: " 'I don't get the feeling any more. I—don't think I will—get it any more.' " At this point Digby makes the judgment which is crucial to the novel. He

> was struck by something more than familiar in the serious eyes under the broad band of the toque with its red pom . . . That was it—the look upon Brian's face—the same expression that had puzzled him on the Young Ben's: maturity in spite of the formlessness of childish features, wisdom without years. 'Intimations of Immortality,' he thought.
>
> 'Perhaps,' said Digby to Brian, 'you've grown up.'

And yet Brian is certainly different from the Young Ben. Western society defines maturity as responsibility to the social world, as the leaving of petulant childishness for emotional restraint at least in recurring situations, and Brian comes to this, in spite of his years, whereas the Young Ben does not. But for that matter, few of the adult characters in the novel achieve maturity to the extent Brian has done. Bent Candy in his greed and the Abercrombies and Mr. Powelly in their desire for revenge furnish ready examples of pettiness and petulance despite their adult years. Their world, like the child's world, is built around themselves, and basing their actions on material values, they can neither appreciate breadth of mind nor express valid and deep emotion. But the

Young Ben and Saint Sammy, though socially immature to the extent that they, too, live for themselves, do possess a maturity of a different kind. Unlike Bent Candy or Mrs. Abercrombie and although their methods of appreciation remain those of sensory perception, their values are non-material. By reason of their primitive awareness of life and death and existence, by their uninhibited passion, by their oneness with the prairie, they have achieved apparently instinctively the egocentric 'maturity' of contact with the timeless and immortal.

Brian, however, gives promise of coming to a contact with the Absolute which is comparable to this, but of course his methods will differ. The approach of the Young Ben and Saint Sammy to eternal truths is from a material, a physical point of view. They see the Eternal through the senses, by running *with* the prairie wind and watching coloured butterflies and collecting broken glass and labels, and their appreciation of beauty and truth is as if by instinct, whereas Brian's changed approach, his socially mature approach, is not through sense perception but rather through the more abstract routes of emotion and conscious intellect. Staring out at the prairie when he is twelve, he muses:

> It had something to do with dying; it had something to do with being born. Loving something and being hungry were with it too. He knew that much now . . . Some day, he thought, perhaps when he was older than he was now, he would know; he would find out completely and for good. He would be satisfied . . . Some day. The thing could not hide from him forever.

But the day of rebirth to oneness with the perfect and immortal would be a day of death to the physical and mortal, a cycle of existence that is reflected in Mitchell's recurrent imagery of light and dark, summer and winter, growth and decay and new growth.

The realization of the nature of this cycle would bring Brian to the state of awareness—an intellectual awareness—that Digby himself has achieved. Brian does not in the novel come to full knowledge and understanding of the "realities of birth, hunger, satiety, eternity, death." For him are only glimpses, only foretastes of the final order—or perhaps only recollections of early childhood—in Mitchell's terms: "moments of fleeting vision." Maturity involves moving *from* childhood, however, and to acceptance of the responsibilities of a social world. Brian, in achieving the degree of maturity beyond his child's years that Digby recognizes as "growing up," chooses a way of life which is balanced between the isolating extremes of material crassness and private mysticism. And yet he preserves in curiosity and breadth of vision the sympathetic state of mind that will allow at once both acknowledgment of human interdependence and an adult-grown contemplation of the mysteries of existence that activate the world in which he lives. This is the maturity that will allow the new completeness—leading a full life—to replace satisfactorily for the period of mortal existence the old, the childlike awareness of a different order.

David Lang and Keith Maclean and Daddy Sherry are seen in their period of mortal existence, too, and at the end of *The Kite* David realizes that it is Daddy's "awareness of his own mortality" that supplies the completion he needs to live his own life fully. David already has intellect, but as Donald Finlay has told him, intellect by itself is insufficient:

". . . intuition is nearer to life than intellect—or science . . . That's why we have the arts, isn't it? "
"I suppose."
"It's one of the reasons I'm a minister."
"Just what do you mean by living fully? "
"Expressing your whole potentiality—taking advantage of every bit of elasticity life offers and stretching it to your profit . . . Liberty—freedom."

But freedom does not mean indulgence of appetite, nor does it mean disregard of all but the self. Daddy Sherry, for example, has led a full life, has taken advantage of its elasticity, and though in his age he is at times cantankerous, he remains loyal to his ideals (Ramrod Parsons) in spite of the opportunity to turn Paradise Valley to personal material gain. He stays concerned, too, for his family (Helen and Keith), but, as the doctor notes, " 'he steps at will into the past—might even be a form of adjustment for him. His personality may have lost some of its elasticity.' "

Daddy's life, which in Helen's words " 'didn't encourage conformity—it gave him a chance to resist imprint,' " has therefore been a continual expression of individuality within the framework of a given environment. Because it has expressed the potentiality of the man, it has brought him happiness—an awareness of growth and an expectation of the future that will not allow him to die in the spring season. Having achieved the completeness of a full life, Daddy no longer fears death, just as the child, who is unaware of death, also has no fear of it—but different, because the mature approach is a conscious one. No longer fearing death, he must still continue to live fully, however, for once he consciously lets time live for him—once he allows his actions to be governed by the clock—he loses the attunement with immortality that allows him to continue to live. Hence he can say to Keith Maclean:

> "Get to ninety-five an' you're immortal agin—jist as immortal as you are right now—settin' there ten years old on the top my front porch step . . ."

The one does not know death, and the other does not fear it and can therefore destroy time by destroying the clock on his one hundred and eleventh birthday. Unlike the others at the Daddy Sherry celebration, Daddy himself cannot partake in any "propitiation of the god of mortality." He recognizes it, and that suffices.

At these celebrations, however, David Lang achieves a new completion of his own, for here he at last recognizes the necessary relationship between the individual and the realities of life and death. Limbo—surrender to the negating power of time—is a kind of death-in-life for the journalist in him, but elasticity of self within his own environment, in place and in time, will allow immortality and let the artist in him create. Recognition of this also allows him to anticipate a full future —out of limbo—with Helen and Keith Maclean.

Both David Lang and Brian O'Connal, then, undergo a process of growth and development that results in their increased awareness of realities beyond the physical. But though their situations are in a sense complementary—the sensitive boy balancing emotion with intellect and the man in limbo balancing intellect with emotion—the two novels that explore these situations differ markedly.

In *Canadian Literature* No. 14, Patricia Barclay quotes W.O. Mitchell as saying: "When I wrote *Who Has Seen the Wind*, I didn't have an answer. It was just a question, which is a perfectly fine reason for writing a novel. In *The Kite*, there is an answer . . ." The answer in *The Kite*, however, which should have become apparent through the situation itself, is made so explicit by the end of the book as to weaken the effect of the central symbol:

> Now he knew what it was that Daddy had for him—the astonishingly simple thing the old man had to say—and had said through the hundred and eleven years of his life —between the personal deeds of his birth and his death, knowing always that the string was thin—that it could be dropped—that it could be snapped. He had lived always with the awareness of his own mortality.

But *Who Has Seen the Wind* approaches the question merely from a different point of view, and the same answer is implicit here in the development that takes place in the novel itself.

The flaws which weaken *The Kite* do not, however, prevent an appreciation of the concepts that Mitchell attempts to convey. David Lang's intellectually competent approach to living recognizes the truth of there being life in art; only when he tempers his objectivity with emotional intuitiveness, however, can he recognize also that there is art in life. His contact with the forces of life when he visits Daddy Sherry in Shelby allows him at last to see the short period of mortal existence as a continuum that does not "arrive at anything" or "echo anything" except what the individual makes of it. If he orients physical reality towards the self only or if he reacts only intellectually towards life, he deprives himself of values that are inherent in more abiding relationships; and if he indulges in emotion only, he again lives in a world populated by self alone. Only by the balance of objective reason and judgment with subjective concern and contemplation can he enjoy the fullness that mortal existence offers. Brian O'Connal's development is also one that brings him to an awareness of the possibilities in mortal life. His maturation takes him from unimpeded emotional indulgence when confronted with death to a balance beyond his child's years that allows him to recognize intellectually the inevitability of death and yet to appreciate through his emotional sensibility the abiding expressions of transcendent perfection. Here, in *Who Has Seen the Wind*, the answer to Mitchell's question is more subtly revealed; partly because of this, and partly because of the novel's unity, its insight, and its world of suggestion, it manifests the strength of certain artistry.

1963

SINCLAIR ROSS'S
AMBIVALENT
WORLD

One of the most haunting phrases in all of Canadian fiction has to me always been the last line of Sinclair Ross's *As For Me and My House*. The ambivalence of it puzzles, irritates, confuses. When Philip Bentley at that time protests that to name his illegitimate son Philip would be to raise the possibility of not knowing which of them is which, his wife—the central character-narrator—writes in her diary: "That's right, Philip, I want it so." And so the novel closes. At first that "*I* want it" seems to reveal a great deal; it speaks the voice of the manipulating woman who has already almost destroyed her husband by confining his artistic talents, and who even now does not let up. For Philip in such a climate to leave Horizon and the ministry and run a book shop somewhere appears still to be his wife's decision, and the future seems bleak indeed.

The picture's other side—for it has one—is, though not exactly rosy, certainly less bleak. If we can accept that Mrs. Bentley's final remark is a sign of a new-found humility—"I *want* it so"—and this is certainly the received interpretation—then she and Philip have some hope of escaping their hypocrisy towards themselves, towards each other, and towards the towns to which they have been inadequately ministering. Both views are reasonable. This one is supported by the climactic scene in which the storm in Horizon blows down the building's false fronts and Mrs. Bentley angrily reveals to Philip that she knows that their adopted baby is really illegitimately his own. The other view acquires its credibility from the book as a whole, from the character we see self-revealed in the pages of her admirably constructed diary. For Ross has consciously constructed it after all; the calendar system itself is enough to tell us that. But what does he really want us to think at the end then? Which view of his character does he want us to accept? There is a third possibility: that it is neither the one nor the other view, but the ambivalence itself which is desired—not based on an indecisiveness about who his character really is, but emerging out of a carefully constructed web of viewpoints, Mrs. Bentley's and ours, pitted ironically against each other so that we come to appreciate not only the depth and complexity of the narrator and her situation, but also the control in which Ross artistically holds his words.

The scene which gives us some indication of this lies between the storm scene and the final words of the novel. It is their last Sunday in Horizon, and Mrs. Bentley writes:

> After three or four years it's easy to leave a little town.
> It turns out now that all along they've liked us. . . .
> Last Friday they had a farewell supper for us in the basement of the Church, made speeches, sang *God Be With You Till We Meet Again*, presented us with a handsome silver flower basket. It's the way of a little Main Street town—sometimes a rather nice way.
> It's blowing tonight, and there's dust again, and the room sways slowly in a yellow smoky haze. The bare, rain-stained walls remind me of our first Sunday here, just a little over a year ago, and in a sentimental mood I keep thinking what an eventful year it's been, what a wide wheel it's run.

It is the first time she has ever complimented the towns-people or found anything attractive about the small town way of life. But is she sincere now or has she, since the storm, learned another hypocrisy? That ambivalence again.

The importance of this episode for the novel as a whole is not just the revelation of the new attitude, but the image which follows it, that of dust and rain, for if the imagery is structured as well as the events of the novel, it should serve to support the themes and to confirm our interpretation. The simple 'polar opposites' view of Mrs. Bentley, that is, as being *either* success *or* failure at the end of the novel, would be supported if a strand of 'polar opposites' imagery ran through the book, distinguishing truth from falsehood, good from bad. The false-fronted stores come at once to mind— yet after they have fallen we are still left with ambivalent scenes. The dust and rain, then, would seem to fulfill the function of delineating opposites, but they are even more deceptive than the false fronted stores, and to force them into this technical role would be to distort what Ross intends. To illuminate this question, however, forces us back into the novel.

The overall impression left by the book is certainly one of aridity: of dust and heat, the Depression on the prairies and the drought which went with it. And accompanying the unproductivity of the land is the dryness of the people: Mrs. Bentley, who cannot bear a child; Philip, who does not believe in his church and cannot comfort the people; the people themselves, who in Mrs. Bentley's eyes cannot appreciate anything or anyone beyond their own restricted world. Yet this directly conflicts with the view of them she gives us at the end of the book, so obviously 'in Mrs. Bentley's eyes' is the operative phrase here. By extension, we suspect all of her affirmations, finding in them partial truths that ring ironically against the complex realities Ross ultimately allows us to glimpse.

So it is with the dust and rain, which reveal the complexity that several separate points of view create. The image becomes one not of affirming polarities of good and bad, but of exploring what is real in the world. Mrs. Bentley's view is thus not the only one we are conscious of, for the technique of the book, Ross's words in Mrs. Bentley's diary, establishes a linguistic tension that allows us to view the narrator with distance, objectivity, dispassion: and so perceive the irony and ambivalence—the 'jests of God', in a

sense, if we can anticipate Margaret Laurence—which characterize reality in Ross's world.

Although from the very beginning, that is, we come up
against Mrs. Bentley's explanation of things, the false fronts
and social attitudes of Horizon, the first detail of weather we
see is not one of dryness but one of a "soft steady swish of
rain on the roof, and a gurgle of eave troughs running over."
April rains are usually a symbol of hope, of nurture for new
growth, of Christian sacrifice and forgiveness, but here in
this 'disordered house', they (ostensibly for the first time)
leak through the roof and stain the walls. Obviously the rain
in reality does not serve to refresh, just as the 'Christianity'
hypocritically uttered by Philip or by Mrs. Bentley's towns-
people is powerless to affect the environments through
which they move.

We see this most clearly in the Partridge Hill episodes. In
this little country town, beyond Horizon, the people are
experiencing their fifth straight year without a harvest, yet
they continue to place faith in the ministerings of the
Church. Sardonically, in June, Mrs. Bentley writes, "This
was the day out at Partridge Hill we prayed for rain." The
Church ceremony is thus reduced to pagan ritual, and she
and Paul Kirby, the equally sardonic schoolteacher, 'tie' in
their reaction: "Surely it must be a very great faith that
such indifference on the part of its deity cannot weaken—a
very great faith, or a very foolish one." It is just this ambivalence, explicitly enunciated here, expressing at once the
impossibility of taking sides and the human inclination to do
so, which the book communicates throughout.

Paul's continuing habit of uttering etymological facts,
which seems almost gratuitous in the novel at times, is not
thematically unrelated. He has already told us, for example,
"*pagan*, you know, originally that's what it meant, *country
dweller*," and in June in Partridge Hill this echoes through
the scenes we see. Paul's problem is that he cannot live outside his world of arid facts. Whereas he thinks he knows
what's around him and withholds himself from it, others are
encountering, experiencing whatever is there. The problems

that others (like the farmers) do have, however, emerge not just physically from that encounter (the drought, the land), but from a state of mind in relation to the experience that is not unlike Mrs. Bentley's or Paul's own. Mrs. Bentley later wonders if she is "the one who's never grown up, who can't see life for illusions"; the farmers for their part live in one sense in a dream world that does not recognize the present, for it acknowledges only two times, the good harvest and the possibility for one, "the year it rained all June, and next year."

April rains, for the Bentleys, then, had been destructive; June rains do not exist. The persistent faith in rain seems ironic, therefore, and with this in mind we move back to Mrs. Bentley herself. She likes water, wants it, apparently needs to go walking in the rain, for example, and so heads out in it whenever possible. Even snow will do, though then reality gives way "to the white lineless blend of sky and earth." 'Horizon' seems itself to be reality, therefore, just as the present is reality, and like the farmers with their belief in June rains, she comes headlong into conflict with it. Once in a recital she played Debussy's *Garden in the Rain*; now she tries to build one, but water is scarce and all that blooms is a single poppy—while she is away.

Similarly, her view of her husband is founded in this dream of fruition. That he is an artist is what *she* says, but whether or not he indeed has talent, he lacks the milieu that might foster greatness. She sees his artistry, moreover, in terms of her own image, just as he (with his 'sons', Steve and young Philip, as well as with his God) creates in his:

> It's always been my way to comfort myself thinking that water finds its own level, that if there's anything great or good in a man it will eventually find its way out. But I've never taken hold of the thought and analyzed it before, never seen how false it really is. Water gets dammed sometimes: and sometimes, seeking its level, it seeps away in dry, barren earth. Just as he's seeping away among the false fronts of these little towns.

When Philip is ill, too, it is she who says he has nausea—

causing Paul to flinch, because his etymological sensibility is outraged. *Nausea* "is from a Greek word meaning ~~ship~~ sea and is, therefore, etymologically speaking, an impossibility on dry land."

That Philip needs a change of environment is true, but again it is Mrs. Bentley who voices the desire, even acts it out when she walks recurrently down the railway track as far as the ravine. When Philip goes with her, she locates her wish in his eyes, and finds the possibility of escape—the possibility of a fruitful, ordered future—in the train to an outside world.

> At last we heard a distant whistle-blade, then a single point of sound, like one drop of water in a whole sky. It dilated, spread. The sky and silence began imperceptibly to fill with it. We steeled ourselves a little, feeling the pounding onrush in the trestle of the bridge. It quickened, gathered, shook the earth, then swept in an iron roar above us, thundering and dark.

Paradoxically the train comes from, passes through, and heads for 'Horizons', which are realities, not dreams, and must be faced. The 'water sickness' is in a sense Mrs. Bentley's, not Philip's, therefore, a function of her perhaps unconscious dream and a further indication of her imposition of her own point of view onto the world around her.

What Ross does to communicate these ironies and ambiguities is to blur the edges of his images. Absolutes do not exist. For all that the recurrent water images seem to accompany an inability to come to terms with reality, that is, the water is not itself 'bad'—it only becomes so when in a person's viewpoint the dream it represents stands in the way of altering the present. When the dream and the reality come into conflict, the water takes on the characteristics of the desert, the arid land. At the ravine, thinking of Judith, Mrs. Bentley writes:

> Philip and I sat in the snowstorm watching the water rush through the stones—so swift that sometimes as we watched, it seemed still, solid like glass.

Later, knowing of the affair between Judith and Philip, she notes:

> The rain's so sharp and strong it crackles on the windows just like sand.

The similes work in the opposite direction as well. At Partridge Hill, "there was a bright fall of sunshine that made the dingy landscape radiant. Right to the horizon it winked with little lakes of spring-thaw water." But we also hear of "dust clouds lapping at the sky," of "dense, rigid heat" and "planks of sunlight." We're told that the August heat "was heavy and suffocating. We seemed imbedded in it, like insects in a fluid that has congealed." This last image recurs again when Philip seduces Judith, and Mrs. Bentley wakes, listens, and knows: "like a live fly struggling in a block of ice". For her, during the winter that follows, "The sun seems cold." These are not all working to say exactly the same thing. There are times, apparently, when the dream serves a useful function in the mind of a people, but again, when the reality—'Horizon'—is obscured, the dream is frozen, becomes as hard and apparently sterile as the dust and sand.

The ambivalence we are left with at the end of the book is not absolutely resolved by these observations, but they bring us closer to understanding it. In presenting and exploring a single point of view, *As For Me and My House* runs the danger of seeming shallow, of allowing no aesthetic distance from which we can respond *to* the narrator as well as participate in her verbal reactions to the world. Fortunately Ross's technique, his control over the words he allows Mrs. Bentley to use, creates the ironic tension which raises the book from a piece of 'regional realism' to a complex study of human responses. Mrs. Bentley herself is all too prone to approve or condemn, but Ross would have his readers avoid this. By his images and through the other characters, he shows us, in fact, how Mrs. Bentley's polarization of Horizon (this world, arid, sterile, bad) and the Bookstore (dream, water, fruitful, good) is invalid and gradually breaks down. That she and Philip ultimately do leave to try to set up the bookstore is perhaps cause, therefore, for us to see her as a failure, continuing as the manipulator she has been before.

But then we still have her compliment about Horizon's townspeople to contend with, and her acknowledgment in the same breath of both the dust and the rain stains. Here she seems to be aware of reality at last; if so, her future might hold at least some success. But reality to Ross is still not clear cut, and that the book should end so ambivalently seems ultimately part of his plan. The ambivalence is founded in his imagery, founded in the lives of the characters and the nature of their world, germane to the whole novel, magnificently distilling what it has tried to say. When we become conscious of this, we become not only involved in the book, but like the people of Horizon, no matter how apparently sure of themselves, still sensitive to doubt and so to reality as well.

1969

THE GENIUS
OF PLACE
AND TIME:
THE FICTION OF
ETHEL WILSON

To some," writes Frances Burnaby, the narrator of Ethel Wilson's *Hetty Dorval* (1947), "the genius of a place is inimical; to some it is kind. . . My genius of place is a god of water." In her case, the god is kind, for though experience comes to her, no real harm ever does. This does not deny that there are ironies in her life, and ironies in Life, and it is with skill and subtlety that Mrs. Wilson presents them. Frances Burnaby's apparently casual statement, for example, is more than just a statement about what landscapes people like; it is also a revelation of character and of the discovery of that character. Not all of Mrs. Wilson's figures show the perception of Frances Burnaby; not all are conscious of what motivates them. But all are observed in relation to an environment that becomes their 'genius', and the author's balance of character with place becomes part of her exploration of man's relationship with himself, with others, and with the philosophical traps and supports which he invents to trouble and to comfort him. Such concerns do not make the author's works distinctively 'Canadian', but such a demand is irrelevant in any estimate of literary worth. Ethel Wilson's sensitivity and her stylistic restraint have made her one of Canada's most accomplished novelists, and that is enough.

Frances Burnaby, as the title of *Hetty Dorval* indicates, is not nominally the central figure of the story, but as the narrator, the perceiving and focusing eye of the work, she becomes equally as important as Hetty in controlling its direction. 'Frankie' is a twelve-year-old child when the book opens at Lytton, where the clear Thompson River meets the larger and muddy Fraser (and is absorbed by it), in British Columbia. Hetty, with a mysterious Oriental past, is older and knowledgeable. She lives isolated from the community, and though she enjoys Frankie's company, she asks that the visits be secret. The child considers this "unnatural"; the community "knows" Hetty to be "of no reputation"; but Hetty, like the "domestic promiscuous cat," "simply sheds people," and Frankie writes: "I only once caught a glimpse of her claws."

It is in her attempt to understand the morality of this attitude that Frankie grows up. Time takes her away from Lytton to school, and then, at nineteen, still feeling twelve, to England, but Hetty is always a Presence in her mind. By coincidence they also meet again, in Vancouver, and aboard the boat, and in Piccadilly, and the coincidences strain the novel a little. What redeems it from complete artistic limbo is the continuing sense of life which is in turn related to the reality of the characters themselves. This is not to say that Hetty has either the 'psychological reality' of James' Isabel Archer or the 'working class reality' of Dreiser's Sister Carrie. She's much more like Muriel Spark's Jean Brodie, in fact—an enigma whose identity is real to those who know her even momentarily—an identity defined less by adjectives than by events, less by absolutes than by ironies.

The epigraph to the book is the familiar one from Donne's Meditation XVII: "no man is an island," and it is Hetty who attempts to contradict this:

> Circumstances sometimes make it possible to know people with sureness and therefore with joy or some other emotion, because continuous association with them makes them as known and predictable as the familiar beloved contours of home, or else the place where one merely waits for the street car, or else the dentist's drill. Take your choice. But one cannot invade and discover the closed or hidden places of a person like Hetty Dorval. . . . She endeavoured to island herself in her own particular world of comfort and irresponsibil-

ity. . . .But . . . Hetty could not island herself, because we impinge on each other, we touch, we glance, we press, we touch again, we cannot escape. "No man is an Island." Who touched me?

For Frances's 'place' is the domain of the god of water. She changes, she grows up, whereas Hetty, with her silence and withdrawal, simply uses people for her own security and moves on, always the same. She moves through the world, but in silence is her real identity. When at the last she leaves England behind, and Frances and Rick (whom Frances loves and with whom Hetty has been toying), she heads to Central Europe. The book closes this way:

> Six weeks later the German Army occupied Vienna. There arose a wall of silence around the city, through which only faint confused sounds were sometimes heard.

The device is a transparent one, but the *book* is not transparent simply because Hetty is not. She's a power, an influence, even an allegorical sense of political intrigue. Yet her effect is to crystallize the identity of those around her, not to develop herself. What she does serves to make Frankie conscious of her own relationships with others, and if her influence could be inimical, that part of it is offset by the environment which Frankie helps to create for herself.

Though this first novel is both slim and slight, it shows the simplicity of tone and the detached, ironic standpoint that has come to characterize Ethel Wilson's work. It shows also the ability to create vital and credible characters, which is rare enough in any fiction, let alone that in Canada. Her control over character increases, too, and the political implications of isolation still interest her when she comes to write her second work, *The Innocent Traveller* (1949). This, though it reads deceptively quickly, has much greater subtlety and depth to it than the earlier novel, and must be counted one of her finest works.

The title figure is Topaz Edgeworth, daughter of the Victorian world of social establishment and a family that entertains Matthew Arnold at dinner, who travels in one sense only when her family travels, but, in another, entirely on her own. She grows old, though not up, and her father grows old:

> sleeping in security in the sunshine. His world was a good world. His Queen was a good Queen. His country was a good country. His business was good. His health was good. His family was a good family and God was good.

His capsulated mores, too, are neatly reflected in the style the author uses to present them. Topaz's brothers and sisters then marry; she becomes Aunt Topaz, later Great-Aunt Topaz. She moves with her sister and niece to Vancouver and encounters the twentieth century in what to her is a new and fascinating frontier town that thinks itself sedate because it's a seaside town as well. Like Hetty Dorval, however, she never changes; but she and Hetty are totally unlike except in that one respect. Her innocence is of a different kind. Hetty was the promiscuous—and perhaps amoral—cat; Topaz is the moral bird—but 'moral' (as 'innocent') in a very special sense.

> Into her majority and for ever, Topaz took her three loyalties. Not religion, although she had an indigenous faith in God . . . ; not patriotism, although she loved her country; not love for a man . . . . But the Royal Family moved through her life with banners streaming. Mr. Gladstone stood for ever four-square in his integrity . . . and through his spell she adhered in a wishy-washy way to the Liberal Party. And now her loyalty to her father lived as a loving memory . . .

They create her world, her place, and her innocence is possible only because she does not leave it.

Ethel Wilson extends this in three related directions in the course of the book: one concerned with character, a second with time, the third with politics. *The Innocent Traveller,* unlike *Hetty Dorval,* is not written from a first person point of view. Instead, the author manages to combine first and third person in a way that is stylistically reminiscent of

Joyce's *A Portrait of the Artist as a Young Man.* When Topaz is a child, the sentence structure and word choice combine to create the child's viewpoint; later, we are conscious of the older woman seeing her environment. But integrating these passages is Mrs. Wilson's overviewing eye. It is Mrs. Wilson, that is, who tells us that Topaz "enjoyed music as she enjoyed food, with pleasure, but without passion, like a warbling unimportant bird"; that "heavier beings encounter acute sorrow or acute joy or dull despair of which the water-gliders know nothing," and that Topaz was "equipped as lightly as a waterglider of considerable education." But sometimes Topaz interrupts her;

> The private life of Topaz, if life must be compared to a journey, had been like travelling on a canal. Topaz had never said to herself, "My private life is like a canal" ("A canal indeed! Whatever are they talking about! "), but nevertheless when for purposes of recollection or recapitulation she regarded her past and passing life, it was as a canal that she saw it. This canal had been soundly constructed by her progenitors, and was well administered by those now in charge.

The ebullience of Topaz's character makes it almost inevitable that she should intrude this way upon her 'biographer'—as she intrudes irrepressibly, innocently, and arbitrarily upon everyone:

> "Rachel, Rachel, what *do* you suppose," she cried, "there are nine young men swimming about the bay with nothing on, and I do believe that one is Andrew's friend Mr. Morland, and I *do* believe that one of them is that nice young man in the Bank! If they would only turn right side up I might be able to see! I called and called but they did not reply! "
> "I sometimes think, Aunty, that you have no modesty."
> "Me! No modesty! " exclaimed Aunty with indignation. "Well, really! Here I am clothed from head to foot, and they haven't got a stitch on! Who's immodest I'd like to know! "

The book is consistently quotable for its humour and its

quick changes of mood, and any commentator must resist the temptation to quote all and must, instead, simply urge that others read her.

Part of the success of the book is certainly traceable to its use of language, for the shifts in mood and in point of view are neither damaging to the characterization nor unrelated to the imagery. For all that Topaz is extroverted and uninhibited by ordinary social conventions, it is those conventions which allow her to exist. She is the waterglider, unaware of acute emotions—sorrow or joy—and she glides within the limits of a Victorian canal. The irony of this is that others around her are living a 'fuller' life, a 'significant' life—which makes them at once more sensitive and more restrained—while the Victorian world is passing, with time, out of existence.

Time is change. Time is being aware of the world around one. Time is watching love develop and death occur. And Topaz is vaguely unconscious of it all. Her father and the Queen are her guides and promise to be permanent, but during World War I nations become conscious of

> the continuous fusing of Time and Place and Effect everywhere, and people (startled and rallying from shock) in all places found that their lives were not their own and were no longer assured, because the Germans (who had not consulted them) had decided to march into Belgium.

Passages such as this seem at first only part of the novel's setting, but in fact they are adding another dimension to the book. Like Hetty Dorval, Topaz is not affected by life, but Topaz has even less effect than Hetty upon those who know her. When, objectively, we stand outside the novel looking on, we can be delighted by her, but we do not identify. Though the question Ethel Wilson asks—can people isolate themselves from the world—is again answered in the negative, this does not detract from our delight in Topaz or our appreciation of that which is both different and (congenitally, perhaps) independent in her. What it does do is make us see that difference in another perspective, in relation to the environment that allows it to exist.

The Equations of Love (1952), Ethel Wilson's next work, combines two novellas, "Tuesday and Wednesday" and "Lilly's Story." Both are forays into working-class life, and though the stories are again related with a controlled ironic detachment, the sense of aliveness that earlier characters exuded is absent here. The characters in this book are less flamboyant, though their lives are not without incident, but to present grey people is a dangerous course for a writer to adopt. What Mrs. Wilson is trying to convey is the flatness with which flat people will respond to even the most extraordinary events in their environment. Their 'place' has formed them, and their identity once established, it continues, no matter what fate may bring. The danger lies in the fact that readers may respond only to the flatness and not to the reaction itself.

Mort and Myrtle Johnson, in the first story, for example— and Myrtle's wispy, painfully withdrawn cousin Victoria May Tritt—are identified by their respective blundering well-meaning, self-centredness, and shy retirement. The passages that, for Mort and Myrtle at least, present their personalities are obviously akin to those in which Frances Burnaby discovers that she is governed by a god of water, but they are much more contrived, and though witty, are too obvious to succeed:

> Mort's angel had some time ago found out that the insecurity of the quarters wherein it often rocked as in a rough mountainous sea before settling down again facing in a different direction, was due to a weakness in Mort's potentially strong inner structure, but, as it had discovered that it could do nothing about this weakness, had rather given up . . . The two things Mort really loves are his wife Myrtle and himself—the first inconstantly and the second with a varying intensity that sometimes includes his fellowman in some vicarious way identified with himself . . . .
> Myrtle's angel had long since become a nervous and ineffectual creature because Myrtle's various entities

and impersonations were enough to keep any angel thin. Of all people, Myrtle loved herself in whatever guise she saw herself.

The difference between the two is spelled out, and it is this difference, simply, that the story considers. Mort drowns with a drunken friend, and Myrtle reacts with self-pity—thinking herself deserted by a souse, and what will the neighbours say. But Vicky May, who lives, privately, in a movie magazine world, insists he died a hero, and Myrtle, sensing the melodrama of this, adopts another and rather more queenly attitude. It is in character for her, and Vicky May goes back to her own apartment. What briefly allowed them to communicate was one of the equations of love, but they are, at the end, again alone.

The equations of love are many, however, and most of them are implied in this book: love = a casual affair, love = love of *things*, love = love of home, love = marital love, love = parental/filial love, love = appetite, love = sentiment, love = affection. In "Lilly's Story" we see again the opposition between independence and community that Mrs. Wilson has talked about before; here, too, we have a retelling of the "Innocent Traveller" motif, with even a recurrence of some of the same minor figures from that earlier book. Here the central figure is the sluttish Lilly, who, when she has an illegitimate daughter, invents for herself a name—Mrs. Walter Hughes—and a history, in order to let her daughter be "folks" and know a life different from her own—stable, ordered, secure. Lilly does not have the 'canal' that Topaz, for example, has—which makes life more difficult for her. And like Hetty, she is less like the bird and more like "the little yellow cat, no worse and no better." She must therefore create her own place, which she does—as a maid in Comox, a hospital aide in the Fraser Valley, a chambermaid in Toronto—and she pretends a reality, always pretends. The truth always threatens her, almost like natural law—and the scene of eagle-pursuing-robin-pursuing-snake in the centre of the story is symbolic of this—but gradually deceit comes in fact to *be* her life, and eventually (declaring her wig as her only deceit) she marries into absolute middle-classness in, "faint with happiness," the United Church. Mrs. Wilson's tongue is, as usual, continually getting into her cheek, but the examination of the emotion that allows a sense of community ever to exist in a world of isolated people is quite serious.

This becomes even more apparent in her next book and finest novel, *Swamp Angel* (1954), which again focuses on one woman, Maggie Lloyd, who rejects one identity (her middle-class marriage with Edward Vardoe) to be herself. Maggie adopts her first husband's name again, and in a calculated but not callous way, leaves Edward and Vancouver and heads to the interior, to the lakes near Kamloops, where she becomes cook and general enlivening spirit at a faltering fishing lodge. Again we see the effect of one life on another and the effect of environment upon the individual life.

The birds are migrating at the beginning of the book, and throughout we are conscious of change, of movement. The mountains themselves are "fluid," writes the author; the route Maggie takes out of Vancouver is the River Road; Maggie enjoys fishing and is, in effect, fishing for a new life when she leaves Edward; she heads to the city of Kamloops, its Indian name meaning 'Meeting of the Waters'; and after she gets to the Gunnarsens' fishing camp, she finds joy and release in swimming out into the lake. These apparently minor details all contribute to the story, for they are all part of the author's concern for the effect of place and time upon people. They grow, too, out of the earlier works. To design one's future, as Maggie does, was also one of the aims of Lilly 'Hughes', and "Lilly's Story" seems in some ways to have been a trial run for *Swamp Angel*. Even the 'natural law' scene reappears—but this time limited to the contest between an osprey and an eagle for one of the lake fish and hence more organically related to the story proper.

In Maggie's case, the attempt to design the future is a much more intellectual recognition of the nature of her own personality. Like Topaz Edgeworth, she needs 'open country'—but of a particular kind—and her story is her search for her own place. When she is out swimming, for example, she realizes that

> The water, that element that bears her up and impedes her and cleaves and flies away and falls as only water can, transforms her, because she can swim. If she could not swim, ah . . . then . . . it would no doubt kill her and think nothing of it. But, since she can swim, she swims strongly out into the lake, forgetting past and future, thrusting the pleasant water with arms and legs, and then, quite suddenly, she turns on her back and floats. She is contented. She is not a seal. She is a god floating there with the sun beating down on her face with fatal beneficent warmth, and the air is good. . . . The god and the seal are out there in the water. Or perhaps they are not there unless the swimmer is there too.

But acceptance of one's environment must be a positive thing, and not a negative escape from momentary disturbance. If the environment is indifferent, one learns how to survive in it, that is all. Perhaps this is one of the equations of love too.

Maggie's 'place' also bears some relationship with time, and as with *The Innocent Traveller*, the novel acquires another dimension because of this. The minor characters assist here: Nell Severance, with her ties to the past, and to the circus world in which she (with her little revolver, the swamp angel) was a star; her daughter, who reacts to a loveless childhood by refuting her mother's way of life and accepting middle-class values; Vera Gunnarsen, whose shallowness deprives her of even the simplest philosophy of life to sustain her in moments of crisis; her son, whose childhood sensitivities allow him to change identities and merge with the environment he creates around him:

> Along the fallen tree Alan crawled on hands and knees. When he reached the end of the tree he rose and said "I'm a Mexican leopard! " and sprang to the ground. . . .

> In the leopard's mind a joyful kaleidoscope of bright
> Mexico and dark Africa swirled and blended. Both were
> the same to him, and no less real in that place than
> himself . . . .
> "Did you see Alan? " asked Vera . . . .
> "No," said Maggie. She thought That's not fair to Vera
> but it takes God himself to be fair to two different
> people at once. What she had seen was a leopard slipping
> secretly into the forest from which Alan would no
> doubt emerge.

In time, the childlike sensitivity alters in nature if equanimity is to exist at all. If the adult attaches too closely to the past, he becomes Nell Severance, valuing the symbol, the revolver, more than the reality of the life (her daughter) that is around her—not by conscious choice any more, but by ingrained habit.

The alternative is to find one's place, as Maggie does, and then accept the present as a kind of stability in a world of change. When Nell is hurt and becomes acutely aware of her age, she sends the swamp angel to Maggie, who keeps it for awhile and then throws it into the lake: "When all was still the fish, who had fled, returned. . . . Then flickering, weaving, they resumed their way." The image is like that of the migrating birds; here, promising a future and some continuity, it provides an optimistic resolution to · the conflict that Ethel Wilson has observed. For Maggie, "Things were falling into 'place'—she has found some order, and her 'own sphere.'"

The author's subsequent publications, *Love and Salt Water* (1956), and *Mrs. Golightly and other stories* (1961) (a collection of earlier published works), show somewhat less precision and exert much less effect than *Swamp Angel* or *The Innocent Traveller*. Some of the short stories are witty and entertaining; some are rather moodier; a recurrent motif, however—from Mrs. Golightly's attempt to deal in a sophisticated way with her first convention to the attempt on the part of an anonymous 'I' to cope with what appears to be a dead dog on Granville Street but turns out to be just an extraordinarily well-trained one—is the relationship (inimical or kind) between individuals and their environment. The same is true in *Love and Salt Water,* but here the symbols are so overt (the title itself establishes the relationship) that the narrative suffers.

The story depicts a sequence of events in the life of Ellen Cuppy, from the time she is eleven and called 'Gypsy' (an innocent traveller?) by her family, to her impending marriage in early middle age. It is not a simple chronology, but rather a study of several significant moments in the creation of her identity. Early in the story, when she is sixteen, the cabin boy on the boat on which she is travelling is swept overboard into the dark, and Ellen, like everyone in the storm, feels alone. Years pass. She falls in love with Huw Peake, but discovers that love is not enough, that she cannot live with a man who cannot laugh at pettiness. George Gordon meets and proposes to her then, but "This free life-without-an-object, which had become so boring, was suddenly necessary to her security." What it takes her time to discover is that 'most things are dangerous. Nothing is safe.' And what impresses this upon her is another event which brings her close to drowning and to a consciousness of time itself.

Where she goes to live for awhile, to the Gulf Islands off the coast of British Columbia, there seems to be no time: "you do not count by days which slide, shimmer, coalesce, and become one summer day in such a place." And unthinking, she takes her deaf nephew rowing in Active Pass without checking the time of the tides. They are swamped and almost drowned, but what could have led to disaster results only in disfigurement. She goes then to George and to a "happy chequered life"—the "chequered" removing any saccharine quality from the ending—and so again there is a resolution. But this simple plot masks what in Ethel Wilson's work is much more complex: the interweaving of time, place, and people in what ultimately creates a pattern though it is not wholly predesigned.

Love and Salt Water contains one direct statement of this idea:

There is a curious semblance of reality in those of our years which are certainly valid, but seem to elide, and differ from our years of reality. During those years of elision we live, of course, with relative intensity, and those years mark, retard, hasten, improve, or worsen us, and, alas, may affect some of those with whom we come into touch to a degree of pleasure, exasperation or even of damage, of which we are only partly aware; but then the true years of our life arrive—or do not arrive— and we forget those other irrelevant years which may, since Time is an agent, some day stir, and take their unexpected vengeance in a variety of ingenious ways.

It is during such "years of elision" that Hetty Dorval influences Frankie Burnaby, that Edward Vardoe affects Maggie Lloyd, that Maggie in turn influences the Gunnarsens, that Mort and Myrtle Johnson influence each other, and it is these years and their variety and their effects that most interest Mrs. Wilson. The effects are various. For Hetty and Edward and Myrtle Johnson, no "true years" ever arrive; because of death or fear or a restricted imagination they never do break out of the "semblance of reality" and discover the truths that the human heart can understand. Topaz Edgeworth, in a different way, is another person whose years are "certainly valid" but, in time, wholly insignificant. Topaz's identity is one that makes no imprint on the world, and for her, of course, the surface of life is the only reality. For Myrtle Johnson and Lilly Hughes, middle-class values are the only reality. Ethel Wilson does not deny that these are real, but sensitive to joy and sorrow in the human situation and conscious of the possibilities that exist simply because one is alive, she presents in her work another dimension to the world. If some of her people see only surfaces, so does her prose sometimes skitter along, recreating those points of view. But these passages are counterpointed with unobtrusive symbols, and given breadth by the technique of irony, and set in perspective by the presentation of characters who succeed in recognizing their capabilities and in establishing environments that are personally satisfying.

Topaz, Myrtle, Lilly, and even Hetty can all, of course,

be viewed as successes too—provided we redefine 'success'—and in this lies much of the author's irony. Hetty gains a world of silence that is matched by her own personality; Lilly finds security in deceit; Topaz, in her innocence, never questions or has to question the order that allows her to exist. But it is still Frankie Burnaby who sees more, Ellen Cuppy who feels more, Maggie Lloyd who knows more than they. And if *Hetty Dorval* and *Love and Salt Water* are not wholly satisfying as novels, they still form important parts of a canon that examines the many ways of defining human love and of meeting one's world. *The Innocent Traveller* most clearly presents the problem: how do you evaluate a life that does not see deeply into things—and *Swamp Angel* most clearly resolves it: you don't try, you simply sympathize and then go on to realize that in your own life are the same possibilities for acute sorrow and extreme joy, and you find the world that lets you taste what joy you can, no matter what sorrow the active agent Time may also bring. The sympathy is part of the social communication that is another of the equations of love; it must also exist between the individual and the place that lies around him.

There is fluidity in both time and place, and because a person creates his identity in terms of these two, his identity is fluid as well. It is this fluidity that Mrs. Wilson is conscious of and that, through her imagery and her successive explorations of travellers-through-life, she has detailed in her work. In recognizing their 'genius of place', her perceptive characters become conscious of the fact that lives can be moulded, and hence also sensitive to their own potential in a specific place and time. What they must do is locate this world—"create their own system or be enslaved by another's"—if they are to know in their lives not only passion but also some peace. Frankie Burnaby can do this; so can Rose, the autobiographical grandniece in *The Innocent Traveller*; so can Maggie Lloyd, for whom the others are prototypes, in the most successful *Swamp Angel*. This, then, is Ethel Wilson's statement. It offers a strange combination of a romantic vision and an acute perception of reality—which is not distinctively Canadian, but is quite characteristic of Canadian irony. Mrs. Wilson's technical facility in presenting her statement—through character and symbol rather than through simple exposition—raises her work to the level of ordered, vital, and artistically satisfying fiction.

1968

THE IRONY
OF ORDER:
ETHEL WILSON'S
THE INNOCENT
TRAVELLER

When Ethel Wilson's second novel, *The Innocent Traveller*, appeared in 1949, it was almost without exception praised by reviewers—and not altogether for the right reasons. The exception was the *Canadian Forum*, whose reviewer simply found the central character, Topaz Edgeworth, a bore. But whatever else one can say about Topaz— that she's garrulous, independent, scatter-brained, uncontrollable, eccentric, arbitrary, and 'innocent'—'boring' is not an appropriate epithet. The other reviewers confirm this. What they in turn fail to notice is the skill with which the author has created more than the central character. In other words, like all Mrs. Wilson's longer works—*Hetty Dorval* (1947), *The Equations of Love* (1952), *Swamp Angel* (1954), and *Love and Salt Water* (1956)—this is not just a character sketch. Under the surface lie implications which an examination of theme and structure can hope only to suggest. The novel explores innocence, independence, and order, and in presenting the character of Topaz it interprets both twentieth-century life and the necessary relationship that must exist between people in any society whose stability is, like this one, precariously founded in time.

Mrs. Wilson has in various places and in various ways been likened to Willa Cather, Jane Austen, Proust, Defoe, Blake, Butler, Trollope, and Bennett: an awesome group, and somewhat daunting to any subsequent commentator who feels secretly obliged to follow up all these clues to the writing's character. Mrs. Wilson's success in creating live people leads to one of the comparisons; her concern with time, her social consciousness, her irony, and her control of words lead to others. But the observation of likenesses only serves to clarify the nature of individual parts of a novel, and all those listed here exist in *The Innocent Traveller* not separately, like borrowings, but unified into a work of art. Undoubtedly all writers who read are eclectic borrowers. If a writer has talent, however, as Mrs. Wilson does, then the new book ordered out of these details has its own life and its own reality. So with Topaz and the novel in which she appears.

Hetty Dorval, the first of Ethel Wilson's works, studies the nebulous influence which the experienced title character has on a young girl. It is not just an opposition between youth and age, or between innocence and sophistication. What it explores, with reference to the whole question of morality and amorality, is the extent to which Hetty, though using the worlds through which she moves, can be an individual by exempting herself from ordinarily accepted codes of behaviour. The two novellas which make up *The Equations of Love* are also concerned with codes, but they observe 'morality' from other angles, attempting to explore the nature of love by depicting generosity, narcissism, casual affairs, sacrifice, and many other subtleties of human response, in working-class settings. *Swamp Angel* and *Love and Salt Water* focus again on individual women: Maggie Lloyd, in the first book, finds she must escape suburban routine if she is to *be* the individual she knows she has the potential to be; and Ellen Cuppy, in the second, values her independence so much she flees marriage and, for a brief while, fancies she has escaped from time. But time, as *Love and Salt Water* also tells us, "is an agent," and the years of our life that seem irrelevant "stir, and take their unexpected vengeance in a variety of ingenious ways." Time stirs even in *The Innocent Traveller,* where Topaz Edgeworth (with her own private morality and her protected world) moves gaily through life, but its 'vengeance' here is felt in the world at large and only ironically, when at all, in relation to Topaz herself.

Irony is the dominant tone. The book opens when Topaz,

s an infant, blurts out 'shocking' words at an English Vic-
orian dining table when Matthew Arnold is being entertained
t dinner, and then leaves the table to crawl around under-
neath it. Though the narrative is presented from the third-
person point of view, the style continually shifts to embody
the first-person reaction that is at once being presented and
described. Three passages will serve to illustrate here. The
beginning of the book shows the child:

> Underneath the heavy mahogany table sat Topaz in a
> world of shoes. She had recovered from fear and shame.
> Now she crawled from shoe to shoe. Each pair of shoes
> told Topaz a story. Mother had no shoes, no feet at all,
> just a beautiful rustling spread of purple silk. Topaz
> studied the silk without touching. Then she crawled to
> the large visiting boots of Mr. Matthew Arnold. Mr.
> Arnold wore elegant old-fashioned trousers which had
> straps under the feet. His feet were large, impeccable,
> neatly placed together. Topaz touched a leg with a
> friendly tickling finger. Above the table the great man
> checked his speech, smiled to himself, and continued.
> Topaz in the pleasing gloom of tablecloth, legs, and
> feet, crawled on.

Later we meet, with almost every paragraph, the irrepres-
sible woman Topaz has become:

> And a journey to France (". . . and we climbed the
> Eiffel Tower, and *such* a wind, oh, *such* a wind! And
> my skirts blowing above my head—such skirts! And
> John said, 'Topaz, turn and descend this instant! This
> is no place for a young Englishwoman with all these
> Frenchmen about! ' "). And a journey to Italy (". . . the
> ceiling of the Sistine Chapel! Wonderful! And there
> was hardly anyone there, so I lay down flat on my back
> to see better. And John hissed, 'Topaz, get up at once,
> I disown you completely! ' and he walked away. Oh,
> John was annoyed! I thought he'd never get over it,
> but he did, he did . . ."). And a visit to Dartmoor
> (". . . and away went horse and trap down the hill, and
> over it spilled and when I came to, the horse and I
> were lying in each other's arms. Oh, Father *was* sur-
> prised! ").

But not herself: she was surprised by nothing and delighted with the world. Towards the end of the novel, the prose slows again, but Topaz's sprightliness takes another direction:

> Aunt Topaz gathers the rattling newspaper together and with her embroidery scissors cuts out a picture of the King and Queen, an account of a wedding, and an advertisement for garlic pearls because they sound so odd. She may send for these pearls some day. She puts the newspaper cuttings into a large overfull box with a red plush cover on which some sea-shells still remain. She is very old. She will soon be a hundred.

Her character, then, does not substantially change during her life; and Mrs. Wilson's novel gains its subtlety partly in language, partly in managing to create something significant out of an essentially plotless and insignificant life.

The Innocent Traveller is not a novel of plot and makes no pretence of being one. The very first chapters, depicting all the main characters of the book, immediately anticipate everyone's future, completely undercutting any 'suspense'. We focus upon Topaz as she grows, has a brief love affair which momentarily saddens her when it ends but which ultimately leaves her unchanged; we watch as she ages in a childlike way, becomes Aunt and later Great-Aunt Topaz; we see her react when her father dies, go then with her sister Annie and niece Rachel to Canada, grow old in Vancouver, encountering life there with gusto and 'innocence' before she finally dies and is almost forgotten. What has happened except that a life was and then is not? Very little; just life itself. But can any life be insignificant? Or does insignificance only apply to the relationship between that life and the world around it? Mrs. Wilson writes: "Aunty's long life inscribes no significant design. Just small bright dots of colour, sparkling dots of life." It is an accurate description, too, of the method the author has used to present her central character; what we see are 'dots of life', the moments of vitality that seem to have created and to illustrate Topaz's personality. To talk of time and 'significant design', however, raises other questions about the relationship between Topaz's innocence and the world around her that lets it exist. It adds, also, to the depth of Ethel Wilson's novel.

'Innocence' is not a simple term. It refers here to the childish naiveté of Topaz's grand-niece Rose:

> Whereas the ministers of the Gospel to whom she had listened Sunday by Sunday since infancy spoke gently of the love of God, the Rev. Elmer Pratt thundered about brothels. She supposed that brothels were places where broth was made and decided that the broth must be very bad or the Rev. Elmer Pratt would not be so angry.

It refers also to the naiveté and the disarming tactlessness of Topaz herself:

> "I have lately, Miss Edgeworth," said Mrs. Coffin, who was a serious woman, "come under the influence of Ralston's Health Foods, and so has my husband. We are making a careful study of physical health and exercise and right thinking. We eat Ralston's Health Foods and a new food called Grape Nuts" ("Grape Nuts! That sounds delicious! " said Topaz) "twice a day. Already complexion is brighter, our whole mental attitude is improved, and I *may* say," she lowered her voice, "that faulty elimination is corrected."
> "Faulty elimination! Well, well! Fancy that! " echoed Aunt Topaz, and wondered "What on earth is she talking about? "
> "I also made an appointment with Mr. Fortes for a swimming lesson and I hope very soon to have mastered the art. This is my third lesson."
> "Never too old to learn! Never too old to learn! " said Topaz merrily but without tact.

Topaz's almost Blakean innocence—a harmony with the environment so complete that no sadness disturbs it, no disruption mars it, no experience is incapable of being absorbed into it all—depends, naturally, on a particular kind of environment surrounding her, and it can best be understood by seeing two passages of the book in conjunction with each other:

> Topaz had at last reached open country. British Columbia stretched before her, exciting her with its mountains, its forests, the Pacific Ocean, the new little frontier town, and all the new people. Here was no time limit, no fortnight's holiday. Here she had come to live; and, drawing long breaths of the opulent air, she began to run about, and dance for joy, exclaiming, all through the open country.
>
> . . . when for purposes of recollection or recapitulation she regarded her past and passing life, it was as a canal that she saw it. This canal had been soundly constructed by her progenitors, and was well administered by those now in charge. The banks of this smooth canal were pleasant, and presented much variety to her, not in scenery, but in people who were seen in passing—to whom Topaz eagerly spoke, nodded, or waved when possible, whatever their station or occupation—and objects, which she pointed out with many lively comments.

What she needs is a curious combination of confinement and freedom—or of freedom to do as she is inclined and freedom from all concern about the world around her. She depends heavily, that is, on the world being ordered and maintained for her, but she cannot survive in a society that observes rules above idiosyncrasies. Thus her departure from her brother John's Europe is a move to harmony. She finds *her* world in turn-of-the-century Vancouver, a frontier town that only a few years previously had been called Gastown and that was quickly disguising itself in propriety. Idiosyncrasy (at that time, at any rate—perhaps as in any Far West town) was a way of life, yet out of individuality was fashioned order.

In the irony created when we see this order in relationship with time lies yet another dimension to the novel. Topaz has an innate respect for the "spirit of History," perhaps prompted by the guides in her life which she accepts as touchstones: her father, Queen Victoria, Mr. Gladstone, and ("in a wishy-washy way") the Liberal Party. The trouble with history is that it does not exist just in the past; it is continually being made, and of this Topaz is ("innocently") unaware. The world her progenitors founded for her was the Victorian one, symbolized at the beginning of the novel by Matthew Arnold and the dinner-table conversation. When old Mr. Edgeworth finally dies, that world is symbolically ended. For Topaz, "Life with her father had promised to be permanent, but the promise was broken." What allows her innocence to continue is her move to the new world and the protection supplied by her sister, Annie Hastings. But even the new world is influenced by time. Topaz's "open country" has "no time limit," but in 1914 the world around her knows that the Victorian sense of order and decorum is over. Time is continually operative within life, but in living their individual lives, people are often unconscious of it. They see only the spectacular event—Rose's becoming a woman goes unnoticed; her having become one therefore seems "sudden." The breakout of World War One and the concomitant end of the Victorian era seem comparably sudden, yet retrospectively they seem equally gradual in their development.

This novel, then, has at its base a kind of symbolic structure; by examining events in individual lives, it interprets a series of historical events that led to the twentieth century being what it is. Time is important to people more than ever in a world that changes quickly—and in a world where spatial distance means less and less as an isolating barrier. Its effect is to make any social order or 'absolute' code of morality that people establish seem a little ironic, for the only constant in such a life is change. Perhaps in time, then, is the only order we can know:

> For our existence which we call civilized becomes increasingly complex; so that 3 P.M. next Wednesday week has an entity and form and prognosis before ever it arrives; and instead of living in polar time and space like free Eskimos, we make prisoners of ourselves by

appointments which we arrange for ourselves for 10 A.M. on Tuesday week and 5 P.M. on Thursday fortnight, and the first two weeks in July, and thus, between us, we murder our peace. The only thing in our changing world that we can now regard as being safe and sure is that next Monday will certainly be Monday, next Tuesday will be Tuesday and nothing else, and that Saturday afternoon will always be Saturday afternoon and for this much stability we should be thankful.

It is not a gloomy view, but it is a serious one, and its undercurrents stir in the depths of the novel, occasionally rising to remind readers that life, with all its frivolity, all its possible harmonies, is a mortal thing, and therefore, for most individuals, a Blakean Experience as well.

The two recurrent metaphors which Ethel Wilson uses to explore her subject both involve oppositions: peace and war, and surface and depth. Topaz's harmony is both peaceful and superficial; the world around her, by contrast, knows war and knows suffering. And so Topaz herself becomes a symbol of a certain kind of life. Those who accept codes of another world or time may find, as Topaz does, contentment, but only if the actual world around them loves them sufficiently to give them the same kind of protection given to children. Her individuality is protected only because she lives in an environment that accepts it; in other words, for all the fact that it is individuals who create an ordered society, it is society that lets the individual survive, and any concept of individual 'freedom' is ironic in its expectations if it does not take this into account.

Though Topaz lives for herself, she cannot even try to live on her own as Ethel Wilson's other characters Hetty Dorval and Maggie Lloyd do; Hetty's amorality removes her from ordinary social codes, and Maggie, when the city does not satisfy her, possesses the skills and the intellectual strength to leave for the hinterland and create for herself the world she needs. Neither of them, however, can isolate herself from the human race; their actions all touch others, and the books reiterate what the epigraph to *Hetty Dorval* borrows from Donne: no man is an island. In *The Innocent Traveller*, Topaz cannot isolate herself either, because she does not have either the wish to do so or the ability to survive should she have tried. In another sense, however, she is more isolated than Hetty Dorval or Maggie Lloyd could ever hope to be, for the fact that she lives a perfectly moral life that is not necessarily out of date but quite certainly out of touch with the present makes her influence upon her world negligible. A society should gain from individuality in its midst, but Ethel Wilson's book makes it quite clear that though Topaz delights, her particular life is, in time, of no importance. Why then write about her? Because her gaiety has value even if it is not useful, because her possibilities are those of Everyman, and because a comprehension of her life tells us something about life in general and about our own.

In the course of her book, Ethel Wilson uses several images to try to capture some of the qualities of Topaz's personality: the "warbling unimportant bird," the "small invisible wind which ran rapidly along the surface of the water and made its presence known by the sudden pretty dimpling and wrinkling of the stream, and by the deflection of some dry leaves whose time had come to fall," and (most characteristic) the waterglider

> which we see in summer running about on the top of pleasant weedfringed pools. Unencumbered by boots or boats they run, seldom wetting their feet and, one supposes, unaware of the dreadful deeps below them, in which other beings more heavily weighted are plunged, and swim or sink, caught in the mud or entangled by the debris of circumstance and human relations; and sometimes these heavier beings encounter acute sorrow or acute joy or dull despair of which the watergliders know nothing.

The world is delightful, innocent, harmonious to Topaz precisely because she does not respond in depth to experience. She travels on, anticipating new scenery, even to the end—

but reacting to it only in her own terms: " 'Quick, get me some fresh lace for me head, someone! I'm going to die, I do declare! ' Evidently she is pleased and confident. What an adventure, to be sure! Away she went." She is, as John Donne says we all are, " 'transported, our dust blowne away with prophane dust, with every wind.' " But her terms are not the world's, and though we delight in Topaz, though we participate in life as she does, we cannot become what she becomes, for though she by and large escapes sorrow, she also evades the extremes of joy, which others, responding sensitively and emotionally to the world, cannot do.

Ethel Wilson's own sensitivity shows in her successful creation of character and her acute and evocative use of language, not just in this book, but in her work as a whole. *The Innocent Traveller,* which is partly autobiographical (Mrs. Wilson is in large part Rose, Topaz's grand-niece) and historically accurate in its depiction of Vancouver, demonstrates this admirably. Just as the image of the waterglider applies to Topaz, however, so can it also apply to some of the book's readers, for, because of its apparent simplicity, it is deceptive. Under its surface lie deeps of emotional impact and intellectual perception which a careful reading will gradually reveal. It is a witty and sensitive book, too—stylistically apt, gently ironic, and quietly humane.

ending
the liberal
pageant

THE STORM
AND AFTER:
MACLENNAN'S
BAROMETER RISING

Hugh MacLennan's first novel, *Barometer Rising* (1941), is important in Canadian fiction for its interpretation of the national character and for the narrative technique which it uses. Its structure is allegorical; the two generations into which the central characters divide, for example, represent the young Canada and the controlling Great Britain; the explosion which figures as a prominent event in the story represents both the First World War and the political severance between Canada and Britain, which historically accompanied it. The novel is also a work that can be read with interest outside Canada, for the conflict that it depicts is ultimately not limited by national boundaries.

The most vivid writing in the whole book is that which concerns the explosion, but ironically this is in a sense an artistic flaw, for it fixes attention on an event that, albeit spectacular, is not organically the climax of the novel. The book is set in Halifax, Nova Scotia, during the winter of 1917. At that time a munitions ship did blow up in the harbour, destroying much of the town, and this was in fact followed by a severe snowstorm which impeded rescue operations. The novel is concerned with the week of these occurrences and with the lives of the characters as they become related, yet the climax to which it builds is not the explosion but the invading storm. Throughout the novel, MacLennan carefully establishes the conditions necessary for a winter storm, but this does not ultimately result in artificial and manipulated scenes. The records of weather assist in the evocation of mood, and the four related strands of imagery—weather, war, diurnal change, and seasonal change (which includes an opposition between desert and garden)—assist both in the delineation of character and in the outline of the conflict to be resolved.

The force of the explosion is such that it suggests not simply a political separation, however, but a revolutionary break. To focus on the explosion would be to emphasize revolution, yet this was neither Canada's experience nor what MacLennan suggests is a valuable course of action. It is not, that is, the pattern of development which the characters themselves in this novel, or the young nation, work out as a resolution to their conflict. The break itself is therefore still preliminary to the activity that will mean success or ruin. The explosion is disastrous but does not totally destroy the city; the snowstorm, by contrast, is ravaging, and its corollary could easily be desolation rather than freedom. What happens at that time is what allows an evolutionary development and what offers a hope for the growth of a valid national consciousness.

The young—perhaps the potential—nation is represented by four characters: Penny Wain, a ship designer whom the war had liberated from outdated and constricting attitudes, her energetic but hotheaded cousin Neil Macrae, their illegitimate daughter Jean, and Penny's brother Roddie. The old order in Canada is the older generation: Penny's father, Geoffrey, whose experiences in war have all been aimed at his personal aggrandizement, and her aunt and uncle, Alfred and Maria. The cast of central characters is completed by a third group, which includes Jim and Mary Fraser and Angus Murray. This exists on the periphery of the main action but, as a reservoir of liberal thought, it must necessarily be present if evolutionary development is to occur. When the novel begins, Neil is presumed killed in the war in Europe, but he has in fact just returned to Halifax to try to clear his name. The mission on which he had disappeared was a stupid one, and of Geoffrey's design, but Geoffrey has transferred the blame for its failure from himself to his nephew. The young man therefore faces court martial if he is discovered, and his isolation, partly self-imposed and partly imposed upon him, prevents him from at once approaching those who could really help him.

Isolation is not his affliction alone. It is also that of the other major figures and of Halifax itself, which, when Neil returns, has been set up as a garrison town. To find an internal harmony is their common problem. The people must come to co-operate with each other; the harbour, which "is the reason for the town's existence," must re-establish a code of marine courtesy when darkness, fog and storm disrupt it. The winter wartime setting at once connects two of the major strands of imagery. The city can defend itself against a naval attack, but when the invasion that takes place is one of weather, the defences are of no use.

A key to the function of the weather imagery is found early in the book when Angus Murray considers

> the way Halifax had of seeming not so much a town as a part of the general landscape; its chameleon-like power of identifying itself with the weather. There were fine days with westerly winds and you could smell the odour of spruce trees . . . . But there were almost as many wet days when Halifax was worse than any town he could remember, when the fog isolated it from the ocean and the forests . . . .

The isolation prevents an appropriate course of action from being either adopted or even clearly perceived, and when Neil wanders aimlessly through his town, he experiences the same problem; the "wind had changed and now it was bringing in the fog." By juxtaposing scenes, MacLennan shows a comparable situation elsewhere; Penny stands at the Shipyards, "watching the evening draw in over the water. It was invading the Stream like a visible and moving body . . . . She stood quite still, alone in her unlighted office." As it moves in on the harbour, it moves in on her, for "this harbour with its queer congeries of the very new and the very old . . . was . . . a part of her life . . . ." Angus recognizes a similar relationship in the Wain House itself: "in its silence he could hear the rhythmic pulsating of the fog signals coming in from the harbour which had given this old house its reason for life." But with change, the order of both the house and the harbour is being challenged.

Order exists in summer and in light, therefore, but at the beginning of *Barometer Rising*, in the early winter of 1917, this light exists essentially only in memory. When Neil returns, for example, Halifax "seemed to have lost all its graciousness, and yet nothing was actually changed. Then he realized that he had been remembering it as it was in the summer with the . . . limes towering their shade over the roofs." The attunement between Penny and Neil that is made explicit later in the novel is even now worked out in the imagery. In her attitude and her occupation, Penny is alone without Neil, and her present war work seems shallow and monotonous when compared with the stability of the past:

> The anaesthetic of hard work could never compensate for the feeling of life and growth that had departed from her; and now, like a man in the desert obsessed by thoughts of green grass and running water, she remembered things as they had been before the war . . . . She recollected the odour of lime trees heavy in the streets on close summer nights when there were shooting stars, and how those evenings as she walked alone it had been possible to imagine an aeon of tranquillity broadening out like a sea under the sky, herself growing old gently, with children about her, the land where she had been born mellowing slowly into maturity.

Both Neil and Penny, then, at the beginning of the novel, are living in the past; what the conflict that forms the story does is force them away from this attitude and into another. Neil's "peculiar tenacity which made him determined to preserve himself for a future which gave no promise of being superior to the past" is paradoxically founded upon his memory of the summertime happiness, and the future is not secure until his present existence is established legally. Even then it is Angus Murray's action rather than his own that secures it. At the end of the novel, however, Penny and Neil are together, and in that moment is a consummation of all past and all future.

Before that time, there is only separation—caused by preconceived attitudes and presumed death, by darkness, by fog, and by temporal distance from summer's growth. When Penny looks out from her father's home, the darkness will not let her see clearly:

> the earth was frozen hard and the flower beds were stiff with frost. It was impossible to see the details of the garden with its stone wall separating it from the street, its great lime trees like buttresses beside the house-walls, its benches and summer-house in the distant corner. The garden was the only part of the property she really loved; to her, the rest of the house was an incubus.

Again the relationship to summer is underlined. In the attack on the incubus, too, is an implication that true love contains the life and the growth which seem to have departed. In this lies the basis for the denouement of the novel.

The garden imagery is extended in two directions in the "Tuesday" section of the novel—one episode concerning Penny, and the other, Neil. Prince's Lodge, the home of Jim and Mary Fraser, is a sort of perpetual garden, one with the stones and the forest from which it was cut, and part of the life of those who dwell there. It is to the Frasers that Penny can turn for a home for Jean, to them that she can look for support and sympathy in her relationships with Neil and Angus. Prince's Lodge becomes, as it were, the resting spot in her desert, for it seems "an oasis of yellow light in the brooding and heavy darkness of the forest." Neil, too, is further involved both with his memory of the summer garden of love and with the present bleak winter: "the strange sense of peace grew as he watched the sun roll over the line of trees by the Wanderers' Grounds and disappear in fire . . . . Even as he stood and watched, the colours were dying, and by the time he had reached Spring Garden Road again it was dark." For Neil as for Penny, darkness threatens the vision, and the knowledge of fullness, which they had found in love in Montreal "at the zenith of the [summer] season" and "in the dawn together" is only a transitory peace when they are apart.

An ironic twist is given to Penny's relationship with Jean during this particular episode at Prince's Lodge:

> Penny was bending over her, beginning the evening tale. "When the winter comes and Jean goes out in the woods, she can't see a thing but the white blanket of snow that covers everything. But underneath the snow there are all sorts of things happening. The rabbits have cities in the ground with tunnels all made like little streets and big holes where they live, warm like you are now, until the spring comes and the snow melts. . . ."
> "Bees and bears, Aunt Penny? "
> "Oh, when the snow falls they just go sound asleep and they never wake up at all, not till after it all melts away."

The peaceful blanket of the tale is soon to come in reality as a blizzard, and sleeping is soon to be a grim euphemism for death—all this unknowingly on Penny's part and therefore ironic in its foreshadowing. Almost immediately, Angus and Penny leave in the night, and a hint is given as to the course that disaster will take: the "forest was hushed on the verge of winter storms." When Penny then turns to Angus upon arrival back in Halifax and says, "Thank you for giving me this afternoon," the ambivalence of image and heartfelt commonplace underlines the portent of difficulties to come.

Penny, of course, is aware that what she tells Jean is superficially unreal, but what she does not recognize is that her own dream of the past—a never-never land of the has-been and the might-have-been—has similar qualities of the fairy-tale about it. In a different way this is the same difficulty that attends the attitudes of Geoffrey, Alfred, and Maria Wain. They apparently live in the present—and even for the future, as the Colonel's plan for a military oligarchy would seem to indicate—but the basis for their thinking belongs to the past. It emanates from nineteenth-century Britain rather than from the land and the time in which they live.

This division is that on which MacLennan builds the emotionally involved didactic passages in the novel. When Neil moves down Spring Garden Road in the darkness, the point has already been made that he has only two choices: complete success, with legal re-establishment, or failure. For him there can be no part-way, and this situation is also worked out in the imagery:

> He wished it were spring. But the trouble was that Canada had no proper spring; that season was always skipped when winter leaped right into summer. One week there would be snow-flurries and then, toward the end of May, it would be blazing summer with the leaves unfurling on the trees . . . .

When he comes, then, to consider the future possible for himself and his nation, he still does so without having established the present securely. Until this is done, any plans for the future, though important, remain to some extent as idyllic and ironic as Penny's fairytale. But the future he envisages is one that contains both darkness and light; it is one where an infinite diversity is still held together by a potent binding force. He becomes eloquent in praise of the country he hopes to see established, but the importance of the passage is fictional rather than political. He contemplates the "railway line, that tenuous thread which bound Canada to both the great oceans and made her a nation, (that) lay with one end in the darkness of Nova Scotia and the other in the flush of a British Columbian noon." The new nation must in some way be able to survive not only in the light, but also in the presence of acknowledged darkness. To complete the fictional pattern in *Barometer Rising*, each of the central characters must also come through his conflict to a new light, or else be destroyed.

There is a structural relationship between Neil's observation of sunset at the Wanderers' Grounds and Murray's visit to Mamie's brothel. Murray's pessimism at this time, however, is in sharp contrast to Neil's awakened enthusiasm, and it serves to illustrate an essential difference between them:

> "What do you think of this country . . . ? Everyone comes and goes around here, eh? So, like the wanderer, the sun gone down, darkness be over me, my rest a stone—that's your Nova Scotian, if you've the eye to see it. Wanderers. Looking all over the continent for a future. But they always come back."

Yet Angus moves away from both irony and his own isola-tion when he involves himself positively in bringing Penny and Neil back together. Neil's isolation, too, must of course also be ended before any unity can be established. He must believe in Penny as she believes in him; he must trust Angus Murray; he must not let preconceived attitudes prevent a concerted effort to establish the truth about his military experience and thereby secure a basis upon which to build a future. Penny recognizes this, but when she invites Murray to talk to him, Neil reacts with anger and distrust. Mac-Lennan's imagery is consistent: " 'Neil,' Penny said, 'please don't stand in your own light.' "

The loneliness of Colonel Wain is another matter. In his self-imposed, anachronistic, colonial attitude to Canada, he does not and will not admit that development is taking place. His own house reflects this refusal; from 1812 to 1917 no-thing had changed; "the Wain fortune had remained station-ary." Yet this occurs at a time when the traditional British dominance is giving way to a growing cosmopolitanism in the Halifax harbour—and, by extension, in the life of the town's younger generation. When Penny recognizes that the harbour "was so much a part of her life," she is watching a

> freighter sliding upstream: a commonplace ship, cer-tainly foreign and probably of Mediterranean origin, manned by heaven knew what conglomeration of Levan-tines, with maybe a Scotsman in the engine-room and a renegade Nova Scotian somewhere in the forecastle. The war had brought so many of these mongrel vessels to

Halifax, they had become a part of the landscape.

The new world is a changing one, and in the lives of Penny, Neil, Angus, and even the modified Aunt Maria, the spirit of change finds, in varying degree, an appropriate environment. Unable to admit the truth of change, however, Geoffrey wants to get away from what he considers colonial and—therefore—second-rate. Yet paradoxically he can also perceive certain values in the Nova Scotian, and despite what he says, he is disturbed when these are slighted. Nova Scotians "faced danger every day in the foggiest and stormiest tract of the entire Atlantic, and apart from the Scandinavians they were almost the only seamen still left under sail." The ability to move unscathed through darkness, fog, and storm is the very quality he himself lacks, and inwardly he had recognized but at once rejected this on the day that his ill-planned military operation failed. That he should be found dead after the explosion in the middle of the night and during a blizzard seems, though a trifle too convenient for a successful novel, a singularly appropriate end.

The blizzard, besides being a matter of recorded historical fact, is a focal point for the novel and is neither anticlimactic nor extraneous to the imagery and the action. MacLennan tabulates the weather for each day,[1] and the climax of the blizzard brings together all four major strands of imagery. The Sunday of the book's opening suggests that weather from the west is more clement than that from the east. The mirage of summer which is observed there, however, is accompanied and modified by the colours of blood and disaster. Both foreshadow the course that the story will take: "Above the horizon rim the remaining light was a turmoil of rose and saffron and pallid green, the colours of blood and flowers and the sheen of sunlight on summer grass . . . . This western land was [Neil's] own country." Fog then sets in for the night. On the Monday the wind, "baffling slightly but cold and northerly," is predominantly from the cold polar high rather than from the south. It is still shifting on the Tuesday, with the marine high taking precedence and the clouds blowing to the east: "The morning was dry and crisp, the ground frozen hard, and white clouds rushed through a glittering sky out to sea." On the Wednesday, air currents begin to rise, and along the front—the war imagery being congruent here with that of the weather—conditions for the low pressure area and the storm are establishing themselves: "A pack of cumulus cloud was building up over the land across the harbour and the wind was hauling toward the south."

When the munitions ship explodes on the Thursday, the weather is still fair, but with the sun comes a strange calm that Mary Fraser thinks "almost like Indian summer." But "Jim looked at the treetops, motionless in the still air, and then he sniffed loudly. 'There's east in that wind.' " Under these conditions the energy of the explosion is released, damaging property, killing and injuring thousands. Its importance here—like that of the war it represents—is that apparent logic is suspended. Back parts of houses blow down when the forces come to the front; those that escape the initial impact of wind damage are injured by debris falling from the sky; stoves which are lighted to protect people from the cold are overturned and ignite destructive fires. But the forces of the explosion are in a long view momentary, soon spent; what demands more attention is the disillusionment that can accompany a post-war period. What requires more time is the process of rehabilitation. Here, for survival of the peace, both logic and love are vital.

It is probably at the allegorical level that *Barometer Rising* would be of most interest outside Canada itself. The political ideas embodied in the work may overlap those of other developing nations, for example, but, more important here, MacLennan has demonstrated a competent use of one fictional technique for expressing them. His work insists not that a new nation be established, but that the establishment of the new nation take into account both the pangs that bring it into existence and the subsequent difficulties of salvage, repair, development, and change. The necessarily heterogeneous group that is the new nation can work in voluntary harmony only for a time; after that, the capacities of each individual must be exercised. In fictional terms, this is worked out during the blizzard when Neil considers his city:

> It occurred to him how solitary an organism Halifax had been . . . . Now in the North End nothing remained but snow and an anonymous death, . . . no lights but an occasional lantern flickering in the darkness. There had been one splendid, full-throated bellow of power: the earth had trembled, houses fallen, fires arisen. There had been a few hours of brave and passionate co-operation of human beings labouring in a single cause; then a mechanical routine; then exhaustion and hunger; then finally the primal solitude of snow . . . obscuring the quick and the dead, . . . of handfuls of men too tired to speak standing mutely in a ruined house . . . .

But if the breakdown of harmony leads to insularity, then the society ceases to be productive. Hence the last part of the novel shows the three major characters moving out of their loneliness into participation in the new order.

Each of them survives the relatively superficial injury he sustains during the explosion. Penny is the most seriously hurt, but the image that is used at this time at once indicates that she will survive: "She was on that old sofa they always set up in the garden in summer and kept in the storeroom in winter." A new order is set up in the Wain household; furniture is changed about, strangers have a freer access to those who live there. But it is only at the time of the snowstorm that Angus accepts his role as doctor again. Only then does Neil realize that he does not desire revenge; only then does he demonstrate his ability to lead. Penny, too, faces at this time the deaths of her father and the Frasers and survives because of her love for Roddie, Neil, and Jean. This development is reflected in the storm imagery itself, for the brilliant sunlight that shone at the time of the explosion soon dulls, and the dullness rapidly develops into snow. The darkness, the desert, the weather, and the war are brought together climactically: "The wind shattered the snow high in the air and when the flakes reached the ground they had the consistency of sand . . . . The snow fell invisibly in the darkest night anyone in Halifax could remember." Invasion has come: "In the dawn the harbour was bleak and steel-coloured, extending into the whitened land like a scimitar with broken edges . . . ."

The implications of the explosion—of the political break—are not realized until it is a *fait accompli*. Only Neil's capacity to lead and Murray's ability to mend and to strengthen allow the new order then to survive. Squalls continue throughout the weekend, but certainty of future success comes late on the Saturday night, when Angus anticipates in dream a coming summer: "He saw green trees under the sun and heard locusts shrilling at high noon and there was no more snow because it was midsummer . . . ." Such an expectation counteracts not only the fact of the storm, but also the reliving in memory of past summers, which had formerly been the sole way to apprehend life. On the Monday night, the weather clears.

MacLennan then goes on to underline once more the idea that has been revealed in the structural patterning of imagery throughout the novel: that in love there is a solution to the separateness of the individual. In 1941, when *Barometer Rising* was published, the author could not end the conflict completely. Penny, for example, "could see nothing clearly ahead. To force one's self on into the darkness to keep one's integrity as one moved—that was all that mattered because this was all there was left." But together, in love, in unity, Neil and Penny can maintain their new world. When, in the garden of Prince's Lodge, Neil looks beyond her "to the patch of moonlight that broke and shivered in the centre of the Basin, and heard in the branches of the forest behind him the slight tremor of a rising wind," the total darkness of the winter night is behind them, the harbour is quiet, the storm past, and the barometer can rise once more.

The images involving weather, war, and the oppositions

between light and dark, summer and winter, and garden and desert are consistently and subtly patterned to support the political level at which the novel can be interpreted. Yet a control over structure is not equivalent to great art, and a perception of a structure is merely an assistance in coming to understand an author's position. Though the imagery here also contributes to a comprehension of the characters, Penny and Neil particularly are not thereby brought fully to life. Though the imagery assists in the evocation of mood, the quality of the prose tends to shift the reader's attention from the climax to the more sensational event which precedes it. In spite of its flaws, however, *Barometer Rising* contains some excellent dramatic narrative; it demonstrates an accomplished incorporation of a political idea and a humanitarian principle into a fictional form, and it retains its importance as a landmark in the development of fictional technique in Canadian literature.

1967

NOTE

1. There is perhaps some need to clarify the nature of the meteorological occurrence that is being described. Much stormy weather in the middle latitudes is associated with areas of low barometric pressure, and much fair weather with areas of high pressure. The Bjerknes theory of polar fronts explains the formation of low pressure areas in the northern hemisphere as the counter clockwise pivoting action that is begun when a cold northern high pressure area meets and interacts with a moist southern high pressure area. The air current action of rising and cooling then causes precipitation, and squalls continue until the front is occluded or dispersed, at which time the barometric pressure rises again and more stable conditions ensue.

THE APPRENTICESHIP
OF DISCOVERY:
RICHLER AND
MACLENNAN

The publication of Mordecai Richler's *The Apprenticeship of Duddy Kravitz* and Hugh MacLennan's *The Watch that Ends the Night* makes 1959 one of the important years for recent Canadian fiction. The two works seem at first to be strangely paired. One is a pungently ironic comedy, the other a serious metaphysical study that verges at times on the sentimental. Richler relies on a sprawling picaresque method, and MacLennan on a muted allegory. Even their flaws are different. The tendency to verboseness that afflicts the end of MacLennan's book is nowhere found in Richler's, but Richler will sacrifice the overall balance of his novel for the sake of big comic set scenes. Fortunately his novel survives because his wit is successful, just as Mac-Lennan's work succeeds because the reader becomes sympathetically involved in the reality which the author has created. Yet for all their differences, the two works have the same basic situation. The discovery and habitation of a new land becomes a metaphor for an attitude of mind, and that attitude is at the forefront of present literary thought.

Richler's novel is concerned with the apprenticeship, the voyage, as it were, that ultimately takes Duddy to a new world and gives him the power to create there a recognizable individuality. His childhood position is analogous to that of Jerome Martell in *The Watch that Ends the Night*. While Jerome has known no father, Duddy at the age of fifteen has been unable to find in his father the qualities he wants to admire, and he invents an extra brother Bradley to satisfy this need. While Jerome has not experienced the ordinary expressions of love from his mother, Duddy has not known his mother and is therefore unsure of ever having experienced that love himself. He "couldn't bring himself to risk" asking about this, a key phrase, considering what he will risk, for his incomprehension either of love or of relationship awaits his discovery of an acceptable self. Like Jerome he has a journey to go through part of life, not only inevitable but necessary.

Exactly where the journey should aim and should end is Duddy's problem. When he was only seven he had been told by his grandfather: "A man without land is nobody. Remember that, Duddel." To find and own land becomes in time, therefore, equated in Duddy's mind with the identity for which he also seeks. But to be a somebody is more than this; to be a somebody is to be adult, not only in the self, but also recognized as being adult by a world to which the self bears some relationship. Maturity does not occur with the discovery of a new world, for this tends not to be a satisfactory end in itself. The dimensions of the new world are greater than the old identity can fill out, and there must be a realistic matching between an individual's potentialities and the place he can occupy. Duddy notes that "South America . . . could no longer be discovered. It had been found." But in re-enacting not only the Canadian but also the twentieth-century conflict, he can find a smaller niche elsewhere.

The humour that pervades the book is not gentle and it serves a quite different purpose from that in, for example, Mitchell's *Who Has Seen the Wind*; there is no necessity here to prevent sentimentality from repelling the reader. Duddy moves through a complicated but essentially extra-human sequence of events which, because incongruous, excites laughter. The laughter is directed at an outsider to the ordinary human predicament whose conflict is yet typical of it, and because he can surmount his difficulties in unorthodox and cumulatively extravagant ways, he wins, like Donleavy's Ginger Man, a sort of admiration without respect, a sufferance without approval, an attraction without sympathy, and an attachment without involved concern. At once more than the conventional society and an inherent element in it, Duddy follows a course of life in order to locate an appropriate pattern for it. Though this is pursued in iconoclastic— but innocent, and therefore laughable—terms, it illustrates a growth to maturity which is fundamentally parallel to the serious situations involving MacLennan's George Stewart. The changes that take place in Duddy prepare him for the discovery of Lac St. Pierre, and the discovery is an essential step in his growing up.

Duddy is a comer; he pushes his way to success not by having any idea of a reasonable means to do this, but rather by not having any idea and so using every means as though it were a reasonable one. The losses he incurs in a crooked roulette game stem from his naïveté, and they recall his earlier loss of a much smaller capital invested in a stock of obscene comic books. His earlier reaction had been to burn the stock for fear of being caught with it; the reaction at Ste. Agathe is to run away; yet both are childish in a way that Duddy cannot be if he is to emerge from his apprenticeship in his own terms. The novel has its limited success because the reader will let Duddy have those terms; they reverse standard values, but they become values in themselves.

Because he is a comic figure, a sort of latter-day *picaron* seeking ruthlessly and ultimately successfully for social promotion, Richler must not cultivate for him the reader's pity. If there were a total identification between the reader and the central character, the comic effect would be destroyed, for it is the sense of apartness, of differentiation between the character perceived and the concept the reader has of himself, that is part of the ironic comedy. Duddy, that is, must remain innocent even in success, even though he moves through his failures to a triumph that he does not fully comprehend. The identity that he finally achieves, successful in spite of its disregard for social convention, is both typical of the society he has been scorning and yet beyond it. The 'maturity' he reaches by the end of his apprenticeship is a recognition of a place in relation to society that will probably through time generate social acceptance as well; at that time, perhaps, reader and character could move closer together, but not until. His solution is distinct, then, from that found within a social code by George Stewart, though it is related to the individual one formulated by Jerome Martell.

Duddy's childishness concerning the comics and the roulette must be avoided not because it is socially irresponsible but because it does not contribute to the self for which he aims. Because he has been reared in the St. Urbain Street world of Montreal, a sort of Jewish enclave of low average income, he has been brought up to expect defensive protection as necessary. Several choices are open to him as routes to success: immersion in the Gentile world with concomitant loss of identity, continuation of the St. Urbain Street world of his childhood, participation in the establishment of the new Jewish state of Israel, or the achievement of an independence that will let him be himself in any situation. An attempt to achieve independence, however, makes Duddy uneasy and suspicious because he is insecure. The very defences that protect against any envelopment by the 'alien' culture preserve the St. Urbain Street childhood identity as well. Duddy's brother Lennie removes those defences in his contact with the Westmount Gentiles, but that society only consumes him. He thinks he finds there a freedom that his own deliberate childhood existence did not supply: "They're just themselves and glad of it. Nothing scares them . . . . *They're young.*" But Duddy voices the truth later when he says: "It's hard to be a gentleman—a Jew, I mean—it's hard to be. Period."

To achieve independence in the Gentile world, Duddy assumes he needs money. When he was a child, the identity he had wanted was bound up with his appraisal of Jerry

Dingleman, the Boy Wonder, the Mr. Big of a narcotics underworld. "Duddy wanted to be a somebody. Another Boy Wonder maybe. Not a loser, certainly." But the Boy Wonder is exactly that, a *boy* wonder, because in spite of his power in a localized area and in spite of his wealth, he does not achieve recognition by the Westmount world. Before Duddy recognizes that the Wonder is "only famous on St. Urbain Street," he is used, unaware, to smuggle heroin. Dingleman says of him: "The boy is innocent. He's perfect." The innocence that Dingleman sees in Duddy is a naiveté perfect for being exploited. Because the boy seeks to masquerade in an imagined sophistication, he will avoid questioning what he does not understand when questioning would be the very act that would bring him real knowledge. To come out of apprenticeship, Duddy needs not only to discover truth in the world in which he wants to live but also to know what to do with truth. Dingleman can be defeated not by confronting him with fact (which he has known and disregarded all along) but only by an independence that can afford to disregard him. Duddy's various schemes for achieving the wealth to purchase Lac St. Pierre give him a measure of the experience he needs to be independent of Dingleman; what he needs also, in the way of position, achieved through a recognition by self and by others, he has yet to find out.

Duddy must both extend trust and be extended trust before he can achieve recognizable adult status. For this to be part of any development in him in Richler's comic terms as well, it must be his extension of trust that brings him knowledge of the nature of this relationship but the extension of trust to him that in fact brings with it the success that is maturity and mastery. Duddy's grandfather, Simcha, is an adult of the old order; he merits trust in his neighbourhood and is given it, and it is a measure of his position. But for Duddy the estimation of that world is insufficient, and though one of his plans in securing Lac St. Pierre is to please his grandfather, this must ultimately give way to the more basic need to fulfill himself. He cannot live in Simcha's world; no more can Simcha live in his. The final recognition of their separate identities is prefigured when early in the novel Abramovitch says to his father: "this is modern times."

When Duddy trusts others, his comic naïveté takes him into situations that more experienced persons would avoid, but it is simply because he is naive that he can emerge unscathed, though more knowing, developing cunning in the process. He lets Dingleman use him for smuggling heroin, for example; he unknowingly lets Peter John Friar make *avant garde* films of a *bar mitzvah* ceremony for him; he purchases Lac St. Pierre in Yvette's name, saying, "A friend is a friend. You've got to trust somebody...." But it is in his central and significant relationship with his brother that the difference between intelligent trust and foolhardiness crystallizes for him, that he learns he must make a choice of enemies. Lennie had tried to become part of Westmount society and in so doing was gulled into foolhardy action; he is a promising medical student, and yet he jeopardizes his career by performing—and botching—an illegal abortion, and then running away childishly, to hide from the act. Duddy, however, can not only diagnose the cause but also prescribe the cure: "Don't you know better than to go bareback? " If mature life is a healthy self-possession, then the life lived prior to maturity must be based on self-protection. When Duddy then takes Lennie's problem from him and solves it, earning Lennie's trust, he has achieved part of the relationship that will ultimately give him his final position. Lennie finds his own identity by breaking with Westmount and participating in the building of Israel, by taking his doctor's capacity for healing to a new world that he can inhabit; but Duddy's place remains in the Gentile world. He is therefore different from Cohen, who says: "We're two of a kind, you know. . . . A plague on all the *goyim*, that's my motto." He is different because, for Duddy, this is not a satisfactory guide; he cannot choose to align himself on religious terms. When his film of Bernie Cohen's *bar mitzvah* shows "the pregnant moment, the meeting of time past and time present, when the priest and his initiate reach the *ho'mat*," and shows it, in a hilariously funny scene, by techniques of symbolism and montage, the orthodox apprenticeship to position within the religion is contrasted with Duddy's unorthodox but vigorous apprenticeship to an identity all his own.

Though the story is related in terms of a Jewish boy's rise to adult status, its implications go beyond the strictly racial-religious extension. Duddy's Uncle Benjy is wrong when his estimation of the boy begins and ends here: "Because you're a *pusherke*. A little Jew-boy on the make." What Duddy comes to and in fact must come to if his apprenticeship to life is to be successful is *a* self rather than *the* self. He cannot accept an order that is established for him by race or religion or duty or family, and when Benjy leaves him a letter—which Duddy must be ready to read, somewhat like Nick Adams or Ike McCaslin having to be ready to fish or hunt—the warning it contains to the boy must even yet undergo seachange within him before he can become a man: "You've got to love [the family], Duddel . . . A boy can be two, three, four potential people, but a man is only one. He murders the others." The relationship of family love is only valid for him up to a point. Inheritance of family ties—in individual or even in political terms, for the 'ghetto', for Montreal, and for the Canadian society of the story—must not interfere with the establishment of individual identity. Lennie and Riva find their "God's Little Acre" in Israel, but though this satisfies them, it cannot become *ergo* a necessary reason for Duddy's embracing the same solution. His own little acre lies at Lac St. Pierre, neither in Israel nor in St. Urbain Street, and love that enmeshes him elsewhere than in that self deprives him of his full potentialities and ends by being no love.

He has to become a Somebody, and for this to occur, the demanding love that had attempted to form the child's identity must be exchanged for a trust in the identity that the adult forms for himself. Lennie has to trust Duddy in the matter of the abortion; Max has to trust him with a thousand dollar loan; Benjy has to show his trust by willing Duddy his house. Duddy's particular personality causes a change when the comic reversal of intent takes place; not only does he avoid all other selves in his master of one, but he also turns to his own development the trusts that are placed in him by others. The abortion affair leads to his business ventures with Hugh Calder of Westmount, for example; the house that Benjy leaves him, tied up as it is by legal limitations so that Duddy can only own the legacy and not profit in his own cash terms by it, he empties of its furniture in order to raise money anyway and invest it in the acquisition of his own land. What Yvette will not willingly give him is the opportunity ultimately to be adult; she wants a cessation of imaginative investment and practical energy which is objectified in her care for the paralytic Virgil. Whereas Duddy finds himself by expending, Virgil remains fearful and in need of protection by trying to save intact a bequest that has been left to him. When Duddy sacrifices that tradition to his own effort, he brings the traditional world—albeit weak and by now impotent: Simcha, Dingleman, Virgil—into opposition against him. But when he is recognized as the Owner of the new world, his apprenticeship of discovery is over. He is given a trust that makes him at last the Somebody he wants to be ("That's all right, sir. We'll mark it.") adult, individual, and master in his own terms in his own land.

Success is therefore possible in Richler's fictional world, though his ironic eye builds it only out of breaking traditions. This seems at first to be so partial as to deny adequate scope to the novel, and in Richler's other works this is essentially true. The acrimony of *The Incomparable Atuk*, for example, makes that work merely repellent instead of provocative. *A Choice of Enemies* and *Son of a Smaller Hero* offer only fragmentary views of society, and hence the reader never quite believes in their reality. But the world of Duddy Kravitz is whole, and Duddy himself, while not particularly likeable, is very much alive. He wins readers to his side, moreover, because his reaction to traditions is a positive one. His iconoclasm is of value not for itself, but because it is a route towards inhabiting a new world and fulfilling a social individuality. As he is a comic figure, his apparently destructive tendencies can paradoxically be a means for constructing life, but the fictional tone and technique are necessarily different for depicting this than they are for showing a comparable process of discovery in *The Watch that Ends the Night*. MacLennan's study is of the crossing of political and metaphysical frontiers and it ends in peace, whereas Richler's novel, of a different kind, ends in a comic triumph. That both might be empty victories was a view that hindsight would support; in 1959, they seemed the culmination of a tense but strangely expectant decade.

By the end of Richler's *The Apprenticeship of Duddy Kravitz*, Duddy has come to own an individual property; he has located a new land that he has yet to inhabit. Though the novel implies that Duddy is both highly individual within society and yet highly typical of it, the concept is made by no means as explicit as it is in Hugh MacLennan's *The Watch that Ends the Night*. Each man here must be exactly that: each man. The separation of individuality is basic to both these works. For MacLennan, however, each man in fulfilling himself as an individual becomes Everyman as well, which is a tenable position only as long as the fundamental separation is acknowledged and accepted. Inevitably this moves into metaphysical spheres, and that the conflict should be resolvable here in a profound and moving peace is an indication both of the health that the author sees to be an achievable end, and of the human and humane balance possible for the individual even though conflict and illness persist. Part of the contrast between the peace discovered in this book and the iconoclastic volatility in *The Apprenticeship of Duddy Kravitz* can be related to the age of the authors in 1959, the year both books were published. Richler was twenty-eight, MacLennan was fifty-two. That they should vary in their approach is an indication of markedly different back-grounds; that they should be concerned with such similar questions, however, is an indication of the attitudes and in-terests that by this time had become the focus of the twen-tieth century. Both of the two men who are central to Mac-Lennan's work, Jerome Martell and George Stewart, must make voyages of discovery, and, when they have found their new lands, they must continually modify themselves in order to shape an appropriate life and order for their place and time. The book equates the mature life with creative separa-tion, and it differentiates this from defeatist resignation, from aimlessness, and from apathy.

The Watch that Ends the Night is a large and complex book, by no means flawless, which is, nevertheless, one of the finest accomplishments in recent English-Canadian fic-tion. One of the flaws is paradoxically one of the great strengths of the book—a set piece concerning the boyhood and the first voyage of Jerome Martell that is superlatively written in itself and yet seems insufficiently subordinated to the whole work. It is, however, thematically and structurally related to the concerns of the novel and serves as a key to an understanding of the development that takes place. Jerome is the fatherless son of a loose-moralled cook in a New Brunswick lumber camp. When he flees this environ-ment, his action is typical of that which people in search of a new land undergo, for the search itself begins in escape. Yet in escaping, Jerome is moving from the scene of his mother's murder to a life elsewhere, and his motive is there-fore distinct from that of the killer, whose aim in flight is merely to avoid the responsibility that the murder has placed upon him. In escaping, too, Jerome becomes aware of a new life that is almost like resurrection; it comes when all the skills which he has developed in boyhood are brought into a concerted effort to achieve an end beyond that boyhood. But the new innocence is not yet an end, for it does not make use of Jerome's full potentialities.

Jerome serves as a sort of catalytic agent in the novel, for the characters with whom he comes into contact are allowed to mature because of their relationship with him, and yet he, too, changes through time. His initial journey down river becomes a microcosm for the development in both of the major characters in the novel. Immaturity precedes the change, for Jerome's first canoe is boy-sized and he is not allowed into the main current which would sweep him irrevocably away. But here there is no father to give him a name, and he must ultimately move. The 'entire world' seems to open up as he heads towards Moncton, but when he is found there and adopted by Giles Martell, his world is still childish and prepared for him. No matter how well he fits it, he cannot merely inherit it if another part of his nature remains in conflict with it. The two pictures that are hung on his bedroom wall in Martell's Halifax home foreshadow further change, therefore; one is Reynolds' "*Age of Innocence* and the other was a sailing ship in a storm." The contained metaphor indicates that Halifax is only a temporary harbour in the quest for a larger new world.

The Martells' world is one of faith, an acceptance of accepted religion, and it satisfies Jerome only until the First World War. Religion then seemed to sanction hate, and when guilt after participating in the war only forces him to seem hypocritical to himself, such a religion as a guide for life is no longer valid. That innocence is comfort for an older order—exemplified here by the people and towns of the Canadian Maritimes—an order that has grown "old without ever growing up." His own child life is like part of a nameless and half-asleep New Brunswick town. Jerome says: " 'Kids who looked like me were a part of the landscape.' " When Giles Martell then says to the boy he has just adopted, " 'You'll be proud of Halifax, for it's a fine town, a fine place to grow up in and—well, even for a grown man it's not too bad a place,' " he merely underlines the content he feels in his life and which he offers the boy. The war changes Halifax, however, a phenomenon that MacLennan was concerned with in his earlier novel, *Barometer Rising*, and unless the old order adapts to the change, it has nothing to offer the new generation. The innocence that has been known before is disrupted; for the young people, therefore, the old identity no longer serves, and out of the world they then enter, intending to inhabit, they must fashion a new self. Jerome is hollow after the war—placeless and Godless—and hope lies only in finding a self that will relate him both to infinity and to mortality.

The voyage that George Stewart takes to find God and self, from childhood to full maturity, is the major development of the novel. Because his background is different from Jerome's, he is not forced as early into feeling a need to escape. Born into an old order, he has an identity ready-made, waiting for him merely to inhabit it. But like the Halifax establishment, this, too, is only a boyhood in which his age of change will not allow him to remain. The summer he meets Catherine, for example, is the time of his first attempt to move in a pattern distinct from the established one. Childhood "is a garden," but they are both from then on outside it. Both belong to the "English-speaking garrison of Montreal . . . in the heart of the French island in North America," but neither of them fit it. They must leave if they are to come to terms with the island of self in the midst of an apparently foreign world. Their 'Fern Hill' of childhood, as it were, and the 'dappled green' of youth, must be exchanged for a world that lies, as it does for Steinbeck's Adam Trask, east of Eden. Together and alone, they are apart from the old order of innocence that instinctively knew its God. Catherine has said to George: " 'Grow up and go,' " but he has not yet the ability to withstand tradition. Unlike Duddy Kravitz with Yvette, he cannot bring himself to love Catherine physically and thereby discover a new world. The 'frontier' of knowing that love is related to death awaits his crossing, and in his overlong adolescence his role as a news interpreter is ironic when he has no recognizable identity himself. By the implications of allegory, George is Canada, but he is not limited to this; MacLennan's control over his method here—as opposed to its control over him in such bad novels as *Two Solitudes* or *The Precipice*—gives the work a much greater scope than a rigid one-to-one correspondence would allow.

Like Duddy Kravitz, George and Jerome must grow around the restrictions imposed by a past culture. As Duddy also has to strive against his social income level, so George and Jerome must fight the world-wide depression of the thirties. Each of them is at once part of this phenomenon and yet not typical of it; attitudes of the time become theirs, yet this is only a transient stage in the development of their selves. It is during this period that George and "millions of other young men" undergo the change that came to Jerome during the First World War: "I lost my faith in religion; I lost my faith in myself; I lost my faith in the integrity of human society." The initial change, however, must take place not in the social system, but in the self. Jerome's support of schemes of social union is merely a charade of life. He is trying to escape his guilty self, and when he heads to the Spanish Civil War as a doctor, he is trying to expiate his participation in the earlier one. But it is also part of the encounter with death that is apparently necessary for his coming-of-age. His daughter Sally cannot appreciate his action, for it has not been necessary for her, and later she says to George:

> ". . . he really fitted in and symbolized that whole awful period. Those appalling adolescent he-men like Hemingway and all those naive idealists thinking they were so terrific because they went to bed with each other to prove the capitalist system stank."

To a large extent, it is only after The Depression is over that George and Jerome can grow up completely.

During this period, they and their generation had reacted in varying degrees inwardly upon themselves even when they seemed most to move outwards into the world. Knowing themselves to be alone and empty, they sought love desperately and futilely. Hence Catherine ultimately says to George: " 'Love can be such a terrible torment. . . . People

break loose into sex because it's so direct and simple.' "
Like politics, it is an escape. When a minor character, Norah
Blackwell, invites George to join the Communist Party—
" 'stop running away. Become one of us! ' "—she unknowingly invites him only to further flight. Immersion of the
self in a political system becomes a sort of suicide, an
attempt to substitute a theoretical responsibility for others
for an actual responsibility for self. Because Jerome can never
be fully absorbed into political activity, he must ultimately
face himself and either accept his identity or find a means of
destruction. "The canoe in which he had issued from the
forest had now taken him out into the ocean . . . with a
hurricane rising. Jerome, Myself, Everyone." Only years later
when George must go through a comparable discovery is the
problem formulated rationally. When a child has grown to
middle age, he writes, the father's role of approval is left
vacant. In the thirties, "we tried to make gods out of political
systems, and worship and serve them"; like logic, ability,
success, wife and children, they do not abide, and then
"comes the Great Fear." Such thoughts relate both to individual development and to social history during the twentieth
century, and they read like a commentary upon *Lord of the
Flies*.

For George, Catherine and Jerome are the parent-substi-
tutes and the escape from the self:

> I have never seemed mature to myself. The young seem
> more so because they know nothing of the 1930's. The
> young have the necessary self-confidence and ignorance
> to feel mature, and that is why I like them so much bet-
> ter than I like my own generation. Was there ever a
> crowd like ours? . . . Was there ever a generation which
> yearned to belong, so unsuccessfully, to something
> larger than themselves?

George is behind both Catherine and Jerome in his development; his adolescence is prolonged beyond the time when
both the others have perceived their relationship to a reality
they find unpleasant, and yet have chosen to accept. George's

teaching job is an attempt to regress to the stable world that existed before change: "Nothing in this world is so permanent as a school. . . . Forty years on is today when you return." Even Catherine is attracted by such a view: " 'It would have been so much simpler and safer to have kept the old rules.' " But to avoid progressive change is like suicide, and when George accepts his move, he begins "to grow up. The depression was over at last so far as I was concerned, and I came out of its deep freeze . . . ." His marriage to Catherine when Jerome is presumed dead, however, is not yet a facet of maturity. A necessary reappraisal of his position in relation to others he only gets from his next contact with Jerome.

Jerome is a doctor, and it is allegorically suitable that it should be through contact with him that George should find the health that is maturity. The muted allegorical implications that run beneath the story are specifically Canadian, and it is not surprising that the concept of the Frozen North should enter into the imagery of the book. The imagery is patterned, not random, and it contributes to a comprehension of the concept of identity. The winter imagery is connected with youth and innocence, and the snow of a northern land is a sort of primeval and almost archetypal childhood that any person encountering twentieth-century life has long since left behind. The passing of this former time must be admitted, just as George must accept that the winter world of his own childhood has gone. George is a product of old Montreal as well as of the depression, and it is the old order of the city that appears as a child-like world, a child's dream society, the embryo of a utopia never realized. This must give way before adult health can be achieved.

Even after the depression is over, the old order still attracts George. The cold air "had come down from the germless, sinless land," and George enjoys it. Torn by the desire to retain the memories of his youth, by a feeling that it would be better to forget and merely live in the present, and by an apparent inability to forget, he is faced at this time with

Jerome's return. In disruption he realizes that his happiness with Catherine is only a temporary new world, and his insight takes him into another discovery. Even his city becomes the potentially threatening environment, and he writes:

> I kept staring at that ocean of light that was Montreal. Then fear came back to me. . . .

> Then a man discovers in dismay that what he believed to be his identity is no more than a tiny canoe at the mercy of an ocean . . . Little man, what now?

To show an empty man where fullness lies becomes Jerome's task as friend and as doctor. His medicine aims not, like Richler's Virgil, to preserve life, but rather to help people to look at life more as Duddy Kravitz does and "to get the most out of what life they have."

Through the course of the novel, Catherine is slowly dying, and as George recognizes his relationship to her he feels that he is dying as well. Jerome too, exists in him, but Jerome has been as it were resurrected from the dead. In reconciling these identities George comes to find that death is a part of life just as decay is a part of new growth or as mortality is a part of immortality. Jerome had once said: " 'The only immortality is mankind.' " When he comes back and ministers to George, he extends the idea. Full acceptance of the self involves acceptance of both the infinitude and the edges of self; to be equal to individual fate is to be equal to the knowledge that the limits of individuality are the limits of fullest meaning and yet that because the patterns of identity are common to all, individuals can know love. In the self lies the potentiality of combating the forces of negation. As George can at last write: "I say again that this mysterious thing which creates, destroys and recreates, is the sole force which equals the merciless fate binding a human being to his mortality." In conversation with George, Jerome brings him to an acceptance of the self that can be vital, the self that through passion comes to know both creation and destruction and can, because of this, face time and yet live. Tragedy is wrought to its uttermost only when the individual accepts that he is living his own death. If he thinks of his life "as done," then there is nothing left to fear. He can be aware of a relationship with men without this being an escapist union; he can know the continuity of self in all mankind in spite of mortality and the end of fear because of the knowledge of immortality. He can then emerge from isolation with a sufficient separateness. Any struggle necessitates endurance, but endurance alone will not satisfy human dignity, will not be a vital mode of existence, until the struggle appears worthwhile. George says: "All of us is Everyman and this is intolerable unless each of us can also be I." When the struggle moves within, the capacity to endure becomes the ability to face time knowledgeably and to achieve peace thereby, forever.

For Richler's Duddy Kravitz, the discovery of a new land and an individual tradition is not specifically related to a Canadian search for identity. For MacLennan's George Stewart it is. But it is more than this; it is struggle of men anywhere, beyond the boundaries of politics but not beyond the boundaries of time. In a land that changes in an age of change, the search for identity, for the distinctiveness of self, becomes a search for an emerging maturity, and the converse quickly becomes true as well. Such a poem as Earle Birney's "Case History" is based upon the concept of Canada being an adolescent land, the child of a loveless wedlock, struggling for maturity in an unstable home. What MacLennan does with the theme is to take it beyond the regional borders, to apply it to the universal question of man experiencing change in the twentieth century. His solution is not to accept the traditional source of stability; nor does he sanction flight into union with another. Maturity lies in the ability to remain one self, yet know the self at the same time to be not less than the whole world. Change that happens to the self, therefore, is not merely part of a greater change but in fact is that greater change, and mature man is both self and all.

George's childhood had been that of a winter city, but

as change takes place in the century, so it takes place in the city itself. In spite of the old controls exercised over it, it is turning "into a real world city." Only this will make it mature. No longer controlled from outside its own rules, no longer hiding from the world behind the isolating mask of an identity only as a land of snow, the land can reveal what makes it individual and what makes it vital. The rules that the city knows itself, that govern its intricacy and have kept it alive, that give it cohesiveness in spite of the variegation within, that make it one and yet many at the same time, can at last be accepted as a feature of life germane to itself and necessary to its own continuance. Like man discovering he is Everyman, the city and the society discover that their comfortable security is taken from them and that they are still apprenticing. The masks of tradition or even of isolationism had seemed to satisfy a need, but they were only artificial gods in a time of change. Then comes potential dissolution, the great fear, and George writes: "in the last two years of the 1940's . . . the whole world went over a frontier . . . . In the bleak years we at least were not alone. . . . The bell which only a few years ago had tolled for all, now tolled for each family in its prosperous solitude." Obviously the apprehension of rules by a society of individuals is an ideal, yet it is an ideal within the capabilities of man to achieve. Though the mosaic pattern may not be any more difficult to create effectively than a monochrome perceived in isolation, and though it is subject to much greater chance of disintegration, it is a more pleasing art form.

What remains in man to combat the potential disruption is the will to live, and to love life is to love in the face of time and in the knowledge of separateness. Though every man lives in his solitude, in his individual identity, two solitudes can (to use, as MacLennan does, a quotation from Rilke) protect, touch, and greet each other. In this, love consists. The solitudes must remain, but because man knows himself to be Everyman as well, he can approach another not as supplicant to god but as lover and friend. Knowing immortality in mortality, George can accept death because he can accept his own life, and he can write of Catherine at the end: "What if the ocean of time overwhelmed her? It overwhelms us all." The boy in the canoe has at last grown up and can inhabit his last new world.

The apprenticeship of discovery is a recurrent theme in recent fiction, and though Richler's comic treatment of it in *The Apprenticeship of Duddy Kravitz* differs in many respects from MacLennan's use of it in *The Watch that Ends the Night*, the two novels can still be fruitfully compared. MacLennan's work lacks the vivacity of the other, but it aims for and achieves an entirely different tonal effect. It has been criticized for being autobiographical, yet, if so, it goes far beyond this to create an independent world of its own. George Stewart has been called pedestrian, but he makes a believable narrator. The author has been called old-fashioned, but his ideas and his allegorical technique are abreast of fictional trends elsewhere in the world. One must admit that the ending of the book is weak. Catherine's turn to painting is a sentimental cliché, and a tendency to wordiness accompanies MacLennan's difficulty in voicing the paradox of which he has become aware. Yet the novel is successful partly because that paradox has meaning. The author has at last blended a control over technique not only with the reality of credible characters but also with a pattern of thought that gives substance and dimension to his book. Its people and ideas refer both to Canada and to the twentieth-century world, and its scope will let it therefore be as readable and as involving outside Canadian national boundaries as it is within. For both MacLennan and Richler, the mastery to which the apprenticeship leads necessitates a recognition of the self both by the individual and by others. Where MacLennan's book goes beyond that of Richler is in the equally emphatic insistence on the recognition by the self of its identity as Everyman. This does not deny the other self, the I, for John Donne's concept of man as a piece of the continent is no longer applicable. For MacLennan, man remains an island forever, but an island in position, as it were, as a part of an archipelago; the experience of the one is the experience of all, and each part functions both as an entirety for all and as an entirety in itself. It is here that he reflects contemporary thought and shows himself at last to be a novelist of substantial merit.

1966

WINTER AND
THE NIGHT–PEOPLE:
*RETURN OF
THE SPHINX*

The first sixty pages of *Return of the Sphinx* are among the worst that Hugh MacLennan has written. A blunt statement: but a book like this one, which contends even in fiction with the thorniest political problem in Canada today, is bound to arouse blunt statements. It is not paradoxical, I hope, to add that this is in many ways MacLennan's most important novel too, which makes the faults in it seem larger than under other circumstances they would. The novel emerges not only out of his earlier works and relates to them by both theme and imagery; it also demonstrates a distinct advancement. What before had been nebulous and sometimes even noncommittal in the resolution to his works has here been extended into a tragic vision— for Canada, for the characters, and for the world.

Ambitious? Yes. Worthwhile? Indeed, yes. But successful only on occasion. Briefly, the novel concerns the conflict that assails Alan Ainslie, federal Minister of Culture in a cabinet that seems to have both Diefenbaker and Pearson figures in it (a situation ripe with fictional promise in its own right, but by the way). His French-Canadian wife has been killed by a truck overturning in a freak accident; his daughter, Chantal, is in love with his best friend, an emigrant Frenchman near his own age named Gabriel Fleury; and his son, Daniel, tortured by a Jansenist schooling and by awakening sexual urges, torn between respect for his gentle father and antagonism towards all things and all people not French-Canadian and of another generation, is becoming more and more involved in the Separatist cause. For Alan the problem is only partly a political one; much more so is it emotional—at a national level, where his commitment to the cause of Confederation is both deep and honest, and at a personal level, where his memory of past happiness with his wife is so strong that he has really lost contact with the world that is growing up, here and now, around him. The two are obviously symbolically related. Alan's tragedy is that he does not recognize what is happening until it is too late, until events have taken place that divide him irrevocably from his position in government and effectively from his children. His world, at the end of the novel, is different from the one he has seen at the beginning, although in the background there still broods a hint of the ideal world which Alan has been conscious of and which MacLennan himself has been concerned with throughout all of his fiction.

We have met these characters before in MacLennan's work. Chantal, idealistic, young and therefore confident, at once sophisticated and naïve, intelligent, capable, and determined, has under different guise appeared as Penny Wain in *Barometer Rising* and Sally Martell in *The Watch that Ends the Night*. She performs much the same function here—the representative of the realization of young love—but she is less of a stick figure than the other two and so more satisfactory as a character. Daniel has developed out of Marius Tallard, the young rebel and Oedipally-motivated father-hater in *Two Solitudes*, but again he is more rounded and more credible. Whereas Marius had been shallowly drawn, a shadow figure defeated as much by his own character as by the System he was reacting against, Daniel is by contrast brimful with talent and possibilities. Tragic again is his commitment to an increasingly narrowing cause, for the mistakes he makes in judgement cease to be the excusable sins of youth when they affect the life of the nation itself.

Alan Ainslie is, of course, quite literally the boy Alan (MacNeil) Ainslie from *Each Man's Son*, now grown up—trying, as so many MacLennan characters do, to forget his origins (wandering father, murdered mother), and attempting by this means to attach himself and his family to a kind of order it has never really been his to know. We have seen this in Neil Macrae in *Barometer Rising*, in Jerome Martell, and even to some extent in Paul Tallard. In all the earlier books MacLennan has implied that the order is achievable, that the characters have conquered the major obstacles in the way of their happiness. But in fact there is always another note present as well, which, in imagery involving winter and darkness, hint of isolation and of further conflict yet to come. Neil and Penny, for example, are reunited by the end of *Barometer Rising*, and the Canadian nation of the present has severed itself successfully from the nineteenth-century control of Great Britain. But the language is not altogether joyful: "They paused on the narrow snow-banked platform and watched the lights of the coaches disappear around the next curve and heard the dying echoes of the whistle reverberating through the forest." Similarly, *Two Solitudes* ends with Paul Tallard and Heather Methuen together, with autumn golden, and yet things are not really stable: "Only in the far north on the tundra was the usual process of life abruptly fractured"; the nation is going into war, "knowing against her will that she was not unique but like all the others, alone with history, with science, with the future." *Each Man's Son*, moreover, ends with Ainslie adopting Alan MacNeil—which closes a novel largely about ignorance and single-mindedness, but also intimates the beginning of another phase of human conflict: Ainslie "had no sense of the distance he had walked or what time of night it was. He stood in the darkness outside his own house for a long while, hearing the sound of the broken water in the brook." And *The Watch that Ends the Night*, which closes at the end of a summer with George Stewart discovering a kind of metaphysical peace, ends also with his knowing the world about him as a shadow, knowing politics as an unreal thing in that world, and knowing light only insofar as his life is now illuminated from within himself. *Return of the Sphinx* picks up these darker threads of MacLennan's thought, in a study of the breakup of the order of a single man's family and a parallel disruption of society at large. No answers exist—only the sphinx—and this novel, too, closes with "the long snows" approaching.

The extension of character into political affairs, by a kind of modified allegory, is also a feature of all of MacLennan's books—most demonstrably forced in *Two Solitudes* and *The Precipice*, where the one-to-one correspondence between character and political entity is so defined as to make any proffered solutions seem facile. The allegory is most competently handled where it seems effortless, where the technique becomes an integral part of the message. *Barometer Rising,* for example, is brilliantly structured, yet the reader is conscious less of the form than of the reality of the novel's focal situation; and *The Watch that Ends the Night* succeeds because the political allegory is implicit in the imagery rather than explicitly enunciated by the central characters. *Return of the Sphinx* wavers a little between these two groups, but ultimately, because of its overt commitment, it most closely approximates *The Precipice*, except that large parts of it are better written.

MacLennan uses here some of the same image patterns he has used before, and handles them well. Night, winter, flowers are all important strands in exploring the conflict. The story takes place in Eastern Canada as a hot, humid summer is settling down on Montreal. It is the ripe time for riots in North America. The oppressive climate and oppressive situations (real or imagined) seem to come together then, and if causes exist in the mind of a people, they can manifest themselves in forceful, concerted, mass, and therefore often dangerous and violent ways. Some emotionally sensitive individuals, like Daniel Ainslie, will be used by the power structure that orders any political demonstration, and if this turns to riot, they are consumed. Others, like Alan, will be so committed to a given ideal that they may be overwhelmed by the moment. Still others, like Gabriel Fleury, are taken out of their personal isolation during a time like this; if they discover the real meaning of love, they survive. This last situation is figured early in the novel when we are told that Gabriel "was not a good golfer—he preferred winter to summer on account of the skiing, at which he was very good— but it was the only summer game he knew and physical exercise was the one permanent security in his life." The problem is the same one presented to George Stewart in *The Watch that Ends the Night.* He has to discover that the winter snows—symbolic of an innocence that this country perhaps once knew—are no longer the only identity to be met with. He has to learn the games of summer, in effect, so that in any season he can survive, but in doing so he will learn the facts of heat and discord as well. So with Alan, whose happiness (Constance, the children, a lake and a cottage and summer when "the daisies were like snow in the high Gaspesian meadows") lies in the past; and so with Daniel as well (whose blinding focus on the present is jolted when he discovers not only the identity of his Cape Breton grandfather—the Nova Scotia/French combination in the place name a probably unintentional added irony here—but also how alike they are).

This tension between past and present is given further development in the overtly political passages in the book, but first we must see that Gabriel's character is extended by the imagery of night and flowers. His name, for one thing, and his recurrent association with nicotianas ("they're night flowers and I'm only here at night") are a constant reminder of the possibility of flourishing and of being at peace with one's environment. His union with the younger generation, in his love for Chantal Ainslie, is a happy one for them both, and the last time we see them, though the summer is ending and the country's innocence is gone, the flowers "of late summer were in bud." For Daniel and Alan the contact between generations is more difficult, and when the book ends with winter coming on and with Alan outside the city contemplating the landscape, thinking "The vast land. Too vast even for fools to ruin all of it," we can see that symbolically the ideals of Confederation, co-operation, and stability are still held as possibilities within man's reach. But for Alan it seems more like an insistent belief in the mask than an acceptance of the night and the heat that influence the human landscape.

Daniel, like Chantal, also has the opportunity to respond to both the city and the land, and as his first sexual encounter is with a woman from the older generation, the parallel with his sister is strengthened. Chantal is learning from Gabriel as well as giving to him, however. Daniel is affected rather less by Marielle's wisdom than she is carried away by his impulsive desire for satisfaction and revenge. The 'revenge' is against many things—his Jesuit schooling, his conscience, his father, his mother's death, *les anglais*, the American influence in his society and among young people, and so on. MacLennan's extension of the image patterns into the political sphere becomes obvious in Daniel's reaction to his city:

> It's fantastic, the truth you can see in this city at night. You can go for miles without seeing a single *Anglais*. They know no more about this city than the English knew about India. When I learn more about television techniques I want a program about this city after dark. About *la nation* after dark. The camera spying. The camera working as if it had a mind of its own. The camera just telling me what to do with it. The people speaking in broken sentences. That's where the truth is, in broken sentences. Their expressions when you catch them with the truth on their faces. The people are smoldering. There's not enough room for them any more. They live in the city like a huge African kraal with the forests all around them. The lights on the snow in the streets, the dirty snow in the streets . . . .

In the city, in Montreal, the mask of innocence that the land has heard before itself no longer exists, but it is not a world of sophistication which by and large has replaced it. Gabriel Fleury is sophisticated, is part of the night, and he survives, but in the world Daniel recognizes only negation exists: surrender to material pleasure, decadence, bombing (ironically for the sake of a culture), and rioting simply for the sake of being divisive. Even this is a way of living to which he wants to attach himself, but he cannot. For all his activities, he remains the spectator-television interviewer, trying to escape himself and discovering only another kind of incarceration.

The political problem of *canadien* separatism is of course a particularly grave one in Canada at this time. MacLennan is right to feel that this can be the focus of a work of fiction, but when he writes a work of this kind he is creating something that seems less readily apprehensible by the Canadian imagination than by the American or English one. All those works in Canadian literature that apparently emphasize sociological phenomena, for example—*The Loved and the Lost, The Master of the Mill, Scratch One Dreamer, The Man from Glengarry*—are all much more obviously studies in the psychology of an individual conscience. Such a categorization is less obvious, I think, in works by C.P. Snow or Robert Penn Warren, and the disposition of American writers towards political criticism is what perhaps lies behind Edmund Wilson's approval of Hugh MacLennan's *The Precipice* and the novels of Morley Callaghan. In these works something of man-the-Canadian-political-animal comes closest to the surface. But *Return of the Sphinx*, political as it is, captures only some of the character of either the country or the separatist question.

Canadians seem, in other words, to be much more addicted to the onlooker-interviewer role than most are willing to admit. Daniel and Alan Ainslie are our men, that is, just as George Stewart was in *The Watch that Ends the Night*—no matter how stuffy, thwarted, or unaware any of them might appear. MacLennan is right to set up this kind of character, right to interpret much about the nation this way, and curiously wrong when for some reason he locates a different kind of character in the West. He suggests that Westerners are delighted with Quebec's threatened withdrawal from the nation, for that event would give them a wealthy independence themselves, and he is wrong. Westerners, plain and simply, are the onlookers again, goaded in this decade into calling a plague on both houses, which they locate specifically in Toronto and Montreal, whose perennial opposition is now more than just high school rivalry. It is a continuation of an historic clash of cultures, which MacLennan himself implies in his book, but never makes clear, and it is this local antagonism, misunderstood by both locales, who both erroneously consider themselves representative of half the nation, that has been grotesquely magnified into an almost insoluble problem.

Like Daniel and Alan Ainslie, each side is magnificently sure of the other side's position. In this lies inevitable tragedy, for it demonstrates a previous foreclosure on both imagination and understanding. When Daniel thinks: "Endlessly the French Canadians talked of their deprived past and what did that do except weaken their purpose to make the future theirs? ", both he and MacLennan have seized on a major truth underlying the whole situation. The parallel United Empire Loyalist-Upper Canada syndrome that afflicts some English Canadians, valuing some invalid sense of historic superiority, also prevents some people from preparing adequately for the future. Together these underline the fact that not only is the conflict in the present emerging out of the past, it is also very much of the past, still based on attitudes that most of the nation's people—from whatever cultural source (many young Westerners, for example, do not regard themselves as being *English* Canadian particularly)—do not here and now share. Daniel's immaturity is shown in that he does not trust his perception of truth; instead, he goes along with the riots and the bombs, which solve nothing. Alan's generation is by and large no better, for its members, violent in their own way, talk and talk, and again solve nothing.

It is interesting, at this point, to place the political argument of this book beside that in Peter Weiss's absurdist and terrifying play *Marat/Sade*. Part of the dialogue is apropos:

Sade: Nature herself would watch unmoved / if we destroyed the entire human race / I hate Nature / this passionless spectator this unbreakable ice-berg-face / that can bear everything / this goads us to greater and greater acts / Haven't we always beaten down those weaker than ourselves / . . . . /

Marat: what you call the indifference of Nature / is your own lack of compassion / . . . . /

Sade: no small emotions please / Your feelings were never petty / For you just as for me / only the most extreme actions matter /

Marat: If I am extreme I am not extreme in the same way as you / Against Nature's silence I use action / In the vast indifference I invent a meaning / I don't watch unmoved I intervene / and say that this and this are wrong / and I work to alter them and improve them / The important thing / is to pull yourself up by your own hair / to turn yourself inside out / and see the whole world with fresh eyes
(I, 12)

One of the many fascinating things about this play is that its technique of depicting plays within plays forces us all into roles both as spectators and actors: all implicated in whatever guilts, animal motives, insanities and oppressions may be represented. Towards the end, Roux, the fettered radical, is still shouting out "When will you learn to see / When will you learn to take sides" as pandemonium engulfs him. What we do see above all else is the extent to which both Marat and Sade intellectualize humanity, and therefore, though opposites, how much they are alike. The other opposites— freedom / confinement; sanity / madness—also come in a sense to be indistinguishable, for one cannot identify which is which. But we are actors as well as spectators in such a play, and so if we respond at all these are truths for our own lives as well.

MacLennan's novel bears, it seems to me, enough likeness to Weiss's theme to make this digression reasonable. In Alan and Daniel, and in the views of Canada which they represent, we have just such intellectualization coming into conflict. In the demonstrations Daniel plans, and the resultant riots which destroy Alan as a political figure, are just such unidentifiable motives as those of the revolution and the madmen of Charenton. Liberty? But the Québécois have liberties under federal law now that would be lost to them if they secede. Equality? Fraternity? Yet as both Hugh MacLennan and Peter Weiss show, these motives are not necessarily distinguishable from the desire to exercise power.

The difference between the two writers is partly in technique, partly in the fact that Weiss does not draw a moral; his effect lies in his presentation and in the extent to which that alone can cause us to pull ourselves up by our own hair and see the world with fresh eyes. MacLennan, on the other hand, guides the reader to a point of view rather more deliberately, and the sadness of this is that the novel would have been more powerful had the characters and the images been capable of doing it on their own. For all the novel's political importance and for all the clarity with which the author views some political situations, no novel can absolutely succeed unless the characters come to life. With *Return of the Sphinx* we are up against a problem that has plagued MacLennan throughout his work: much of the dialogue is stilted, therefore lifeless, and the characters, who in other situations can be perfectly credible, will occasionally die. Regrettably, at those times, the novel dies with them. MacLennan can write magnificent monologues; of this there is no question, but so much of the dialogue is simply punctuated monologue that it becomes incredible. Where it is good, the formal language is inherently part of the situation being presented. Some of the arguments between Alan and Daniel, for example, and the passages of House of Commons debate are handled well. But where the conversations should be informal, even if they are not exactly relaxed, the language remains repetitive and starched:

"He's wasting his life."
"Can you be so sure he is? "
"Oh yes, I can be sure."

This sort of thing is so constructed as to be artificial, too formalized to seem natural, and it occurs so often that one's attention shifts from the heart of the book to its method. It is a frustrating novel, because it promises so much and wavers so much too. For MacLennan scholars it will be a key work, one which shows not only his descriptive abilities but also his consciousness of the tragic possibilities in modern life. For many more readers its topic will make it an interesting enough narrative to warrant reading. But for very few, unfortunately, in spite of its potential, will it be the impetus for seeing the world with eyes that have been made fresh.

1968

THE
DISAPPOINTED
DECADE

When *Canadian Literature* first began in 1959, Canada was happily experiencing a traumatic publishing season. All at once appeared an impressive collection of books: Richler's *The Apprenticeship of Duddy Kravitz*, MacLennan's *The Watch that Ends the Night*, Sheila Watson's *The Double Hook*, John Buell's *The Pyx*, Callaghan's *Collected Stories*, and others. They came at the end of a curious decade, one that for all its wars had been basically hopeful, enjoying affluence while its people remembered the Depression, and emphasizing the need for at least the appearance of security at a time when World War II could not yet be spoken of with objective dispassion. But 1959 began a decade too, a rather less satisfied one, certainly less overtly stable, and these books contain within them a hint of the disappointments that writers in the sixties were to worry over and respond to.

Some indication of this changing attitude can be seen in the direction taken by Richler and MacLennan alone. Whereas *The Watch that Ends the Night* had ended in a metaphysical peace, with the promise that Montreal's winter identity would be subsumed in its international role, MacLennan's later novel *Return of the Sphinx* (1967) denies that peace. Seething with political disruption, it discovers a winter not of discontent so much as of a humourless determination to protest. Like Ronald Hambleton (to use the title of *his* 1959 novel), MacLennan has insisted in the past that "every man is an island"—a canoe, on the ocean, with a storm rising. By individually accepting this, his earlier characters, George Stewart, Catherine, and Jerome Martell, could survive the threat of disintegration. They could accept their *selves*, in effect, and "living their own death," let others live theirs. But the characters of *Return of the Sphinx*—Alan and Daniel Ainslie—so much more bound by a preconceived notion of a world order, so much less capable of understanding any other, cannot communicate. Failing, they locate the fault outside themselves: the one, defensive, finding threat in 'winter' rebellion; the other, rebellious, and in his own way equally narrow-minded, trying to announce the 'winter' as the only truth.

Richler's *The Apprenticeship of Duddy Kravitz* similarly closes on a 'dark' possibility, though the ironic treatment makes it seem less foreboding. Duddy, a triumph both because and in spite of himself, threatens to become an extraordinary kind of conservative when he buys land and so acquires a bourgeois position in the eyes of society. It's hardly what he expected, but the irony is a nice touch at the end of his comic progress. The implications are more astringent, however. What happens when rebels, achieving power, turn into inverted conservatives? What can the mild conservative do when he starts to look like a dangerous liberal? Richler's comic gifts turn these possibilities into high camp in the interrupted scenarios that make up *Cocksure* (1968), but again in this later work the characters lose their identity rather than find it. They live lives designed for them by Madison Avenue and the movies so much that real emergencies cannot break their stance; humanity disappears along with naïveté, and only the brittle would-be sophisticates remain. In another context entirely, Northrop Frye notes: "A provincial society will produce a phenomenon like the tea party described in F.R. Scott's well-known satire, 'The Canadian Authors Meet'. A metropolitan society would turn the tea party into a cocktail party, and the conversation would be louder, faster, more knowing, and cleverer at rationalizing its pretentiousness and egotism." It doesn't mean it will be more worthwhile, and it nicely describes *Cocksure*.

Frye also points out in *The Modern Century* what is a favourite Blakean theme with him: "The child's vision is far behind us. The world we are in is the world of the tiger, and that world was never created or seen to be good. It is the subhuman world of nature, a world of law and of power but not of intelligence or design." This sensibility, with all its attendant frustration, is what characterizes the writing of the sixties. A few works do escape, often through irony, into happiness—Mitchell's *The Kite* (1962), Elliott's *The Kissing Man* (1962), Moore's *The Luck of Ginger Coffey* (1960), St. Pierre's *Breaking Smith's Quarter Horse* (1966). But often a 'peace' that is discovered at the end of a book is possible only after denying a way of life that had been apparently peaceful. Rudy Wiebe's *Peace Shall Destroy Many* (1962) is an obvious example. Set in a prairie Mennonite community, it explores the nature of repression: in young people who are coming to sexual maturity, and in a society that by attempting to deny violence actually breeds it. Yves Thériault's *Agaguk* (tr. 1963) is comparable: the title character, if he is to find contentment, must leave his band and relinquish to his wife part of the traditionally male prerogative of making family decisions. David Walker's *Where the High Winds Blow* (1960), Jane Rule's *The Desert of the Heart* (1964), Brian Moore's *The Emperor of Ice-Cream* (1966), Margaret Laurence's *A Jest of God* (1966), and Robert Hunter's *Erebus* (1968) supply further examples; all five of them, showing crises of conscience that lead to violence or disruption, also suggest a hesitant and uncertain but basically positive future.

In the popular formula books, too (written with varying degrees of imagination and skill), where one might expect saccharine solutions, we find an accompanying kind of muted terror. This perhaps has always been true, from Gothic novels to detective fiction, so it is not surprising to find it in Arthur Hailey's *In High Places* (1961), Charles Israel's *The Hostages* (1966), or in other works by these prolific writers. Though too often the terror can itself become a stance, a stylization exploited for its sensationalism or indulged for its commercial value, it will sometimes be more than this. It will pervade a whole work, as in James Clavell's *King Rat* (1962), and not so much characterize its tone, or be in conflict with even a comic tone, as it will underlie the situations and provide the sensibility by which we understand them. A Victorian example of all this would be Edward Lear's "The Jumblies," which for all its comic surface presents us with a frightening world. The decade of the 1960's is not so far from the Victorians as it has often liked to think, and its conflicts involving identity, order, chaos, religion and science have their roots in an earlier time.

The works of Marie-Claire Blais, one of the best of the new writers of the decade, illustrate this exploration of the 'psychology' of the present day. *Mad Shadows* (tr. 1960), *Tête-Blanche* (tr. 1961), and *A Season in the Life of Emmanuel* (tr. 1966), all present 'abnormal' families wending their way as quickly as possible towards decadence. But as writers around the world in the previous decade had shown—*The Aunt's Story* (1948), *Catch-22* (1955), etc.—'madness' in a mad world that fancies itself sane comes to be a kind of sanity. Leonard Cohen's now famous lyric "Suzanne takes you down" is a perfect extension of this. Cohen, George Bowering *(Mirror on the Floor*, 1967), and Gwendolyn MacEwen *(Julian the Magician*, 1963) have all been concerned with developing new techniques for Canadian fiction, and with breaking down not only the barriers between poetry and prose but also those between the sensual and the spiritual. It is one of the things "Suzanne" is about, and one that the madness/holiness/innocence/guilt complex tries to evoke.

Political protest is a different kind of extension of this same problem of chaos, and (also characteristic of the 1960's) we see the psychology of it examined in Robert Kroetsch's *The Words of My Roaring* (1966), and David Lewis Stein's fine first novel *Scratch One Dreamer* (1967). We see the political encounter between youth and age, Quebec and *les anglais*, raised vividly in MacLennan's *Return of the Sphinx* (1967), but extended into violence more frequently in French-Canadian works, as in Hubert Aquin's *Prochain Episode* (tr. 1967), Jacques Godbout's *Knife on the Table* (tr. 1968), or Gratien Gélinas's play, *Yesterday the Children Were Dancing* (tr. 1967). Fortunately there are more and more French-Canadian works being quickly and artistically translated into English, which may not serve the cause of bilingualism, but does give aid to understanding, so there is at least some interim value. And if the translations are themselves artistic, the more reason to appreciate their existence.

Also translated have been works which inform the literature with a political background: Jean le Moyne's *Convergences* (tr. 1966), or Jean-Paul Desbiens's *The Impertinences of Frère Untel* (tr. 1965), which should give English-speaking writers a new perspective towards their land. The venture into political spheres is interesting in Canadian fiction, unusual enough to be noteworthy and noteworthy enough for Edmund Wilson to pick up and even overstress in his *O Canada* (1965), for the political books still work as psychological studies. To ignore this aspect of the recurrent examinations of self, in emphasizing the political, is to ignore what has by now become the typical Canadian mode. The number of works one could list in illustration is not endless, but so long as to be bibliographic rather than discursive. Writers like Peter Taylor, Diane Giguère, George Ryga, Margaret Laurence (in a beautiful 1964 novel, *The Stone Angel*, recreating in retrospect the life of an old woman during her dying days as she strives for a freedom she has never quite realized she has), and Henry Kreisel (with his second novel, *The Betrayal*, 1964) all have come into print. And all are concerned not just with broadly political relationships, but with the individual reasons for them, which is something different.

Freedom has been a key word in the fiction of the decade, a freedom variously defined in political terms, or as freedom from the material minutiae of modern life, or as freedom to act as an individual, or as freedom from the self and the sense perceptions that limit its understanding. How individual a person can be in an age of causes and moral imperatives is exactly the point taken up by so many of the partly political books, like *Scratch One Dreamer*; the hero, here, would prefer to avoid committing himself to anything, but he finds himself drawn into action until he finally chooses to act. Whether or not this is freedom is another question. As Alden Nowlan writes:

> In those days, the vanquished
> surrendered their swords like gentlemen,
> the victors alone
> surrendered their illusions.
> The easiest thing to do for a cause
> is to die for it . . . .

And in Nigel Foxell's *Carnival* (1968), with its German setting, we find just such a choice examined. By choosing to leave the country rather than fight a duel that could only strengthen other people's positions, Walter Phalts gains a kind of personal liberty at the expense of a possibly ephemeral fame. That he still looks like a loser is natural in a world like the one Foxell shows us, but what it *feels like*—from inside Walter Phalts, for example—is what more and more writers have tried to express.

In the process, subjects for fictional examination have widened, particularly with censorship retreating into the background, and expression has become freer; characters do and say things that earlier writers might have known but not written about, heard but not said. The result, as one might expect, is a mélange of licence and art, and the licence is as much an impingement on freedom as it is freedom itself. But readers retain the choice of which books to read, so ultimately we are better off. This does not defend all recent Canadian novels, for many, despite their vivid details, are rude rather than revealing; they exploit rather than attempt to understand. If Stephen Vizinczey's *In Praise of Older Women* (1965) begins delightfully comically, it ends up a sort of

"Rake's Digress", repetitive and in the long run boring. And Harold Horwood's *Tomorrow Will be Sunday* (1966) or Scott Symons' *Place d'Armes* (1967), the one embarrassed, disguising itself in sympathy, and the other militant, displaying the narrator's wilful self-degradation, both encourage not understanding so much as a commercially successful snigger.

Leonard Cohen's *Beautiful Losers* (1966), on the other hand, is a different quality of book entirely. It is written well and it has something to say—all too rare a combination, but welcome when it appears. The narrator, trapped in a triangular affair involving his wife and their male lover, is both satisfied and desolated by his relationships and is anything but free because of them. Constantly losing himself and being made beautiful by his experiences, and constantly recognizing and losing respect for himself, he is torn in opposing directions, seeking at last in metaphysics for an answer to his dilemma. But in seeking a spiritual communion with Catherine Tekakwitha, a 17th Century Iroquois saint, he discovers not the peace that MacLennan's characters could find in metaphysics in *The Watch that Ends the Night*, but brutal sensuality and the kind of accompanying doubt of saintliness, the suspicion of pride, that one finds in an earlier work like Callaghan's *The Loved and The Lost* (1951). Réjean Ducharme's brilliant *The Swallower Swallowed* (tr. 1968), raises a comparable dilemma. The young girl narrator, caught in Arab crossfire in Israel at the end of the book, deliberately sacrifices her companion in order to preserve herself. Is this sense or cowardice? Is amorality possible? The questions stand unresolved. People at large, not aware of the 'facts', consider Bernice a heroine, and she complacently accepts the tribute. It was "what they needed," she adds, and if the sentiment smacks of condescension, it is also honest. Honesty has become callous, and the underlying bitterness shows through. It isn't disillusionment particularly; it's just disappointment, made acrid by a kind of anarchy when love itself seems insular and values dead. When Austin Clarke, in his third novel *The Meeting Point* (1967), examines the prejudice and violence that face West Indian immigrants in Toronto, we are still not far from this feeling. After its wry comedy the book turns 'sour', and the central character, Bernice Leach, becomes less angry than hollow. She ends up listening to "talking and talking"—to words—which are meaningless beside her knowledge of injustice and her more and more futile ache for understanding.

There is no immediate or easy exit from problems like these, no peace untainted by a kind of corruption, no beauty undisturbed by the very existence of the self, which at once allows an individual identity and limits what it can do. Like Cohen's poems in *Flowers for Hitler* (1964), Clarke's novel and Ducharme's speak to their generation of commitment and emptiness. The ironies are dark, the humour is brittle, and any affirmations are a little wistful in an uncertain world.

1969

developing
the textures
of language

SIX
CANADIAN
POETS

Thirty is a precarious age in North America—the terminus beyond which youth is advised by advertisers and other youth not to trust. So it serves as a handy clue to the predicament of Canadian poets who now find themselves beyond thirty and no longer rebels with the fashionable cause. In a poem in a recent issue of *Poetry Australia* (No. 24), for example, George Bowering—once the acknowledged leader of the 'Tish' group (including Frank Davey, Fred Wah, and others), preaching the Black Mountain Gospel—forsakes Robert Duncan to find a world for himself. Having announced that Duncan's "community" wants control and bright packages, and that a man should be able to "cook for himself," Bowering adds:

> Not that I wouldnt
> get tired
> of my own cooking
> I just need to
> reaffirm my ability
> to survive

But his books—*Points on the Grid* (1964) and *Baseball* (1967)—have not really established him as a major poet, however important he has become as a critical theorist.

In fact among poets of about Bowering's age, it is those who have been least associated with groups—Leonard Cohen, Daryl Hine, Peggy Atwood, John Newlove, and Alden Nowlan—who are now emerging as the most accomplished young writers. Hine is possibly the least approachable, Cohen the most popular, with the other three enjoying stages of critical success in between.

Hine's first poetry volumes—*Five Poems* (1954), *The Carnal and the Crane* (1957), *The Devil's Picture Book* (1961)—give some indication of the direction he was to take. The last stanza of "A Bewilderment at the Entrance of the Fat Boy into Eden" shows the ironic distance between body and mind, carnal and crane:

> A little word. Unconsciousness is all.
> But all our wisdom is unwillingness.
> We cannot blink the lightning of the wit,
> Or sink the ego's fragile paper boat.
> We think too much. Our selves are ponderous.
> Only the fat boy bounces like a ball
> The law set rolling into the lawless park:
> Contemptible, unintroduced to art.
> His demon is our muse, when, after dark,
> Each must choose a mask and play a part . . . .

The measured tone of the language mocks, in effect, the private 'bewilderment', for the artist's problem is not so easy to solve. A facility with words might deceive the world, but not the self, or not for long. "In Praise of Music in Time of Pestilence" makes this even clearer: "In the hospital of the particular thing / eternal principles sicken and expire, / and under the deceitful lure of skin / rebellious angels play with fire." The moment becomes increasingly important to him, as his subsequent volumes *The Wooden Horse* (1965) and *Minutes* (1968) demonstrate. Other identities will not serve him, even through his studies in the Classics; "Patroclus Putting on the Armour of Achilles" is a clumsy man, unreal to foes and gods, for he finds "only the chill of evening . . . / Like an arrow piercing where the armour fails to join."

People must therefore face reality as themselves—Canadian isolation expressing itself as usual in terms of individual viewpoints rather than communal ones—which is fine as long as we know what is real. "The Wave" complicates the issue. An 'unexceptional' moment's perception will teach us about the moment, nothing else, but is that enough to say anything about it? "What could I say of an event where nothing happened save . . . ? " And though "Point Grey" affirms plaintively that "A beauty of sorts is nearly always within reach," it is 'of sorts' and there only for the moment. So the poet's 'solution' is an admission of a paradox—the discovery of reality through a failure to find it: "I wear for my variety of reasons / The uniform disguise of a time and place / As much mine as anyone's." Patroclus' armour is transformed *into* the recognition of the moment, and into the recognition that the moment's perception is as much a mask, an inhibition of reality, as any *alter ego*. So we are not so far from George Bowering's home cooking as it might seem.

Nor do we change direction much when we look at the work of Alden Nowlan—who, like Cohen, Hine and Bowering, has published prose as well as poetry for some time, and like Atwood, has won the Governor General's poetry award. Nowlan's award came for the recent *Bread, Wine and Salt* (1967), which followed on five earlier, slimmer volumes, *The Rose and the Puritan* (1958), *A Darkness in the Earth, Wind in a Rocky Country* (1960), *Under the Ice* (1961), and a 1962 book from Contact Press, its title emphasizing the perception that Hine has so much difficulty with: *The Things Which Are.* Ironically, 'realities', real 'things', often only are 'things' to the extent that the mind structures them: "Your body's a small word with many meanings. / Love. If. Yes. But. Death." So language comes to be truth and untruth, and the poems strive to get beyond it to the realities embodied in fairytale and dream—to forces such as sexuality and power, the 'Bluebeard-ness' of people in their everyday acts.

In *Bread, Wine and Salt* the poet looks again at the ordinary citizens of small New Brunswick towns, whose perfectly ordinary but not always pleasant actions are the stuff of poetry. Violence, hatred, prejudice, pride—all can be looked at, if not with objectivity at least with dispassion. And the poet, seeing this, finds a curious kind of escape in his poetry:

"every god has departed / disguised as a babe, perhaps, / into the dark continent: / rum is the only Africa / a man can carry —the portent is repeated / over and over, this escape into a strange country." "Sleeping Out" adds another—even almost mythic—dimension to this process: "where there is no / defence against / the night, / I am no longer / afraid of / the dark." And "July 15," in asking "How long have I lain here," answers enigmatically:

> Well, it is still summer. But is it the same
> summer I came?
> I must remember
> not to ask myself questions.
> I am naked. Trees sing. The grass walks.
> Nothing is happening.

As in a poem by Leonard Cohen, "nothing happening" is itself a just cause for love, however, which may in turn raise a whole new set of difficult realities and ironies, but should still not be denigrated or turned from.

Margaret Atwood's ironies tend to be bitterer than Nowlan's, and more distancing. Even in a poem like "God Sour the Milk of the Knacking Wench," Nowlan can come off as a gentleman suffering an inflammatory bout of dyspepsia, but in Miss Atwood's two books, *The Circle Game* (1966) and *The Animals in That Country* (1968), the world, being human, is a dark and disappointing place. "On the streets / love / these days / is a matter for / either scavengers / (turning death to life) or / (turning life / to death) for / predators . . . ." Kisses become "caustic remarks," and for people in igloos "ice" is "the only thing / between us and disaster." "That country" becomes the world we know, vaguely disparaged by the distancing demonstrative *that*, and the "animals" in it are men. "The trappers" illustrates:

> The trappers, trapped
> between the steel jaws of their answerless
> dilemma, their location,
> follow, stop, stare down
> at dead eyes
>   caught in fur

. . . . .

I can understand

the guilt they feel because
they are not animals

the guilt they feel
because they are

There is no humour here, for the violent world prevents it.
But violence apparently always exists and is therefore ines-
capable. When in "The reincarnation of Captain Cook" all
exploration is over, the captain still has a vision of an "innocent" land:

> I could
> never arrive. Always
> the names got there before.
>
> Now I am old I know my
> mistake was my acknowledging
> of maps
>
> Burn down
> the atlases, I shout
> to the park benches; and go
>
> . . . . .
>
> into a new land cleaned of geographies,
> its beach gleaming with arrows.

The arrows, presumably, could be directional, but (weapons
as well) they imply that man finds direction only in violence.
Humour, like love, is seen more as an escape from this recognition than a means of accepting it, so tension inevitably
mounts and doom seems more and more likely. The poet's
stance is that of observer, presentation manager, rather than
visionary and legislator, but another part of herself walks in
"that country" too. She becomes the observed then, an event
to be recorded as much as any other, and the observed events
in passing become the only credible realities (however brief)
in an apparently fateful and unstable world.

Equally grave, and equally quiet in observing the human scene is John Newlove, whose characters find it impossible to contemplate the future and difficult to accept whole-heartedly the erratic present. "The Hitchhiker," in his most recent book *Black Night Window* (1968), can go out into the cold wind

> through the country
> to no end, only
>
> to turn again at one sea
> to begin it again,
>
> feeling safe with strangers
> in a moving car.

Elsewhere is uncertainty;

> it is imperfection
> the eyes see, it is
> impreciseness they deserve,
>
> but they desire so much more,
> what they desire, what they hope,
> what they invent,
>
> is perfection, organizing
> all things as they may not be,
> it is what they strive for
>
> unwillingly, against themselves,
> to see a perfect order, ordained
> reason—
>
> and what they strive against
> while they wish it, what they want
> to see, closed, is what
> they want, and will not be.

His earlier volumes *Grave Sirs, Elephants Mothers and others* (1963), *Moving in Alone* (1965), and *What They Say* (1967) explored comparable ideas, but a poem like "The Grass is a Reasonable Colour," ironically placing the "sane" man's individual order beside the "madman's world" (each of them painted with "reasonable" colours), celebrates individual man's possibilities, no matter how dull his present. So the last poem in *Black Night Window*, "The Pride," expressing the plight of the American Indian, shows with power the continuing source of vitality in people. As a poem is complete, whole, unfragmented, so are the Indians not composed solely of "the romantic stories / about them, or of the stories / they tell only" but also of the force of their ancestors moving still within them, prepared to emerge "unyielding," to make them whole, when the moment comes:

> in our desires, our desires,
> mirages, mirrors, that are theirs, hard-
> riding desires, and they
> become our true forbears, moulded
> by the same wind or rain,
> and in this land we
> are their people, come
> back to life

In Leonard Cohen's work, too, 'life' is a possibility, as his four books of poems reveal. *Let Us Compare Mythologies* (1956), *The Spice-Box of Earth* (1961), *Flowers for Hitler* (1964), and *Parasites of Heaven* (1966) indicate even by their titles something of the change in direction he has taken. A little disillusioned after the first lyrical expressions of love, he still finds love to be worthwhile. It changes character, however, partly because the world can be ugly. What is permanently real is not the ugliness for him, but the possibility of an individual redemption. "Another Night with Telescope" forces us to face the recurring problem we have, attracted by vision and decimated by inadequacies:

> I know the stars
> are wild as dust
> and wait for no man's discipline
> but as they wheel
> from sky to sky they rake
> our lives with pins of light

So that we become in truth 'parasites of heaven', forced to

recognize the insufficiency of the physical world and the need for freedom from it. The way to freedom becomes a metaphysical one. "Suzanne takes you down," Cohen's famous 'folksong' (now recorded by various singers), explores this, seeking ways of uniting body and spirit. Suzanne and Jesus both take the reader/listener near the water:

> And you want to travel with him,
> you want to travel blind
> and you think maybe you'll trust him
> because he touched your perfect body
> with his mind.

So all imperfect bodies can with love be transfigured—but to what? The danger of emptiness still awaits. If 'perfection' becomes a mask, a word—and 'saintliness' (as in Cohen's novel *Beautiful Losers*) simply a guise of pride—then all is lost, but if it is not sought after then there is no beauty either, and so the involvement of people with people becomes necessary. Without it is not objectivity, but sterility; not reality, but partial blindness.

To inspire this *immediacy* of involvement, the poet has striven to make poetry an 'oral art' again, as have Bowering and Newlove and others. Records of Canadian poets reading their works are becoming increasingly available; some writers, like Bill Bissett, have even striven to discover poetry in *sound* rather than *word*, and to sing, chant, or even intone syllables. This is a logical extension out of concrete poetry, it may even be a personal discovery of transcendental meaning and a new frontier; certainly in redefining the nature of the poetic experience it leaves the 'reality' of *language* completely behind. But even those poets who still work with words cannot particularly be called 'traditionalists'. Their poetic forms vary, ranging from ballad stanza to Black Mountain 'rime-thought', and their ideas emerge directly from their involvement in the here and now.

Their poetry would have had more difficulty coming into print, of course, had an environment in Canada sympathetic to these ideas not been fostered by older poets. But Earle

Birney, Raymond Souster, Irving Layton, Dorothy Livesay, Margaret Avison, and Phyllis Webb are all still producing fine works, still developing as poets in their own right, responding also now to the new writing and the poetic vitality it has allowed. And the half dozen writers briefly examined here, having established their names, are in turn creating a fertile environment for still younger poets—writers with the promise of bp nichol, Michael Ondaatje, André Scheinman—some of whom have already produced first volumes, others having appeared only in the little magazines that have flourished astoundingly in Canada and elsewhere in recent years. From little presses like Contact, Delta, and Fiddlehead came the poetic experiments that led to writers of the quality of those discussed here. From the newer ones—like Coach House, Talon, and the House of Anansi—are coming the newest poets, with glimpses of what to them and hopefully to many readers will be a fresh way of locating the world.

1969

A FICTION
CHRONICLE,
PART I:
ART AND
POLITICS

Charles Israel's *The Hostages* should
prove (justifiably) to be popular in paperback, but it so depends on topicality for its effect that it is likely to prove
ephemeral as well. Easily readable, suspenseful, and giving
the impression at once of absolute values and relative standards, it has all the virtues of the fairytale, the thriller, and
the adult western. The fairytale emerges in a kind of Hansel-
and-Gretel story of Innocent Children discovering Fear but
prepared to attack Evil. The accoutrements of the Western
include a good-but-tired hero and a bad-but-sincere villain,
who, here, encounter each other when the children are kid-
napped, and establish the conflict that the book in thriller
fashion successfully resolves.

Apparently, then, the skeletal parts of the novel are all
borrowed, but the suspense itself is real. What, exactly,
causes suspense in any book is not just the plot, of course—
the arrangement of events; also involved is the ease with
which the reader will accept the plausibility of those events,
and *The Hostages* depends for any success at all upon our
willingness to believe that extreme right-wing and extreme
left-wing beliefs *can* lead to extremist actions. So far, this is
so straightforward as to appear superficial. But Israel offers
us specific events.

The book opens with a school bus collecting sons and
daughters of various international U.N. employees, but it
quickly reveals that something is not right. The driver is
different; the bus itself is different; the route to school is

followed for only part of the way. One mother alone is suspicious, but bureaucracy stands in the way of her enquiries being answered satisfactorily—a bureaucracy which shows itself not only in the self-protective verbiage of the school, telephone, and bus company officials, but also in the working of the U.N. itself. An unwilling Red China has just been allowed a seat in the General Assembly, and, though it secretly plots war against the western world anyway, the delegation is presently on its way to New York. A group of schizophrenic right-wing Americans, meanwhile, kidnaps the children, planning to hold them hostage till the U.N. indicates it will reverse its stand and bar entry to the Chinese, or if not, to kill them. The time-honoured suspense device of the whodunit combines, then, with the timely question of moral choice. There are values: the children are good, peace is good—yet to make any choice is to deny one of them. To opt for the delegation makes the chooser an accessory to murder; to bar the delegation would lead inevitably to international war. A kind of Aristotelian sense of 'fear' builds up, and the reader becomes involved in making the decision.

But all this works only up to a point—strangely enough, only as long as Israel deals in groups. The U.N. delegations are fine as long as we can leave them in the abstract, but the author has to create individual people, and when he tries, the types lose their credibility and become trite. One must put up with a Haitian delegate shrieking at (naturally) a Dominican Republican: " 'He steal my daughter! He kidnap her! ' " Then there is a (typical) Arab versus a (typical) Israeli, and a (typical) drunken American virago with a (typical) milktoast husband. Even the children cease being credible when the author looks at them individually. The ostensible adolescent jealousy which is supposed to divide Arturo and Steve, for example, simply makes them ostensibly adolescent. The novel departs too often from the reality of its generalizations, and too often, therefore, losing the vigour of its opening pages, it bogs down in maudlin detail.

To work acceptably with types is difficult, for the general-ization and the cliché do not radically differ from each other. Some difference does exist, however, and unfortun-ately—and all too obviously—Christine van der Mark, in *Honey in the Rock*, has been unable to make use of it. To reread her earlier novel, *In Due Season* (1947), is to reac-quaint oneself with the promise she showed, the ability she had to evoke a sense of place and to create a strong central character. This new novel is also about southern Alberta, and about religious bigotry, but it has none of the power of Rudy Wiebe's *Peace Shall Destroy Many*, nor any of his care-ful way with words. None of Miss van der Mark's characters break out of the language surrounding them—not Fenna, the most rebellious and most unhappy of the five Leniuk sisters, who at one point, "chilled and lonely," "wept bitterly, the hot tears burning her freezing face." Nor the humanitarian and more likeable Reuben Zwick, who is made to look at everything "with his clear intrepid gaze." Nor Dan, the naïve teacher, who has "a skinny arm, wiry and strong," and who, with such words as " 'Time will help' " and " 'Get some sleep,' " supports Philip, the naïve preacher, and causes him to respond " 'There's a light in you, Dan Root' " before his heavy lids drop and he turns his face to the wall. Not any of them. And so none of them truly exists as a person, nor does the novel acquire any life.

Even Robert Kroetsch, in *The Words of my Roaring*, bur-dens himself with imitative and hackneyed phrases, which is sad, because his work is a worthy accomplishment in most other respects, and it clearly demonstrates a capable talent. The plot is slight: Johnnie Backstrom, the young undertaker, politically opposes Old Murdoch, the coun-try doctor who had delivered him, in an Alberta pro-vincial election during the Depression. But the plot can *be* slight when the central character is as interesting as he is here. We see everything from the undertaker's point of view, and the quality of the irony can be seen in such a deceptively flat statement as this: "I said something about old Doc bringing you into this hellhole mess, but what was he doing to get you out of it? " All the political acumen of an old campaigner, and all the innate rural conservatism of the electorate are on Murdoch's side, but the time, and naïveté—and the sanctimonious radio perorations of the new leader, significantly named Applecart—are on Johnnie's. So, somewhat unwillingly, are we.

The reservations are all caused by the stereotyped catch phrases we keep stumbling into. J. Backstrom is really Holden Caulfield in disguise, grown older by twenty years, but not having traded in his vocabulary in the meantime. "I have this amazing set of teeth," he tells us. "I was trying to protect her. I really was." "I have this magnificent set of teeth." Even (so help me): "I'm an undertaker . . . . I'm dead serious." Fortunately Kroetsch overcomes this, and Johnnie survives it all to become a real figure—cynical, bawdy, brash, and profoundly innocent. Maybe this makes him even more like Salinger's character, but it relates him also to the tragi-comic figures in several recent films: *Morgan, A Thousand Clowns, Georgy Girl, Midnight Cowboy*. What begins as farce takes on another tone, another depth, and another sensitivity to the dilemma of being human.

Johnnie, like other contemporary 'heroes', is really a little man who finds he has to choose, who commits himself without thinking, who thinks too late and discovers that all choices have effects. Specifically, he has averred, in the midst of drought, that rain will fall before election day, and finds to his mixed horror and delight that his claim is accepted as a campaign promise. The delight is part of what propels him forward: "Good God, life is short . . . my body cried. So live, it said. Live, live. Rage, roar." The horror is his consciousness that he also destroys. As Helen Murdoch, the doctor's daughter, tells him: "You talk. You hunger and thirst. You stride and thunder and roar . . . But in the end you smash." He knows he lives in chaos, and for that reason his stability lies in hanging on to "the old chaos"—yet he finds he has promised change, rain, instead. The rain comes, and with it, ironically, a death which, as undertaker, he must respond to. With the rain, too, comes his certainty of election and his growing sensitivity to what people are like—truths which he could perhaps have found anyway but which have been related to the rain and so related to a kind of deceit. They bring, therefore, not a joyous illumination but a sense of despair. Coupled with an equally strong sense of duty, this promises a future for the man with huge hands and the magnificent teeth, though a paradoxical one—inevitably related to his need for chaos and his ability to survive it. If this doesn't exactly seem rosy, it does seem real, and the words of his roaring—racy, flippant, simple, and sad—ring true.

The commitment to political action that underlies Kroetsch's novel, moreover, defines an attitude that many young Canadian writers have taken as their ground. Although Charles Israel and Arthur Hailey, for example, had capitalized successfully on exposing the political/moral dilemmas that exist 'in high places', providing carefully *vicarious* adventure, writers like David Lewis Stein and David Helwig have insisted (often sardonically) on the *everyday* necessity of moral choice and the *ordinariness* with which political action enters private lives. Their writing is generally less flamboyant in event and less predictable in characterization but truer to life, which makes any discord or dubiety in it a lot more grim. Stein's *Scratch One Dreamer,* for instance, concerns Joe Fried, middle-class Jewish liberal individualist, whose family and friends are committed to political activity—in the form of unionism in one generation and peace marches in the next. Joe wants simply to be free of his ties to them, but he soon discovers that freedom means something other than the avoidance of commitment. He has been antagonistic to his uncle, the union hero, and impatient too with his cousin, who is leading a peace march against an Ontario missile base. In thinking that he is faithful to himself, he says:

the code of a private individual . . . [is] the exact oppossite of the kind of thing that Leo's always stood for. Leo's a public man and everything's on the surface, everything's for show. What matters most is what people think and how much you can influence them. What you do in private, whether or not you keep your word, doesn't really matter as long as you look good to the people out front. Inside the party, Leo was a hatchet man, did you know that? . . . I'm saying it doesn't matter what happens out front, as long as I hold true to my own personal code.

Boag, his mistress, promptly gives him a C- and orders more booze. And Stein manages to maintain this balance between the sentimental and the comic, with the result that he has written a fine novel.

Only the immediate conflict, however, is tentatively resolved. Joe finds that he is influenced by both his environment and his personal responses to it, which leads him in turn to commit himself to a political action that, done, seems pointless, but, not done, would rack his private conscience and deny him the kind of maturity he thinks he's already found. The book has a level beyond that of the individual characters, but here the conflict is not resolved, it is simply presented. What happens if you scratch a dreamer? Do you find an ability to act . . . or words . . . or vision . . . or nothing? And who is the dreamer anyway? Is it the individualist who thinks he can exist apart from others—or the group leader who equally erroneously thinks that his group is acting as a single unit? David Lewis Stein has created a book that explores these ideas and that speaks directly to his generation; what makes it doubly good is that it also speaks *about* his generation and, in a sympathetic, involving, and concrete way, about some of the problems that any person today will meet if he is—in the broadest sense—politically alive. Just as an author's intellectual seriousness does not inherently demand that he write humourlessly, however, so does the presence of a sardonic tone not always mean a book provides keen insights into political behaviour.

At first glance Jack Ludwig's most recent novel, *Above Ground,* reads like *In Praise of Older Women* rewritten in order to praise only slightly older women. The central character/narrator is a young man, Joshua, who recalls his early ill childhood and, beginning with the hospital nurses, recounts his subsequent flight from woman to selected woman. He exempts a spastic girl from his attentions; and Ludwig is a little unclear about the extent of Joshua's relations with the mad sister of his friend Gersh; and if we add the fairy chemistry professor to the list, it still leaves Joshua with a lot of running room for his active organs. There is Maggie, whom he marries; Zora, the dark passion of his life, who grows older; Alvira, the fat girl who obsessively loses weight for him, and when he is not permanently attracted, puts it back on in order to hate him adequately enough; Nina, who abandons him for politics; Gyla, who is all women and all suffering Russian Jews to his all guilty (because of Hiroshima) American maleness; and Mavra, a curiously wistful sad case of a woman, whom, like the others, Joshua says he loves. So goes the book, and it would be magnificently forgettable if all there was to it were these (what the book jacket calls) "stunning characterizations." Some of them are clever, certainly, and Ludwig knows a smart phrase when he sees it, even if more of them should have waited for another book. But 'stunning'?

What the many portraits are supposed to do, if we judge from Ludwig's recurring use of a word like 'palimpsest', among other things, is join together to illustrate the Eliotian epigraph: "so all women are one woman." The trouble is that even Joshua knows it isn't true; they all grow old separately, and they all must die alone. Even the spastic girl, who first seems a casual aside, apparently haunts Joshua's imagination through the course of the book, till he is forced into announcing as a kind of expiation that she died long ago, in her sleep. Death frightens Joshua; he doesn't like talking of it. And so his father's sudden death, and the spastic girl's unplanned one, and the fat girl's reckless fatness, and the birth of his own child all force him to recognize his own age. And age can seem as much of a trap as the hospital in which his youth was expended. Hence the present hectic activity. Hence the girls.

All of this is told at a breathless pace, which is admirably sensitive to Joshua's frantic transcontinental life. Dangerously, however, it tempts readers to parody. The very first page produces passages like "The first strange man in my life was a doctor. He came to ask me what hurt. I said my throat." and "My father came in. I was bleeding. He fainted." The Dick-and-Jane innocence is so real by the end of page one that we expect Spot and Puff to bound into the novel on page two. Fortunately they don't, and though it is predictable that Joshua remains 'above ground' at the end of the story, hoping to welcome the sunrise, having encountered the problems of life but not having solved them, Ludwig's overlong book is still one of those rarities that a second reading will improve.

Difficulty with clichéd situation is what also afflicts Robert Hunter's first and (that unfashionable epithet) promising first novel, *Erebus*. It amasses, in fact, just about every variation of the *Bildungsroman* that the twentieth century has contrived. A young man recalls his first sexual experience; he participates in a gang bang; he gets drunk; he almost has a homosexual relationship; he does have assorted heterosexual ones, including a Great Fulfilling one with an Older Woman; he manfully withstands a seductive attempt by an attractive drunken Indian girl, who later thanks him; he saves the marriage of a friend, who subsequently writes him a confessional letter; he is desolated when another friend, a gentle political liberal, is viciously blinded by some small-town reactionary, hulking hicks; he runs home to Mama, which is No Good; and he finally commits himself to teaching in a Progressive school, learning what he can from his sensitive blind friend, Konrad, and plunging forward through the icy water. So this is Winnipeg? And the reader is left at the end of the book conscious of all the clichés, conscious of all the sentiment, and wondering why the Dickens he's been so moved!

Obviously what Hunter wants from his readers is a gutsy reaction, so (presumably) he uses the situations he does because for all their triteness they are humanly true. What most disturbs his characters and himself is not the animal part of man at all, though that alone is not much—a small and insignificant "spastic shudder," the narrator thinks. The narrator is shown to be both sensitive and insensitive to other people, dirty and concerned about cleanliness, lustful and moral, stupidly jealous and conscious of friendship, or in other words, normal. 'Realism' doesn't deny aspiration here, however, nor does licence replace freedom; for all the impoliteness of the novel, it doesn't advocate immorality or chaos.

What does disturb these people is rigidity, in its many forms: masks of piety and righteousness, which hide narrow minds and inhibit sympathy; or intellectualism which in the throes of categorization grows sterile; of "philosophic, political, emotional, and ethical" refusals "to accept *change*"; or sight which is blind. Konrad when blinded, for example, becomes even more sensitive to the world than he was before; Darryl when he finds his marriage more important than his book of criticism becomes more of an intellectual giant; the narrator himself when he tries to help others to see the world can see it better too. Hunter would probably feel that these statements themselves were 'rigid', that the 'life' of the book lay in the response to it, rather than in the attempt to talk about it or in any attempt intellectually to comprehend one's response. So be it, for one does respond. But that doesn't make the book better than it is; it still leaves us conscious of huge purple patches of prose, largely in the first half of the book, when the "ovate orange sun" rises, the "day batters itself into a stunned silence," the sunrise "stains the sky into a great red membrane," and the narrator "floats belly-up in the steaming red-soup of dawn." Maybe so, but all the characters sound like the same character, and hopefully in his next novel, Mr. Hunter will make his people speak like the individuals he says they are.

Then there is Mordecai Richler's novel, *Cocksure*, which from its title sounds as though it ought to turn into a similar sort of book, a Great Quest for Initiation, phallus leaving Wonderland for a Happy Hunting Ground. Yet Richler, whatever else he does, eschews the cliché. His central character is a good-looking married father, beyond adolescence, who has discovered that his moderately liberal views make him thoroughly square in a with-it world. So Richler has it out with with-it-ness. Mortimer Griffin, denying he is a Jew, is charged with anti-semitism; his wife, conscious of his good looks and morality, attacks him for being an unliberated product of Madison Avenue standards. Their pre-teen child is sent to a school so progressive that sex and swearing are on the curriculum and the Christmas play is *Marat/Sade*. And Mortimer's old strait-laced schoolteacher, Agnes Laura Ryerson, turns out to be giving her little boy students blow jobs to keep them in line (but is fired because this encourages competition), while his boss, a saintly publisher who excuses the Nazis because of their tenderness, sells out to Star Maker, an American mogul whose immortality is guaranteed because of the efficacy of kidney, heart, skin, eye, and other transplants. Mortimer is being eyed for his "marvy lymph system," in fact, and the novel ends with him being besieged, his one hope for survival depending on a recently-acquired girlfriend summoning the police in time. She won't, because she lives in a Hollywood world, more conscious of the reel than the real and so is unable to appreciate a personal threat. There are even more characters, all eloquently differentiated, and all in the same extravagant vein. And all ought to be gloriously comic, whereas after a while the book just wears. Richler, obviously having a go at assorted sacred Canadian cows, mostly succeeds in milking them dry, and the readers who have already encountered bits of the novel in *Tamarack Review* may find them better the first time round.

The difficulty about the book is the sort that the ironic ending of Richler's 1959 work, *The Apprenticeship of Duddy Kravitz*, implies. At that point, Duddy's unorthodoxy has got him some land; he becomes an Owner, wins Recognition, and presumably for all his idiosyncrasies obtains a seat in the establishment. But to extrapolate further: what then? Is he contented with himself, does he rock conservative boats, or does he become the resident joker, accepted and despised? Richler's stinging satire, brilliant as it can be, swings in two directions—against the old conservative world which he's had to do battle with, and against the new crowd of pseudo-sophisticates whose very with-it-ness is simply a new brand of narrow conservatism. Robert Hunter can see this; so can Jack Ludwig, though he's a little more cynical about it. Richler seems a lot more trapped than either of them, for his book suggests that he's at once conscious of the recognition he wants, aware of where the 'important' recognition comes from, attracted by that group, and repelled by even the genuine tinsel that lies under its shallow false surface.

In "Portrait of the Poet as Landscape," Abraham Klein talks about the poet's predicament and the temptations that face him:

> *Fame*, the adrenalin: to be talked about;
> to be a verb; to be introduced as *The*:
> to smile with endorsement from slick paper . . . .
> It has its attractions, but is not the thing . . . .
> Rather it is stark infelicity
> which stirs him . . .
> to walk upon roofs and window-sills and defy
> the gape of gravity.

Either way it's a vulnerable position. Richler's book, which will prove screamingly funny among the cocktail set and be *The* Richler to appear on shelves and side tables, is neither as human a book as Hunter's, as comic as anything by Günter Grass, nor as stirred by stark infelicity as Bellow or Barth. Maybe in the short run this doesn't matter, but for those who walk constantly through slick paper, a different gape of gravity awaits.

A FICTION CHRONICLE, PART II: ARTIFICE AND EXPERIENCE

The technical range of contemporary Canadian novels indicates not simply the degree of experimentation of which their authors are capable; it suggests also the multiple guises in which "reality" can be recognized. Consider, for example, the opening passages of a few recent books:

> The ladies of Tollemarche, Alberta, were always wonderfully clever at disposing of their menfolk; so that these gentlemen, if not already in their graves, were encouraged by their wives to depart northwards in search of business . . . .
>
> (Bhatia: *The Latchkey Kid*)

> It is early in April but the snow still lies on the ground, shrouding the vague contours of the landscape. My emotions of this morning are like that, pale and tenuous, a simple line drawing . . . . Our lives have been brutalized beyond belief, reduced to a bleakness impossible to express.
>
> (Adams: *The Trudeau Papers*)

> Later that evening, Anna left by the same door, the weighted hinges dragging it closed behind her. Ibiza again, bare feet in white dust. She was back, back from Paris . . . .
>
> (Haggerty: *Daughters of the Moon*)

> Heavenly reader, let me anticipate your two most serious objections to *Bartleby*: the first that it is a work of plagiarism; the second that it employs too many gimmicks, stocks in trade, and clichés of the writer's imitative art.
>
> (Scott: *Bartleby*)

June Bhatia's gauze ironies reveal her acceptance of an empirical view of society, while Ian Adams's portentous alliterative utterances make us conscious of the rhetoric of his story more than the story itself. Joan Haggerty, by contrast, relies on image and rhythm, to focus on two women's dislocating responses to their sexuality. And Chris Scott, ingenuously probing the artifice of language itself, circles again and again over the reality of the creative imagination.

The most easily approachable books are certainly Adams's and Bhatia's, and they might seem at first thought to be the most 'real' simply because of that. The ladies and gentlemen of Tollemarche, Alberta, have their counterparts in material society, that is, and if in creating them, their author exaggerates social prejudices for the sake of her ironic tone, she remains pictorially descriptive in her exploration of human behaviour. Yet 'human behaviour' is not ultimately illuminated by such a book. When it ascribes motivation to any of its characters, it does so with such abruptness as to deny life its complexity and subtlety. And the resolutions possess all the credibility of the average television show, geared to the timing of the commercials more than the pace of the drama.

Mrs. Bhatia's commercial is announced fairly early: "In this war amongst the teacups, the worst sufferers were the children." However admirable the sentiment, the constant urge to reduce experience to epigrams makes stereotypes out of her characters. Hank Stych, the 'latchkey kid' of the story (or child with a housekey round its neck, to obviate the need for a parent or babysitter at home), grows up to resent his parents' involvement in Moral Causes rather than Human Beings. At about age eighteen he therefore writes a scandalous, best-selling book to discomfort them, dislodge them from their social niche, and demonstrate the deeply-felt truth that he Really Cares. His mother belatedly discovers that Tollemarche's mentally retarded children need her as a volunteer. In such humble circumstances she finds true reward, for a travelling princess visits her. And Hank, who is given to saying contemporary things like "Jeepers" when he isn't writing dirty books, heads off to England (apparently the spiritual home of every Albertan), marries the widow who used to live next door, enjoys his money, writes another book, and gives promise of Some Day being reconciled with his family. Hence what could have been a very witty book is punctuated with so many clichés that it trips over its own technique. As critical views of 'Albertan' moral legislation, Robert Kroetsch's *The Words of My Roaring* and *The Studhorse Man* pierce pretentiousness and provoke indignant laughter much more readily; they use language coruscatingly and wittily to an artistic purpose: *The Latchkey Kid* merely romanticizes, and however much it attempts to represent daily life and attack superficial social conventions, it simplifies experience too often to do other than escape life, and ends up the prisoner of conventions of another kind.

Avowed thrillers like *The Trudeau Papers* or Llew Devine's *The Arrow of Apollyon*, by contrast, openly admitting their use of a conventional form, manage to convey a certain rough vigour. Both books, moreover, use the suspenseful swift narrative to probe as urgent a moral issue as that which lies behind *The Latchkey Kid*: the impact of money on conscience. Devine's book opens with a murder associated with the Toronto Stock Exchange and investigates the manipulation of people and currency that lead to and follow upon it. The greed of one man, the weakness of another, the amorality of a third: all bear upon the way in which the Market works and ordinary people are unknowingly affected. We respond to the characters in exactly this dehumanized way, however. Two-dimensional, they are not 'real'; only their greed or weakness or amorality is, as though the author were writing a latter-day morality play in which virtues and vices contend for the soul of modern society. Indeed, the central presence of the book, an archer-financier and international mystery allegorically named Max Bowman, is drawn in such deliberately larger-than-life terms as to become a counterpart to the mediaeval *deus ex machina*. Myths collect around him.

Beyond close acquaintance, he is therefore beyond knowledge; beyond knowledge, he contains all possibilities and acquires any powers that the imaginative minds of ordinary men accord him, either for good or evil. Whether people thus relinquish their will to control their own affairs, or eternally require a saviour, or are inevitably controlled anyway by some external force remains unanswered. And the book's closing ambivalence counters any easy resolutions that might readily have sprung from Devine's literary form.

It is still neither more nor less than capable escape fiction, a rendering of social pressures in such a way as to make them both comprehensible and bearable. Any such form is beset by the dangers of oversimplifying, sentimentalizing, and such distancing that the book's presumptive relationship with actual life may go unnoticed. *The Latchkey Kid* fails in part because it pretends its radically simplified characters are real. Devine's is openly allegorical. Ian Adams's *The Trudeau Papers* demands that we accept as 'real' a world of the near future when nuclear 'accident' over Canada causes an American 'peacekeeping' occupation and engenders divisive internal fighting. Such imaginative speculation acquires its fictional credibility in two ways: through the author's journalistic amassing of data and through the rhetorical bias he gives his narrator. The motivation of behaviour and the sequence of events are worked out with the clarity of a well-written news story, and the effect of that documentary sensibility is to imply the truth of non-fiction—just as in Brian Moore's recent *The Revolution Script*—even when the force of the author's argument lies not in the logical arrangement of empirical facts but in emotional intensity and interpretation. Adams has a shrewd sense of what makes convincing detail and a knowledge of how to use political rhetoric to underline his message. He is concerned not only with the insidiousness of American influence in Canada but also with the insidiousness of power itself. Hence his guerilla nationalists turn out to rule as corruptly as did the Old Guard. Idealism fails to flower in such a desert, but it does not thereby cease to be, and if the novel accomplishes its underlying aim, it will provoke a number of readers into questioning the nature —or the very existence—of the ideals that motivate Canadian society in time present.

In concerning himself manifestly with the superficially subdued present instead of distancing cataclysm into the future, David Helwig writes in *The Day Before Tomorrow* a less spectacular book than *The Trudeau Papers* but an even more disturbing one. The impact of the kind of violence he describes depends on controlled use of understatement, and the novel has more of the brooding nightmare about it than does Adams's overt object lesson. The dangers to society that Helwig explores are not those of Foreign Invasion and Atomic Holocaust, but the invasions of the sanctity of the individual mind. Cast as a variety of spy story, it follows the political awakening of a character named Jake Martens as he grows tired of the attitudinizing of simple Canadian protest groups, becomes involved in London locating his career diplomat brother John (who has committed treason out of desperate disaffection with government policy), and tunes in at last on the moment in history in which he lives and must act.

The two meanings of the word 'act' contribute to the tensions of the book, for if its ultimate commitment is to *action* as a way of confirming one's individuality, it distinguishes constantly between that and *acting—seeming, appearing to do*. The protest groups signified for Jake just such a lack of substance, and for all the flamboyance of his brother's disappearance, so does the exchange of affinities that his treason represents. Instead of coming closer to reality, John enters an unstable realm of 'nightmare sequence' in which an anonymous 'They' that had sought his aid now fails to identify or help him. Thrown back upon himself, he discovers he has forsaken himself, that to have once said "I have given myself to the future, I must put myself in their hands" is to render oneself completely powerless. Somehow Jake intuits that understanding, and realizes that *now* is the only point where action and individuality can coalesce. And *now*, being 'real', is imperfect and therefore frustrating for those who serve an ideal in it. Too often such service imprisons rather than enfranchises people, for in *appearing to act* they embrace the perfect future or the perfect past. The one has the insubstantiality of dream, the other the artificiality of history; both have their impact on Helwig's present moment of active existence, but neither takes its place, and to distinguish among them becomes the task of all who live.

In another way it is also the task of the writer, whose contrived literary techniques must convey these disparate apprehensions of the nature of truth. In the chapters evoking John Martens's discovery of his life's continuing emptiness, therefore, Helwig's style breaks into fragmentary sentences; he distorts observations and dislocates time. Jake, contrarily, operates within a strict linear, moment-by-moment frame of reference, and Helwig records the conversations he takes part in almost without apparatus, in order to allow readers—as Callaghan had attempted to do in the 1920's—to overhear them directly and so become involved in the character's/author's moment. Counterpointing these two styles is a third, a compulsion to speak in aphorisms ("The future is perfect because it does not exist," "An aphorism says everything and means nothing.") which seem to epitomize the characters' experience. The 'seem', however, is important. As Alice Munro spells out in *Lives of Girls and Women*, art can only approximate (for all that it can intensify and distil) a life that is lived. To accept the aphorism rather than the substance, would be to equate the intellectual and emotional distillation with the empirical event. For Helwig's characters it means a blurring of life and theory; for Helwig himself, the challenge was concurrently to demonstrate the blurring and enunciate the distinction, and despite its somewhat unvarying tone—which works against his stylistic differentiations—his book manages intelligently to grapple with the art and experience of life.

The same cannot be said either for Joan Haggerty's *Daughters of the Moon* (for all its sensitivity to explicitly female experience) or for Graeme Gibson's fantasy about the "sexual, . . . lyrical and . . . nightmarish" possibilities of one's life, *Communion*. Both books take rhythmic pattern as their basic stylistic technique, which carries particularly strong sexual overtones in Haggerty's novel. *Daughters of the Moon* concerns the emotional links between two women, Anna and Sarah, who each marry, recall family experiences, suffer marital breakup, and come to bear children. In the process they discover their love and their separateness, the concurrence of their experience and the identity of death, and as the prose patterns recur and the story steps in and out of dreams, signs, and daily events, we approach an understanding of the pressures that affect their lives. Yet so consciously is the language made into a sexual rhetoric that the novel ultimately seems arch, a defective Woolf-Lessing-Drabble set-piece that contains illusions but cannot seed them. The style manages to catch at the heat and doldrums of the Mediterranean setting, and to capture some of the emptiness of the lives being lived, but none of the characters ever proves very interesting.

Presumably the rhythms—as Gibson's book jacket advises about *Communion*—are meant to be "haunting" and "mesmerizing" and "rise to a harrowing and purgative intensity"; in them lie the "truth" of the identities to which the characters lay claim. Certainly for Gibson's Felix Oswald, a veterinarian's assistant identifying with a dying husky—feeling violent, beautiful, angry, animal, caged, controlled, uncontrollable, and superior to authority—the recurrent but interrupted visions of passion blend conquest and defeat into an ambivalent portrait of an ordinary man. Both avatar and servitor in his own imagination, Felix consumes himself with each new 'communion'; his identity is lost, therefore, with each fulfilment—reminiscent of Cohen's *Beautiful Losers*. The trouble is, his imagination is too tiresome to arouse much sympathy; as an advance on the barren 'realities' of the 'veterinary' world, his visionary glimpses seem curiously negative; and seen as an absurd dilemma, his predicament neither engages nor dismays.

Much livelier and wittier—though sometimes overwritten and far too long—is Chris Scott's *Bartleby*, and in it, we take the next step out of fictional realism. A shaggy Shandyan funhouse, *Bartleby* recognizes as 'real' not the life presumably devised on the page but the process of devising artifice itself. In life, life is real, but in a book, only the book is. Within such a framework, anything is therefore possible, and Scott contrives to write about the Writing of Book in such a way as to reveal the impositions of an author upon his characters, the independent vitality they manage nonetheless to acquire in readers' minds, and the control they (subsequently, paradoxically) exert upon the creative abilities of their author. Taking the form of a burlesque quest story, the characters' search for their creator and for creativity takes them into bouncing bawdy adventures, into conflict with a Protean figure named De'Ath, and into innumerable quarrels with the author at his typewriter over what they may or may not do, and when. If he consigns events to the wastebasket on occasion, they steal his chapters and only release them long after they're needed. And when he needs all his characters at one point and they disappear, he is forced into writing *The End* abruptly, in the middle of his book—only to turn about on a fresh page, equally as abruptly and artificially, with a continuation:

> ———*The End* of Book One, that is, because I have just hit on the explanation———forget about the end, reader ———and amazingly simple it is: the fog, the *fog* from the last chapter has filtered through to this chapter!
>
> "There is no fog," said Damon Gottesgabe.
>
> "Extraordinary," said I. "That's extraordinary, Damon, but I have just read your words"—I will not allow myself to be drawn into that trap, reader. Nevertheless, I read what he said and read it aloud: " 'There is no fog,' said Damon Gottesgabe," but there is, there is a fog!
>
> "It seems very clear to me," he continued while I searched the MS, "that the fault is yours . . . . you have

forgotten what day of the week it is, see fogs where there are none, and now to cap it all you have lost not just one or two of the persons in the book, but all of them."

"Enough, enough, Damon," I conceded, "the narration has not been without fault."

The ironies and exaggerations of this admitted Cock and Bull story demonstrate a shrewd sense of comic timing, and introduce the finest parodist Canadian literature has for a long time seen. Scott's style keeps pace with a huge cast of characters, some his own and some borrowed, all speaking in the syntax their original author gave them and grumbling at it, and his knowledge of literary archetypes and analogues allows him to move gamely through a range of allusive techniques.

The end of all this flamboyance is not merely to bewail the rigidity of the straightforward narrative process of modern realistic fiction but also to affirm the joyful, invigorating spontaneity of the spoken/written word—and not merely to berate the categorizing impulses of the modern society that are epitomized by the realistic novel, but also to insist on the continuing human capacity to utter the idiosyncrasies, potentialities, aspirations, and unpredictable forays of the creative mind. "Upon the very principle of beggary" does "The Narrative Age founder," Scott writes. It was June Bhatia's and Ian Adams's intention simply to use the language of narrative; it is Scott's intention (like Robert Kroetsch's or Abraham Klein's) to revitalize it. In the process of attempting to do so, he explores a principle that Malcolm Lowry had absorbed from Ortega: that an author is created by the works he writes as much as he creates them, and they, therefore, have an independent 'reality'. He also rediscovers what Stephen Leacock averred in "Fiction and Reality" as early as 1916:

"That accusation is," repeated Mr. Pickwick, "that *we are not real, that we are caricatures,* that not one of us, and I beg the company to mark my words, not a single one of us, ever existed, or ever could exist; in short, my friends, that we are mere monstrous exaggerations, each of us drawn in a crude and comic fashion from a few imaginary characteristics!! "

. . . the truth was that from the time of the Romans onward Art had of necessity proceeded by the method of selected particulars and conspicuous qualities: that this was the nature and meaning of art itself: that exaggeration (meaning the heightening of the colour to be conveyed) was the very life of it . . . : that by this means and by this means alone could the real truth—the reality greater than life be conveyed.

Such praise of the artist's craft describes a willingness to render experience innovatively rather than photographically, and to hold faith in imaginative truths rather than strictly empirical ones.

THE
STUDHORSE
QUESTS

Names like Demeter and Poseidon in a book about Alberta provide a fairly obvious hint that all may not be what it seems on the surface; the Classical deities ride ironically through such a landscape, and any author who puts them in it is trying less to recreate the order of the Greek pantheon than to demonstrate the contrary attractions of contemporary life and art. Robert Kroetsch's *The Studhorse Man* amply illustrates this position. Full of conscious parallels and explicit contrasts, the book plays wittily with the tensions of post-World War II Canadian life, moving at the end away from bizarre comedy into a half-bitter, half-bemused acknowledgement of the compromises that underlie order in modern society. Demeter Proudfoot, the narrator of this saga of Hazard Lepage, does not approve of his subject, but is fascinated by what Hazard represents about modern man's quest for identity. And when he dedicates his tale, like a testament, to Hazard's daughter (also named Demeter), he offers indirect counsel about the interpenetration of dreams and actions, which concurrently insists that discovering an ancestral continuity should liberate rather than enslave a present generation.

Hazard's bawdy story is episodic, idiosyncratic, full of extraordinary coincidences and motivations, but told with a linear simplicity. After surviving the horrors of war in France (1939-45), Hazard returns to Alberta and sets out on what proves to be a continuation of his twenty-four-year quest; he possesses the Lepage line of blue roans, and to assure its continuity seeks a mare to mate with his virgin stallion Poseidon. Constantly he is thwarted. A quarrel over payment leads him to seek refuge in a freight car, which takes him uncontrollably westwards, away from his home (Burkhardt) and from Coulee Hill, where his fiancée Martha Proudfoot has five suitable mares but will not comply. Hazard emerges in Edmonton, absurdly out-of-place among the engulfing commercial and legislative buildings, is bedded by P. Cockburn, one of the museum's assistant curators, and leaves in a Mountie uniform and a borrowed milkman's cart only to enter the Home for Incurables which is run by a little old nun named Sister Raphael. On finally moving southwards on the Calgary Trail, now in a clergyman's costume, he thinks he discovers a suitable mare for Poseidon, but at the moment of empty triumph is arrested and offered the option of nine days in jail or three days and nights pigsticking for, and incidentally bedding, ugly Widow Lank. His stint accomplished, he encounters Eugene Utter (a smooth-talking confidence man for all seasons), attends a wedding of one of Martha's kinfolk, and eventually comes to rest in the home of Marie Eshpeter, who stalls him along while secretly selling Poseidon's seed to an artificial insemination firm. Another flight follows, to the home of Mrs. Laporte, and here Hazard seems to be destroyed along with his hostess's house. Though he revives when Martha at last 'mounts' him, it is Demeter who finally brings Poseidon and Martha's mares together at Burkhardt, and it is Utter who finally gets Martha. For Hazard, trampled at the very end, the quest remains essentially unfulfilled.

The result is an entertaining and clever narrative. Seen more closely, *The Studhorse Man* also appears as a kind of freewheeling adaptation of Homer's *Odyssey*. Hazard thus becomes Ulysses, Martha Penelope, World War II the Trojan Wars, and the quest for Poseidon's mare an equivalent for Ulysses' doomed ventures, willed by the angry sea-god, across the western oceans in search of Ithaca. Kroetsch makes the bilingual pun (mare/*mer*) explicit when he has his Cassandra-character, an old woman on the French battlefields, prophesy to Hazard: *"La mer sera votre meurtrière."* And if Burkhardt, the decayed mansion in which Hazard and his horses once lived, seems an odd Ithaca, the fact that it is spoiled, besieged, full of ancestral rolls (in this case stud books), and inhabited by Martha's suitors makes the equivalence roughly parallel in form if not in style or intent.

The episodes, too, have their Odyssean counterparts. The passage aboard the train, when Hazard loses hold of reality and lives with a dream of Martha in a "perfection" of "darkness," is a kind of Lotus-land which he is freed from only by a visit to Hades:

> "Where in hell—," Hazard began again.
> "No." The brakeman laughed encouragingly.
> "In Edmonton."

But Edmonton, the city of 'monstrous' armoured troop vehicles, Woodwards' Stores, the R.C.M.P., and the Museum of Canadian History, is also the land of the Lestrygonian giants, and from the Cyclopean embrace of P. Cockburn in her Polyphemus' Cave-museum bed, Hazard must flee to live. She would give him place and order, but would destroy his vitality in so doing. Already there are six life-size wax figures around her bed:

> on one side the resplendent figure of an Indian chief, the buckskin of an early explorer, the red coat of a North West Mounted Police constable; on the other the black robe of a missionary, the coat and tails of an early premier, the black gown of a university president...
>
> "Wait a minute," Hazard cried out . . . .
>
> Hazard did battle: the dear ninny was terrified of history. But in the end and finally, that which he wrestled most was the image of himself for which the hands of P. would seek to take measure. He would not be seduced, he was resolved, into that immortality.

Seduced physically nonetheless, he manages to leave when he takes the clothes from the Mountie model and leaves the wax replica in bed in his place. When life weakens, art carries on—raising in the process, however, a question about the duplicity of both of them.

Circe calls next, in the unlikely form of Sister Raphael, when the word "Come" echoes through the shadows of a barn; she is a domineering woman, despite her gentle exterior. Maintaining a perpetual game of rummy in her basement which she runs by an aberrant form of Roberts' Rules of Order, she is surrounded by the swinish card-playing Incurables. Hazard is absorbed by the game and finds it difficult to leave. But that episode over, he is immediately involved in others. The choice between jail and Mrs. Lank offers Hazard his Scylla-Charybdis option. Marie Eshpeter becomes the detaining nymph Calypso, and Mrs. Laporte becomes the stimulating Nausicaä. Yet all these identifications are themselves unimportant. What Kroetsch is doing with them is building up a view of art, life, history, and immortality, in which the contrasts between Canada and Homeric Greece are as telling as the formal similarities.

The Studhorse Man, deliberately employing epic conventions, constantly subverts them. Hence catalogues become breeding lists; epic similes turn into outrageous puns (it is no accident, surely, that horse-lover Hazard's surname should be that of a great Canadian glue company); heroic battles descend to vituperative verbal exchanges, like the occasion at the exit from Edmonton's High Level Bridge, when Hazard and a trucker do combat by hurling at each other at least eighteen synonyms for penis; and so on. In particular, Kroetsch's style captures the implicit distinction between heroic and ironic possibilities that the book as a whole exposes. The narrator speaks constantly in an elevated tone, but his details are frequently Sarah-Binksian; his sentence structures are sophisticated and complex, his vocabulary urbane—yet this style is peppered by quotations from vernacular speech, and words like 'boobies', 'pecker', and 'arse' appear unadorned and unmolested in its midst. Instead of themselves being elevated, they sharpen the contrast between the artificial world of art and the physically real one of everyday experience. Throughout the novel ART is revered as though in capital letters. But from Sister Raphael's name and P. Cockburn's waxworks to the patterned wallpaper at Burkhardt and the idea of artificial insemination, that art establishes a rigid pattern without admitting the supple and flexible beauty of actual life. When Poseidon lashes out in Edmonton at a statue of a bronze stallion, for example,

> A man of ministerial voice announced the bronze horse to be superior: "The artist has done it. In bronze. Forever."
>
> The man's colleagues repeated these words and nodded: "Forever. In bronze." They applauded briefly.

The antiphonal lip-service these people pay to art is merely subservience to propriety, to the mask of order they have imposed on life to keep their incurably animal impulses and equally unquenchable thirst for romance from upsetting the status quo.

Hazard's quest—announced by one of Poseidon's nicknames—insists in such a civilized wasteland on the flesh-and-blood vitality of 'Poesy'. It is a deceptive belief, for if it takes him through the comic reversals of his life, urging him on towards an ideal consummation, it also prevents his responding discriminatingly to artifice and frequently traps him in sensuality. Poesy kills him in the end, for it always stays beyond his grasp and understanding. But to realize that is to infer that Tennysonian and Joycean odysseys affect Kroetsch's world as much as the Homeric one does. His focus is not on the exile who re-achieves his kingdom, but on the outsider who can't find it, and in this light the narrator becomes as central a studhorse man as Hazard Lepage. Demeter—thirty-three years younger than Hazard—is cast in a Telemachus role, but Ithaca is not for him either; Burkhardt and Martha fall to the suitor Utter, and the spiritual wasteland continues. For Demeter there is only the madhouse in which he is confined, where he chooses to be 'unhypocritically' naked, to cast off the material world, and to write his history in a bathtub. He insists that it is a pose, the only guise in which he will be allowed to speak truth:

> I myself prefer an ordered world, even if I must order it through a posture of madness . . . . I am by profession quite out of my mind.

For him, artifice controls everything. In his case, too, the reversals, though absurd, are anything but comic, and they supply a perspective from which to judge Hazard's progress. Somewhat pretentiously, Demeter points this out:

> The biographer is a person afflicted with sanity. He is a man who must first of all be sound of mind, and in the clarity of his own vision he must ride out the dark night, ride on while all about him falls into chaos. The man of the cold eye and the steady hand, he faces for all of humanity the ravishments and the terrors of existence.

Both men are the prisoners of their visions, however, and for neither the man of flesh nor the man of word will absolute freedom be possible. If Hazard cannot recognize the artifice of Poesy, Demeter cannot accommodate himself to Hazard's unabashed sexuality. The one, shouting "Stop", "No", "Wait", and "Never" throughout his life, rejects all order and is therefore constantly upset by social and artistic conventions; the other, seeking order before life, cannot rest in the ordinary world with which he strives to communicate.

What the exploration of this polarity amounts to is both an aesthetic credo (form rooted in life, life shaped by artifice) and an analysis of the impact of myth on social structure. Hence overlaying the Odyssean parallels and the comments on art is yet another thematic strand. Poseidon's second nickname is Posse, a term which carries overtones of a celluloid West. The ranch brawls and Demeter's defence of Burkhardt as though it were a fort compound the stereotype, but whatever superficial similarities there might be, the American (or even the Hollywood) frontier is not identical with the Canadian. Although Calgary, for example, sports frontier trappings, these now serve largely as a mythic disguise; they provide insiders with a sense of overt distinctiveness and outsiders with a readily identifiable image. In other words, despite the realities that gave rise to chuckwagons, stetsons, and what W.O. Mitchell elsewhere calls Alberta's 'horse snobbery', the current image represents not the dreams of chaotic frontier freedom but a civilized, organized, and comfortable convention.

The Studhorse Man thus circles over the difference between the spiritual impulse and the artificial fabrication that both go by the name of myth, and the distinction affects both the study of art and the study of history. When Demeter asks:

> Is the truth of the man in the man or in his biography?
> Is the truth of the beast in the flesh and confusion or
> in the few skilfully arranged lines . . . . ?

Kroetsch links the technique of his novel with its major theme of artistic/sexual creativity. When Demeter goes on to liken himself with Louis Riel, the analogues in Western Canadian history become clearer. Riel's 'madness' was defined by 'Eastern' courts of law, in which the separate 'truth' he sensed and fought for went unappreciated. The conflict a radical faces, however, lies not just between his vision of freedom and the conservative order it refutes, but also between the free mythic essence of the vision and the restricted existence in which it always takes form. Thus Demeter is content to live in the order of a vision that organized society calls mad, while Hazard constantly rejects the 'mythic' structures (epitomized by the wax statues around P.Cockburn's bed) that society organizes to preserve its present identity. In both cases their generative urgent dream goes unrealized, though the dream itself, empirically amorphous and spiritually clear, hovers insistently beneath the ordered surface of the nation's daily life.

It is in the potency and unleashed character of Poseidon, that is, and in his 'passion to possess', that the novel finds its ultimate core. The 'Poesy' and 'Posse' that are variously associated with myths of the West are both disruptive powers—

and are the impulses which motivate the book's action in the first place and eventually lead to its violent conclusion. At the end, moreover, the themes of art, life, and social history are brought together in a single image. Besides trampling Hazard, Poseidon kicks a hole in the mansion wall which had long before been papered in a pattern of "white and blue and gold with alternating lions and fleurs-de-lis." The design is emblematically Canadian, but for Kroetsch no emblem can contain the nation's integral indigenous vitality, nor can the mask described by the rigid English-French alternation adequately define its continually evolving character. In fact, if Poseidon is enchained, the nation is not free; it acquires liberty only by constantly confronting chaos and pursuing relentlessly its fundamental dreams. To surrender Ithaca to the suitors is to surrender independence through apathy, not to discover a Golden Age of calm. In adapting the Odyssean quests to explore this cultural and aesthetic proposition, Robert Kroetsch has written a wittily ironic book about Canadian society—allusively textured and full of mordant discoveries. He has also contrived a provocative fable for modern man.

voices
for the
soundless
fugue

LOWRY,
THE CABBALA
AND CHARLES JONES

As we are reminded by Stephen Leacock's pointed satire "The Yahi-Bahi Oriental Society of Mrs. Rasselyer-Brown," the Theosophist movement attracted charlatans as well as serious students, particularly when it became a fad. Considering the number of people involved in theosophy from the 1880's into the 1930's—or into the 1960's, for that matter, with occultism becoming fashionable again—this can hardly be unexpected. Good, wealthy, uncertain people are often persuaded out of their money by the strong-willed, and are often coincidentally attracted to philosophies that offer them 'answers'. Conditions are thus ripe for the con artist. The 'converts' accept him, abandon their homes, and enter communities of the 'elect', whose sole function seems to be to await Armageddon and in the meantime praise their self-styled prophet/priest. One of the most blatant examples in Canada of this particular variety of the con game is recorded in a curious 1967 memoir by Herbert Emmerson Wilson, entitled *Canada's False Prophet*. It concerns the career of the author's brother, Edward Arthur Wilson, alias 'Brother Twelve', who attracted people from all over Europe and North America—generally former theosophists—to follow him in 1927 to the Pacific Coast. There he bought Valdez Island and additional thousands of acres with his community's funds, and his 'Aquarian Foundation' flourished. The Eleven Brothers in the Void spoke irregularly to Brother Twelve on matters of faith, and the 'prophet' led his flock to believe what he chose. At least for a time. Wilson goes on in his book to describe the bizarre sexual practices of the group and the increasing sadism of Brother Twelve's cohort, Madame Zee, which ultimately led to its disintegration.

My point here is simply to emphasize that in Vancouver in the late 1920's and 1930's, interest in this strange society, and in hermeticism and the occult generally, was particularly strong. Not all of it was eccentric, of course, nor were all the writers and teachers in the field mountebanks. Some were serious thinkers, whose search into the signs and symbols of black and white magic was for them a way of trying to fathom the unknown. One of these was 'Frater Achad'—Charles Robert Stansfeld Jones—a portrait painter from 1899 to 1910, the author of six books, a resident of Vancouver for many years, and undoubtedly one of Canada's least known writers.

Unlisted at the Vancouver Public Library, Jones's virtually unobtainable work seems recorded only in a brief article (3 October 1936) in the now defunct *Vancouver News Herald*. All of it is concerned with the occult—from the early *Crystal Vision through Crystal Gazing* and *XXXI Hymns to the Star Goddess* (a volume of poems), through a commentary on the cabbalistic numerology of Wagner's *Parsifal*, called *The Chalice of Ecstasy*, to the three commentaries on the Cabbala itself, all written during the 1920's, on which his reputation among metaphysical societies now rests: *Q.B.L., or The Bride's Reception, The Egyptian Revival*, and *The Anatomy of the Body of God*. In them are to be found a detailed analysis of the numerical, chromatic, and alphabetic correspondences associated with the states of mind depicted by the Cabbalistic 'Tree of Life', and an exploration of the theory that the universe is constantly progressing or expanding "while still in accord with the One Order which prevails from its most minute atom to its inconceivable vast circumference." Both ideas were to attract the attention of Malcolm Lowry and (therefore) to be absorbed into his fiction.

In her recent book, *The Private Labyrinth of Malcolm*

Lowry, Dr. Perle Epstein of New York University makes a great deal of Lowry's meeting with Jones, as being a turning point in the creation of *Under the Volcano*, the moment when Lowry had the mysteries of the Cabbala opened to him and thus acquired a pattern for the novel's symbolism. To stress this diminishes the importance of Lowry's previous reading, however—in Melville, Ortega, Poe and other literary figures whose romantic imagination stimulated his own—and in the rhetoric of Charles Fort, and in the expository works of P.D. Ouspensky and J.W. Dunne. It also overlooks the general climate of interest in the occult that was already established in Vancouver by the time Lowry arrived in 1939. It is not that on moving to Dollarton he joined any psychic associations, but rather that he was interested in and (to some extent, at least) knowledgeable about hermeticism by the time he actually met Charles Jones. In 1941, Jones was a census enumerator in North Vancouver who called at the Lowrys' cabin in Dollarton as part of his route. The chance meeting was followed up by a series of arranged ones, as Lowry subsequently became one of Jones's pupils in the symbology of the Cabbala. Obviously Lowry found in Jones's work a structure on which to hang some of his more nebulous feelings about coincidence and fate; the diagram of the Tree of Life at the end of *Q.B.L.*, for example, could serve as a key to a number of the symbols in *Under the Volcano*—more illuminative, in fact, than the *Zohar* itself, which Jones was *interpreting*, and which Lowry never read. But in other cases, the discovery of Jones's work merely supplied an additional rationale for a design that he had already basically worked out.

Miss Epstein's thesis, quite simply, proposes that the Consul is a black magician (misusing his cabbalistic powers and so doomed to perdition), and that the consistent way in which the symbolism of the novel is based on cabbalistic motifs supports her contention. She gains some justification for her position from Lowry himself. Writing in 1950 to Derek Pethick, he points out certain features of Geoffrey Firmin:

> The consul has been a Cabbalist . . . . Mystically speaking, the abuse of wine is connected with the abuse of mystical powers. Has the Consul perhaps been a black magician at one time? We don't know . . . . a black magician is a man who has all the elements . . . against him—this is what the Consul meant in Chapter X (written in 1942) enumerating the elements . . . . The implication is that an analogy is drawn between Man today on this planet and a black magician.

But Lowry's emphasis is constantly on the *analogy*, the *possibility* of the identification, rather than on the identification itself. As he specified in his 1946 letter to Jonathan Cape, the number of chapters in the novel—twelve—is significant partly because of its cabbalistic importance. He adds:

> The Cabbala is used for poetical purposes because it represents man's spiritual aspiration. The Tree of Life, which is its emblem, is a kind of complicated ladder with Kether, or Light, at the top and an extremely unpleasant abyss some way above the middle. The Consul's spiritual domain in this regard is probably the Qliphoth, the world of shells and demons, represented by the Tree of Life upside down . . . .

But then he says further:

> all this is not important at all to the understanding of the book; I just mention it in passing to hint that, as Henry James says, "There are depths."

There are indeed, and Miss Epstein's book patiently explores one of them. She is conscious, moreover, that it is only one approach, and thus her position is distorted when the book jacket announces that "Once and for all, *The Private Labyrinth* . . . clarifies Lowry's intention in his masterpiece." To have attempted that would have been to narrow the book, to deprive it of depth, however much intricate fretwork it might add, but final answers are not Miss Epstein's intention.

The Private Labyrinth opens with a history of the Cabbala from Jewish mysticism through to the present, but unfortunately (though for the layman it will prove a quick guide to mystic thought) this part of the book reads rather like a chapter from a dissertation; it is factual, earnest, and flat. What it does most clearly is demonstrate the force that the Cabbala exerted not only upon the Hasidic movement (Miss Epstein is herself descended from the eighteenth-century Hasidic philosopher Baal Shem Tov) and upon Christian philosophers like Cornelius Agrippa and Jakob Boehme, but also upon such movements as Rosicrucianism, Freemasonry, Romanticism, and Theosophy. Along the way many other influences were absorbed until the Cabbala becomes, in Miss Epstein's phrase, "unrecognizable amid the bric-a-brac of Oriental philosophy," but its importance (however intangible) can hardly be denied.

Among the literary works, other than *Under the Volcano*, in which the influence can be perceived, are *Faust, Parsifal,* and *The Magic Flute*. Partly because of the Faustian association, it is curious to discover that Miss Epstein's bibliography omits such critical studies as A.R. Kilgallin's essay on the Faust motif in *Under the Volcano*, or Jack Hirschman's idiosyncratic note on Lowry and the Cabbala in *Prairie Schooner*. The exact basis for the bibliography, in fact, is somewhat unclear. As a guide to Lowry criticism it is erratically selective; as a guide to studies of the occult it is similarly uneven. Jung's *Psyche and Symbol* is included, for example, but *Psychology and Alchemy* left out; Mme. Blavatsky's *Secret Doctrine* is in, but none of the works of Annie Besant (which Lowry read) are mentioned.

Yet for all this, the main body of *The Private Labyrinth* provides a good example of an exegesis carried out in industrious detail. The cabbalistic correspondences of numbers, colours, animals, and names are all explained; the sexual implications of the Cabbala are examined in relation to the novel; and the author goes on to associate various of the symbols—animals, wheels, gardens, elements, beverages, etc.—with the Consul's progress as an adept. If by meditating on his "spiritual self," that is, Geoffrey may at one time have hoped to "transcend his condition and become divine," it becomes increasingly obvious that possessing the mystic powers not only promises the hope for equanimity but poses a threat to his existence as well. 'Heaven' and 'hell' are thus the same place, perceived by persons either in harmony with their environment or not. As the tarot 'fool' is actually the 'supreme intelligence', so paradoxically is the abyss of hell also the height of understanding and illumination. A 'white magician'—Sigbjørn Wilderness, for example, or Kennish Drumgold Cosnahan—can emerge from his contact with the occult forces not simply unscathed but with a new perception of harmony. (Lowry's previously unpublished notes to "Ghostkeeper" and the "Outward Bound" section of *October Ferry to Gabriola*—attached as appendices to *The Private Labyrinth*—make his awareness of this process quite clear.) But from the same encounter a so-called 'black magician', for reasons of ego or whatever, will emerge misusing his powers, and he is ultimately overcome by his knowledge. The alchemical and mystic balance which would allow harmony is for him—for a man like Geoffrey—impossible now to achieve.

If the specific *identification* of the Consul as a black magician does not quite convince, the sense of the unknown that is evoked by such a consideration is absolutely faithful to the tone of Lowry's own perception of the world. As he pointed out to David Markson in 1951:

> you could with some justice 'rationalize' the Cabbala itself . . . but you can't rationalize . . . the unknown depths of the human psyche . . . . More or less popular and dry half-gobbledegookery though [Jung's "Man in search of his soul"] is— . . . you nonetheless might find it soundly full of the wisest kind of speculation . . . .

In his own later reading, he moved on from 'Frater Achad' (even though in 1956 he was writing to Harvey Burt to have *Q.B.L.* and *Anatomy of the Body of God* sent to him in England) and back to other works that bear on the occult and that continued to influence him: J.W. Dunne's *An Experiment with Time*, for example, which caused such a stir in the late 1920's, influenced J.B. Priestley among others, and is felt in *Dark as the Grave*. Or P.D. Ouspensky's *Tertium*

Organum, which influenced "La Mordida." Or Charles Fort's *Wild Talents* (like the other two, recommended to Margerie Lowry's mother as early as 1940 as books concerned "with enlarging the frontiers of the mind"), which is central to at least one of the episodes of *October Ferry.* Or the Tao and the *I Ching.*

It is impossible, however, to separate out individual strands without doing injustice to the whole; what influenced Lowry was really life itself, with its complexity, its fatefulness, its coincidences, and its hidden potential. If in his later novels he was heading acutely consciously in a metaphysical direction, it was a path which his earlier reading and writing prepared for him. *Under the Volcano* expresses one stage along the way. It remains his greatest book, and in exploring one of the dimensions that makes it so, Perle Epstein makes us even more aware of the centrality of the metaphysical vision to all he wrote, and of the intricacy of his craftmanship.

1970

GABRIOLA:
MALCOLM LOWRY'S
FLOATING ISLAND

It seems odd that more of Malcolm Lowry's works have appeared since his death than appeared before it, but it seems also strangely in accord with the demonic world of metaphysics and fatal coincidences in which he believed. He was being written, he felt, as much as he was writing. The multiple levels of narrating voice that he employed in works like *Hear Us O Lord from Heaven Thy Dwelling-Place* or *Dark as the Grave Wherein My Friend is Laid* were attempts to render exactly that sensibility; he was manipulating not simply time, space and point of view, but also the very processes by which the mind identified itself. To take it on a journey into the wilderness recesses of (alcoholic, demonic, emotional) recognition and back again into intellectual balance became the compulsion of his literary career and his (book by book) overriding theme. The books were to connect into a cycle called *The Voyage that Never Ends,* culminating in the (as yet unpublished, probably unpublishable) manuscript, "La Mordida," now housed in the University of British Columbia library. They were to explore *as a whole* the recurrent attempts of a writer to find paradise, his expulsions from it because of present realities and his mind's fragmenting memories, and his struggle back into stability nonetheless. Each work can be seen as a piece of that journey— sometimes a microcosm of it, as in "Through the Panama." Of all of them, *Under the Volcano* remains the most polished, "The Forest Path to the Spring" the most joyously affirmative, *Dark as the Grave* the most anguished, and *October*

Ferry to Gabriola (the one full-length novel set chiefly in Canada) the most obviously concerned with the intellectualizing process that might turn such anguish back into a kind of joy.

Just as the geographic relationship between Canada and Mexico is important in such a scheme—Eridanus, the Canadian 'paradise', being in some sense merely a mountainous northern symbiotic *extension* of the Mexican volcanic 'hell'—geography emerges as an important structuring device within *October Ferry*. 'Eridanus' is located near Vancouver, on the west coast of the Canadian mainland; Victoria is some eighty miles southwest, on Vancouver Island; Nanaimo, north of Victoria, is more or less due west of Vancouver, and Gabriola Island lies in the Gulf of Georgia between Nanaimo and Vancouver. Lowry responded first of all to the word 'gulf'—which relates to the barranca and golf course images in *Under the Volcano* ("Golf=gouffre=gulf")[1]—but also to the prospect of an island afloat within it. To an exile from Paradise, any Odyssean ship at sea or floating island might seem a potential haven. Nor is the Odyssean allusion accidental. The directional relationships have their exact parallel in Neoplatonism, where the north is the region of intellect, the south of the senses, the west the domain of the demons, the east of the gods. The trip southwest to Victoria thus intensifies the alienating mental exile of *October Ferry's* central character, Ethan Llewelyn; the bus ride he takes north to Nanaimo activates his return to intellectual understanding; and the possibility of a ferry trip east from there to Gabriola (however *west* of Eridanus he will end up) becomes a promise of a new sheltering harmony. That roughly triangular trip describes the course of the novel; to enunciate the implications of the journey's structure, however, is to leap ahead of the complex psychological situation that engenders it in the first place.

Llewelyn is a lawyer, enmeshed affectionately in "the paradoxes and absurdities of the law itself," but more: he is a lawyer pursued by a sense of personal guilt who thus finds himself (in the words of an earlier Lowry short story) afforded "strange comfort by his profession." The guilt arises in part from his lack of sympathy with contemporary judicial values and practice, in part from an undergraduate experience while at "Ixion" (St. Catharine's) College at "Ely" (Cambridge) University. He had, he thinks, not done what he could have done to prevent a fellow-student, Peter Cordwainer, from hanging himself. He thus takes on more responsibility than he can bear, even when his father-in-law later says that such guilt "was of less significance than as if a single hair had gone grey in God's eyebrow," Ethan cannot decide if this minimizes or magnifies its import. Suffering, he is spiritually exiled from the (English) East, heads to Canada, marries, has a son, but is pursued by memories, by the demonic element of fire that sears each resting-place, and by the economic expansion of the Cordwainer empire (which uses Peter's picture in an advertisement for Mother Gettle's Kettle-Simmered Soups) from England to Quebec and then inexorably across the country to the west coast to which Ethan has fled. (St. Catharine's, Ontario, utters particularly strong resonances for him.) Municipal decisions then compound the issue, threatening eviction from the house where the Llewelyns have found retreat and some peace, forcing them to look even further west for safe harbour. Yet to pretend that paradise is possible in such a mental climate is somewhat self-deceiving, and Lowry is at pains to demonstrate the differences between illusion and reality. At the same time, he consciously explores the different kinds of reality that the mind can perceive. In another context Ethan ponders this dilemma; he

> seemed to see before his eyes whole universes eternally condensing and recondensing themselves out of the 'immaterial' into the 'material,' and as the continued visualization of their Creator, being radiated back again. While meantime here on earth the 'material' was only cognizable through the mind of man! What was real, what imaginary?

To evoke the pressures of this many-sided paradox—and to intensify Llewelyn's experience as the isolate in the Chaucerian epigraph: "Al stereless with-inne a boot am I / A-mid the see, by-twixen windes two, / That in contrarie standen evermo"—Lowry draws on the techniques of film and on images related to film. Specific film titles carry their own portentousness: for example, *"Coming! The Wandering Jew"* or *Outward Bound*;

> "—but are we going to heaven, or hell? " the great voice of one of the characters in the show boomed through into the foyer . . . . *"Ah,"* came back the answer, *"But they are the same place*, you see." Had the voice been that of the Inspector, who was supposed to be God, who had come aboard that ship of the dead to judge the passengers? Or was it Scrubby the barman speaking, the 'halfway', destined because of his suicide to commute eternally on that spectral ferry between earth and the unbeholden land?

Ah, thinks Ethan later on,

> the eerie significance of cinemas in our life, . . . as if they related to the afterlife, as if we knew, after we are dead, we would be conducted to a movie house where, only half to our surprise, is playing a film named: *The Ordeal of Ethan Llewelyn* . . . .

'Reality' thus fragments; "the landscape began to take on a sort of reality but it was not its own reality, but the reality of a landscape seen from a train window, in the sunset, in a film." And the image turns in upon Lowry's consciousness of his own fictional method: "Nothing was more unreal than a novel, even a realistic novel." Scenes, events, particular prose passages, chapter titles *recur* through the book—not as the trial runs of an author still assembling his manuscript, but (as in *Under the Volcano*) as deliberate repetitions, designed to happen like the Protean urgings of memory (acquiring new identities in new contexts) and to arouse an appreciation of the almost separate life that the mind is capable of leading. When near the end of the book Ethan and his wife Jacqueline are actually on board the Gabriola ferry, they find surety impossible. Bad weather forces the ship back westward once; then the journey becomes possible once more, without their disembarking: "Beginning: beginning again: beginning yet again." Their whole life together is epitomized by the phrase, allowing a constant flashback or even rerun of both happiness and despair, promising recurrent expulsion but also a recurrent re-creation of hope. The voyage never ends.

The technique carries over into other of Lowry's images. The recurrent flower names, for example, with their curiously ominous overtones—Death Camas, Destroying Angel, Love Lies Bleeding, the Pacific Dogwood (with its Crucifixion associations)—embody a similar tension between 'contraries'. A rip tide, the rough water made "by the meeting of opposing tides and currents," reminds Ethan of the grave marker 'R.I.P.' Life and death blend. References to lighthouses, *farolitos*, Archangel, the White Sea, abysses and volcanos echo passages in Lowry's poetry and other novels. And the many ephemeral houses that the book refers to—the one in Oakville, the Barkerville Arms, the shack at Eridanus, the Dream House on the island, and so on—mark the relationship between the mind and its environment, the novelist and his world. The Barkerville Arms, that is, built in overlaid pieces like a "palimpsest," at once describes the novelist's method and the mind's functioning process. "Scaffolding" and "scaffold" blend to link building and destroying. "Parlour" refers both to sedate living quarters and to the cavernous Calvinist Canadian "beer parlour," the somewhat hellish bar to which Ethan, as a lawyer, is punningly called. But the bar is also "like life"; the barman in *Outward Bound* is an ambivalent source of knowledge; the "creative" bartender in the *Ocean Spray* in Nanaimo, near Hangman's Point, is as much a "magician" as Jacqueline's father, who masters the contraries he contends with. Such balance is for Ethan to discover as he gradually progresses from sentimental reflection to intellectual equilibrium.

Separated from Jacqueline in the *Ocean Spray* (a modern Cupid without his Psyche)—a scene that anticipates the even

more debilitating separation between Primrose and Sigbjørn
Wilderness in "La Mordida"—Ethan sees the room around
him as

> the perfect outward expression of its own inner soul, of
> what it meant, of what it did, even of what awful things
> could happen in it. What made it all wrong was that the
> creatures that inhabited it were alive, though at first one
> was not sure even of this, alive, were moving, or almost
> moving, seemed to be, however cancelled by it, human
> beings.

Moreover,

> life was *like* this bar, from which you could not see
> out; take all that away, he thought, remove the barrier,
> and the verdigris pane, and enter the realm of yourself;
> never mind the beautiful view, the seas are in—

In then tracking his way inwards, Ethan quotes from Her-
mann Hesse's *Demian* a passage on mental, social, and individual puberty:

> In the average person this is the only time in their lives
> that they experience the sequence of death and rebirth
> that is our fate, when they become conscious of the
> slow process of the decay and breaking up of the world
> of their childhood, when everything beloved of us
> leaves us, and we suddenly feel the loneliness and death-
> ly cold of the universe about us. And for very many
> this pitfall is fatal. They cling their whole life long
> painfully to the irrevocable past, to the dream of a lost
> paradise, the worst and most deadly of all dreams . . .

In fact this enervation afflicts Ethan, too, as long as he
thinks of Eridanus as an escape and a permanent habitation.
The harmonious relation with the elements that he and
Jacqueline had found there comforted him; "between the
cabin and themselves was a complete symbiosis. They didn't
live in it, Ethan said, they wore it like a shell." But as Lowry's own commentary on *Under the Volcano*[2] made clear
(a point he picks up in "The Wandering Jew" chapter of
October Ferry), the world of shells is the cabbalistic Qliphoth, the world of demons. Its 'western' dangers implicitly

deny the possibility of godly heaven. To make the point clear, Lowry notes the existence of an oil refinery across the inlet from Eridanus. Its name is *Shellco*, but the company advertising sign, illuminated by night, is missing one of its letters; only *hell* remains. Eridanus, as Jacqueline's Parsifal-like father knows, "apparently wasn't a place to be enjoyed, so much as another test of their love, to be endured heroically, come through." But to know it once is to hold it in memory, with the same potential for recurrence as any curious experience; it "could never perhaps be lost: and yet it must be relinquished." Or as one of Lowry's favourite paradoxical phrases puts it (with echoes in *Ultramarine, Dark as the Grave,* the novellas, and the movements of the ferry-boat and Greyhound bus in *October Ferry*); *punctum indifferens skibet gaar videre.*[3] The ship sails on.

Signs and portents abound in such a pilgrim's progress, for the mind makes of reality what it will. Magazine titles like *Time* and *Life* seem laden with doom, for example; the *Safeway* supermarket chain links semantically with a postwar British Columbia license plate, which had *Safeside* and *Suicide* imprinted on its edges as advice to overtaking automobiles; *Calgary* turns into *Calvary*; vending machines offer *"Your weight and your destiny"*; the Cordwainer billboard pursues; and so on. But as Ethan knows (citing Lamb as his authority), such a pattern of perception describes the process of coming to terms with the mind's unconscious potential: " 'reason shall only visit him through intoxication.' " The problem is to emerge from the intoxicating ('southern') abyss. The Consul in *Under the Volcano* cannot; Llewelyn, intellectualizing ("abye," he notes, "was an Anglo-Saxon word meaning 'to atone for'. But it also meant 'to endure' "), promises just by his northerly progress to reach a kind of temporary equilibrium.

The intellectualizing process is what is least likely to be appreciated in *October Ferry*, however, for it imparts a ratiocinative, ruminative, repetitive quality to the book that seems on the surface to stand in the way of action and characterization. Dialogue, certainly, is wooden. But the kind of characterization Lowry was aiming for, the 'centre' of his book, lies more in the reflective mental processes than in external drama. In one of his letters to his editor Albert Erskine (dated summer 1953), Lowry wrote to describe his manuscript:

> *Gabriola* may not be the artistic triumph I sometimes think it is, but if I have any knowledge of the human psyche at all it is . . . a psychological triumph of the first order . . . . [T]he bloody agony of the writer writing it is so patently extreme that it creates a kind of power in itself that, together with the humour and what lyricism it may possess, takes your mind off the faults of the story itself, which incidentally, are of every kind—in fact it possesses perhaps not one single conventional virtue of the normal story—its character drawing is virtually non-existent, symbols are pointed at blatantly instead of being concealed or subsumed in the material, or better still simply not there at all, it is—or is as it stands—repetitious to the point beyond that which you can believe. It's all done on purpose, and some readers—if they read it once—might have to read it 5 times before they could be convinced anything has happened at all.

What sounds here a little like apology becomes a carefully contrived intellectual and artistic venture when it is seen in the context of *The Voyage that Never Ends*. Authors, characters, demonic forces, God, gods, and men come together then in the fluctuating time-present of creative perception. To 'know' heaven is to know hell; the mind creates it, experiences it. "The lighthouse," as the projected title for his volume of poems put it, "invites the storm." To know past is also to know future. To know 'here' (this physical world) is to know 'there' (a metaphysical afterlife), and Ethan asks himself if

> certain coincidences were really brought into being to remind us that a divine supernatural order exists?
> Could it be that it was rather as if, on our journey

through life, some guardian spirit causes our attention to be drawn, at such moments, to certain combinations, whether of events, or persons or things, but which we recognize, as speaking to us in a secret language, to remind us that we are not altogether unwatched, and so encourage us to our highest endeavour, and especially is this true when we most need help, which is almost the same as saying when we most need assurance that our lives are not valueless? At worst, it is true, we fear it might be the devil. But if beneficent, if not diabolic, then what is it, if it is not God, or of God, this eye that hears, this voice that thinks, this heart that speaks, this embodied hallucination that foresees, with more than crystal clarity, and divine speech.

The question reads like a set of permutations and combinations. To know man, apparently, is to follow the contraries of his mind's eye.

Thus 'retreat' paradoxically becomes a movement forward. *Dark as the Grave*, with its conscious attempt to 'visit' the past demonstrates Lowry's most elaborate application of the idea; the opening image of *October Ferry*, with Ethan aboard the bus, reveals it again:

At times, when the Greyhound overtook and passed another car, where the road was narrow, the branches of the trees brushed the left-hand windows, and behind, or in the rearview mirror ahead reflecting the road endlessly enfilading in reverse, the foliage could be seen tossing for a while in a troubled gale at their passage.

But the "gale" lies ahead of them; "There's a much more dangerous stretch of sea farther out in the Gulf and nearer Gabriola and you never can tell what the weather's going to be from one moment to the next."

Because "it was as if the whole world were beginning to fear eviction," the Llewelyns' predicament becomes society's, and *October Ferry*, like *Under the Volcano*, turns at one level into a social commentary. Much more profoundly it is a study of Everyman's soul. Outward bound for Gabriola, man is also bound to it; it is his cross and salvation together:

Voyage, the homeward-outward-bound voyage; everybody was on such a voyage, the Ocean Spray, Gabriola, themselves, the barman, the sun, the reflections, the stacked glasses, even the light, the sea outside, now due to an accident of sun and dislimning cloud looking like a luminosity between two darknesses, a space between two immensities, was on such a voyage, to the junction of the two infinities, where it would set out on its way again, had already set out, toward the infinitely small, itself already expanding before you had thought of it, to replenish the limitless light of Chaos—

When Ethan and Jacqueline finally dock at the island on the book's last page, it is dark and the stars are out, but "demonic" fires are burning there, too; the island promises to be only another ferryboat continuing the voyage through the Gulf of experience. As the epigraph from George Eliot intones: "There is no short cut . . . to wisdom: . . . the soul's path lies through the thorny wilderness which must be still trodden in solitude". Yet it is a solitude in which readers— perennial wedding guests held by the Ancient Mariner's eye— can share. Had Lowry had the opportunity to polish the novel further, it might have proved as enveloping as *Under the Volcano* or "The Forest Path to the Spring." Its significance as a marker of the development of his thought, however, is undeniable, and (despite some awkward passages, unrealized characters, and undeveloped themes) its complex web even now has the power to engage the mind.

1972

NOTES

1. The phrase reappears in a manuscript short story entitled "Enter One in Sumptuous Armour."

2. See his letter to Jonathan Cape (dated 2 January 1946) in *Selected Letters of Malcolm Lowry*, Harvey Breit & Margerie Bonner Lowry (eds.), Philadelphia & New York: Lippincott, 1965, 65. The Qliphoth, as the Tree of Life upside down, relates also to the substantial tree imagery in *October Ferry*.

3. The short story with this title was reprinted from *Experiment* in E.J. O'Brien's *Best British Short Stories of 1931* as "Seductio Ad Absurdum," and later incorporated into Chapter IV of *Ultramarine*.

LIFE
AND TIME:
LAURENCE'S
*THE STONE
ANGEL*

The opening pages of any good novel do more than just introduce characters and establish setting; by imagery or situations, they also set the tone and give some indication of the problem or the conflict that the book will explore. So it is with Margaret Laurence's *The Stone Angel*. In its opening pages we meet Hagar Shipley, the narrator, and some of her family; we are presented with Manawaka, Manitoba, and with the stone angel in the cemetery there; we are quickly made aware that Hagar can be both sardonic and wry, and that she still has a zest for life which makes her very attractive. And there is more. One of the most striking features about this book's opening pages is the fact that they are filled with empty threats: "If I told they'd—"; "You mind or I'll—"; "You shut up or I'll—." The speakers are children, and thus the threats do not stand out as unusual or incredible in any way; but their irony—the difference between the threatened situation and the actual occurrence— effectively introduces the themes and the tone of the whole book. In exploring the memories of an old woman during her last days, the novel continually juxtaposes desire and reality, expectation and event, what one wants and what one gets. In Hagar's struggle to comprehend why they are different, and in Margaret Laurence's attempt to create her, are sensitive responses to the problem of being alive and mortal; and the two together form one of the most illuminating literary experiences in recent Canadian fiction.

The theme is one that has occurred throughout Mrs.

Laurence's work, enunciated most specifically at the beginning of her travel book about Somaliland, *The Prophet's Camel Bell* (1963):

> In your excitement at the trip, the last thing in the world that would occur to you is that the strangest glimpses you may have of any creature in the distant lands will be those you catch of yourself.
>
> Our voyage began some years ago. When can a voyage be said to have ended? When you reach the place you were bound for, presumably. But sometimes your destination turns out to be quite other than you expected.

With a statement like this in mind, we can make a retrospective judgment about her first book. *This Side Jordan* (1960), set in Ghana just before it became independent, was a promising novel, even though its structure and characterization were a little too unsubtle. Its three main characters—Nathaniel Amegbe, the young African teacher who is caught between native traditions and western society; Johnny Kestoe, the white businessman working in the Gold Coast; and the Gold Coast itself—are each in search of independence, and each must find his own. One difficulty with *This Side Jordan* is that however well we understand Johnny and see that Nathaniel is Johnny with a different skin, we see also that this strategy is much too simple: Nathaniel's problems can only partly be shared by others who are foreign to all his traditions. Ultimately, the novel does not bring us to comprehend Ghanaians and the desire for independence in Ghana; but rather—by an oblique and probably unconscious route—it brings us to understand something more of a comparable but not identical desire in Margaret Laurence's native Canada. *This Side Jordan* gives us a 'strange glimpse of the self' in other words, one which the later novels explore further.

The stories in *The Tomorrow-Tamer and Other Stories* (1963) are also set in West Africa; but the author has by this time made titanic strides in learning how to make characters live on the page. This ability is evident in her two best novels, the two set in the invented but quite credible town of Manawaka, Manitoba: *The Stone Angel* (1964), and *A Jest of God* (1966), the Governor-General's-Award-winning novel about the frustrated creative energies of a woman approaching middle age. This last book, wryly and fatefully titled, does have a few difficulties with making the male characters more than stock figures; and for that reason, it is not as consistently fine as *The Stone Angel*. But the first person point of view in *A Jest of God* explains much of the difficulty and excuses some of it. The narrator, Rachel Cameron, sees the people around her on a flat plane; we see them only through her, and she sees largely what she wishes to. But we are made to see into the woman herself, and when she is forced to recognize that she has been duped by events that she thought she had seen clearly, we are at the core of the book. The irony in this situation is the same as that in a response to an empty threat: a face different from the one that the person has put on is required. This irony raises an interesting question. If an individual has been able to steel himself for one unpleasant outcome, and if another outcome unexpectedly occurs, how should he react? And does he crumble or not? The epigraph to *The Stone Angel*, from a poem by Dylan Thomas, proclaims the alternatives: a person can "go gentle into that good night," or else "rage, rage against the dying of the night." Thomas advocates the fight for life. So does Margaret Laurence.

Even Mrs. Laurence's most recent book, then, takes us back into *The Stone Angel*, into the memories and the viewpoint of its central character, Hagar Shipley, who "often wondered why one discovers so many things too late. The jokes of God." Any mention of raging also takes us to Hagar, for her rages are one of the most vividly memorable things about her. Some of these are roaring reactions against meekness; some grow from impatience with her own physical frailty; but all are connected with pride, and typified by the clan motto her father has dinned into her "Gainsay who dare." Who does dare when Hagar rages? Her husband, Bram, and her second son, John, dare certainly, and in another way, Time itself. In the memories of her men and in reminders of her mortality, Hagar's character is unfolded.

In fact, the novel, told from Hagar's point of view, develops very much as an unfolding. Layer on layer of irony, character and meaning are revealed in the succession of events that the present brings back to the old lady's mind. The way in which present and past are brought together actually contributes to the irony of the characterization. Early in the novel, Hagar momentarily but consciously recognizes and refutes the idea that in aging she sometimes regrets her life: "Oh, my lost men. No, I will not think of that." But she does think, does lament, does remember, and her consciousness ceases to be always in control. The fact that she also rages and, in a special way, comes to love as well, makes her more complex still.

There are several key phrases that help us to comprehend Hagar's exploration of her struggle with life. When she contemplates the difference between an event and its continued existence in the mind, she muses "how small the town was, and how short a time it took to leave it, as we measure time." How else can it be measured? we ask. And the novel considers this question. Again, Hagar has dreamed of the perfect future: "To move to a new place—that's the greatest excitement. For a while you believe you carry nothing with you—." But when you come right down to it, Hagar doesn't really want perfection. Or if she does, she wants it on her own terms: thus, as when Troy, the young minister, comes to pay a duty call on her, she will mentally or verbally lacerate a person who does not accept her reality:

> Even if heaven were real, and measured as Revelation says, so many cubits this way and that, how gimcrack a place it would be, crammed with its pavements of gold, its gates of pearl and topaz, like a gigantic chunk of costume jewelry. Saint John of Patmos can keep his sequined heaven, or share it with Mr. Troy, for all I care, and spend eternity in fingering the gems and telling each other gleefully they're worth a fortune.

However, even when she says this, she is concerned about her years—about whether or not they were good ones, about what one should get for their being "good," about their being "unfair," and about who or what is to *blame* for the injustices of an often bitter and always mortal life. They are the questions disturbing the old lady and us, if we think about them, for they focus ultimately on the problem of human responsibility. How much individuality and how much choice do we have in a world that is influenced by 'jests of God'? Hagar's answer lies again in raging against the night, and in coming by this raging to an assertion of self and to a recognition of the self she has asserted.

Such a process is an essentially tragic one. It is not tragic in the sense of being the fall of a 'great one' (though Hagar's pride can be seen as a kind of *hubris*); but it is tragic in Frye's sense—an example of locating "the centre of tragedy . . . in the hero's isolation, not in a villain's betrayal, even when the villain is as he often is, a part of the hero himself" (*Anatomy of Criticism*). It is not that Hagar was betrayed by pride and fear (though in another sense she is betrayed by her physical weakness) but that Hagar, by obeying her inclinations, by adhering to that which she considers right, finds herself only in alienating herself more and more from other people. She recognizes this late in her life:

> Pride was my wilderness, and the demon that led me there was fear. I was alone, never anything else, and never free, for I carried my chains within me, and they spread out from me and shackled all I touched. . . . Nothing can take away those years.

She will not bend to play a role, for example, even when roleplaying would bring relief to another person. When her brother Dan is dying, it is not Hagar but another brother, Matt, who pretends to be their mother in order to give the boy some comfort. She refuses to play the role because her mother had been meek and frail. Similarly she refuses, early in the book, ever to be a housekeeper like Auntie Doll. But ironically these refusals all reverse themselves. In time Hagar finds herself playing the wounded mother, playing at being in a rage, keeping house for another and then, when she is very old and has fled her family to try to regain her independence and her past, she finds herself playing house by the sea like a child again. At such times, others like Murray Ferney Lees, must play roles to comfort Hagar.

"How can one person know another? " Hagar is constantly asking; but "How can a person know himself? " is the deeper question that Margaret Laurence asks by implication. Even the first of these questions is double-edged. Hagar is not really known by the people around her, nor can Hagar really know them. Only late in her life, when she sees more clearly her relationship with her sons—the favourite, flamboyant John; and the solidly middle-class Marvin with whom she lives—does she come really to see her very self, and hence to see and know her role in life. Only then can she accept for even a moment, for the sake of others, a role that is out of character for her, and discover in it some degree of that capacity for love which she had always craved and which she has always but unknowingly possessed.

At one point in the novel, John is wrestling to re-erect the fallen stone angel on the Currie-Shipley grave above the town. Hagar wants to see him as Jacob, but she does not really know him yet. John in wrestling with this angel is only himself, sweating, grunting, swearing. It is Marvin, visiting her in the hospital and holding her tightly, who

> is truly Jacob, gripping with all his strength, and bargaining. *I will not let thee go, except thou bless me.* And I see I am thus strangely cast, and perhaps have been so from the beginning, and can only release myself by releasing him.

Her response, her expression of a kind of love to him and to others in the hospital, leads to the denouement of the story; but the Biblical analogues thus referred to give another dimension to the book. The *Genesis* story of Abraham's two families is well known: the passionate marriage with Hagar, giving him a son, Ishmael; and the marriage with Sarah which, by a promise from God, gives him a son in Isaac, grandsons in Jacob and Esau, and a dynasty. But Margaret Laurence's story of Hagar is based not so much on the *Genesis* story as it is on St. Paul's reference to it in *Galatians* 4 : 22-27 :

> For it is written, that Abraham had two sons, the one by a bondmaid, the other by a free woman. But he who was of the bondwoman was born after the flesh; but he of the free woman was by promise. Which things are an allegory: for these are the two covenants; the one from the mount Sinai, which engendereth to bondage, which is Agar. For this Agar is mount Sinai in Arabia, and answereth to Jerusalem which now is, and is in bondage with her children. But Jerusalem which is above us is free, which is the mother of us all. For it is written, Rejoice, thou barren that bearest not; break forth and cry, thou that travailest not: for the desolate hath many more children than she which hath a husband.

We have already noted how Hagar was not free, and the numerous desert images in the book, together with the references which liken this story to the Biblical one, are many-sided: the prairie in drought is a desert; Hagar is called the Egyptian, Pharaoh's daughter; she wanders through wildernesses; her relationship with Bram, her husband, is of the flesh—"his banner over me was his skin," she says; and so on. The significance of such allusions is not simply that Margaret Laurence is exploiting Biblical archetypes, but that, having seen Hagar as an essentially tragic figure, she has placed her in a modern setting and explored her point of view. *Genesis*, in effect, gives us Sarah's viewpoint; St. Paul tells us his; and beyond those two lies Hagar's predicament, which we as readers are asked to understand. The son who takes after Hagar can never be Jacob, and is always the outcast without a home. Nor is she a Sarah, and though she is cast as the angel for Marvin's Jacob, she knows this can never be. When, at her request, Mr. Troy sings to her in the hospital—

> All people that on earth do dwell,
> Sing to the Lord with joyful voice,

> Him serve with mirth, His praise forth tell;
> Come ye before Him and rejoice.

—she knows the bitterness of her life and she experiences the moment of truth which is the deepest point of tragedy: "I must always, always, have wanted that—simply to rejoice. How is it I never could? I know, I know." Joy is for the Sarahs of the world; but she is Hagar. Her identity will not allow it.

Hagar does have some kinship with the stone angel on the grave, of course; but this is not the angel from Milton's *Lycidas*, looking homeward with compassion, for it is eyeless in its wilderness and for a long time so is she. The irony of such a situation is picked up by the other images in the book. In her rage for life Hagar is partial to flowers, but the prairie is dry, the houses are grey, and the flowers that are around her are always lilac and lily-of-the-valley, spring flowers that are associated with death and with funerals. She is partial to flowered silks, but Doris, Marvin's wife, who tends her in her old age, is always in rayon and acetate, brown and grey. Doris's hat, moreover, is made of artificial flowers, and her one unchallengeable talent is ambivalently and (ironically) described: she can make gravy that is "always a silken brown." But some of Mrs. Laurence's ironies are defiant with life: in the cemetery, cowslips grow

> tough-rooted, these wild and gaudy flowers, and although they were held back at the cemetery's edge, torn out by loving relatives determined to keep the plots clear and clearly civilized, for a second or two a person walking there could catch the faint, musky, dust-tinged smell of things that grew untended and had grown always before the portly peonies and the angels with rigid wings, when the prairie bluffs were walked through only by Cree with enigmatic faces and greasy hair.

And Hagar herself, at the end of the book, is also as defiant as ever. She has discovered who she is, discovered that she is alone; there is no greater tragedy for her and yet no greater satisfaction. Her final words, "And then—," uttered in the novel at the time of her death, are part of a chronology and therefore part of time. But by leaving the sentence unfinished, Mrs. Laurence closes the book in ambivalence; it is possible that time stops, but possible also that it goes on, and is merely measured in a different way.

Though life has been bitter for Hagar, it has been precious as well; and in raging against the dying of the light she finds her only defence against servility and against a passive resignation to what she considers injustice. Her reaction to death is one of both defeat and triumph, for as earlier she has been continually surprised by the suddenness and shortness of life, so is she at the last assured that death is "quite an event." She meets it as *an* event, as a next episode in her story, but it is an episode which, of course, we are unable to observe (another of the jokes of God).

So sympathetically has Margaret Laurence created Hagar that we see the world through her. In following the track of her mind as it travels back and forth in its personal narrative, we are moved—not only with her, but also by her—and we come at least to understand a little more about being alive. In controlling the point of view, and in unifying character with the method and the formal structure of the book, and in wedding the whole to her vision of independence and human responsibility, Mrs. Laurence has created in *The Stone Angel* a fine novel and an absolutely human world.

1967

EQUATORIAL
ZONES AND
POLAR
OPPOSITES

Every country inherits a national cliché, each as inexact as it is widespread. Brazil, for example, is known as a land striated with coffee plantations, and Australia as a desert of kangaroos. Canada was baptized by Voltaire's pat phrase "quelques arpents de neige," and Africa (its nations undifferentiated) long ago became the 'Dark Continent' to all outside it—a savage jungle of multifarious poisons, whose dangers were offset only by the challenge of survival, the hero's manliness, the heroine's brave frailty, and the prospect of hidden treasure. Such archetypes allowed *King Solomon's Mines* its appeal; nineteenth-century adventure writers consciously built upon their readers' preconceived notions, fulfilling them by finding yet another twist to a hackneyed plot. White missionaries/explorers/treasure-seekers headed into unknown territory/river jungle/mysterious mountains, were attacked/imprisoned by fearful/corrupt natives, but were then saved by trusting/righteous/kingly natives, who bestowed treasure on their white friends as the dawn of understanding/twilight of peace brought all together at last. The Imperial Theme in such adventures is scarcely subtle.

In more recent writing, imperialism has become less overt, though the continued existence of the popular stereotype of Africa prevents its total disappearance. In Canada, as elsewhere, many writers have sought new frameworks for their ideas and new techniques with which to express them, but others have been trapped by conventions. *Their* writing, like

Ralph Allen's *Ask the Name of the Lion* (1962)—subtitled "A modern novel of the Congo"—reflects more accurately the popular imagination than it does any observed event. Paradoxically it is events rather than imagination that most distinctively characterize this kind of writing. *Ask the Name of the Lion* is one of those works that dust jackets call a "thrilling narrative," whose sole appeal lies in the topicality of its plot. Ideas and inventiveness of technique are subordinated to the story, and *character* is less important than *role*. What the novel is about, therefore, is less the internal rebellion in the Congo following independence from Belgium, than the confrontation between Africa and the West *as represented by* a set of stereotyped figures. The rebel Congolese, who are the pursuers and the putative villains of the piece, are conventionally ambitious, animalistic, ruthless, and naïve. But the six pursued characters—Sierra, a U.N. representative; Songolo, the Western-educated federal cabinet minister; Grant, a doctor from a primitive hospital; Mary Kelvin, a Canadian nurse; Chartrand, a Belgian plantation-owner reluctant to leave; and Astrid, his young Congolese mistress—are less the heroes than their own worst enemies. They flee and quarrel; the pursuers pursue; they meet in a climactic and destructive encounter; and the novel ends with the Canadian girl, the most lukewarm of all of them, managing to utter gallant things as she survives.

The gallantry is not the larger-than-life action of Boadicea or Florence Nightingale, however, but simply a way of making the best of a bad job. It is exactly such a failure to discover any real heroism that marks Allen's book as a successor to Rider Haggard's rather than its contemporary; *Ask the Name of the Lion* deliberately finds dubious motives where Haggard found bravery and self-sacrifice. When Songolo and Sierra stand fiercely alone in the final confrontation with Albert Tshibangu—Nkosi, 'the lion,' the self-styled president of the breakaway province—it is not Tshibangu they are fighting, but each other and themselves. Allen's message is clear enough: we have within us that divisive Miltonic pride that violates us; no external attack can weaken as much as one from within. But this being the case, the African setting serves merely as a topical scenario, bruiting a lot of conventional images without in any way requiring them. Theme and form are arranged together but not bound together, and the parcel that Allen has neatly tied up quickly loses its string.

For all its gentility, the work of John Peter betrays a comparable format—less easy to appreciate, perhaps, because the South African settings and the anti-apartheid sentiments are emotionally attractive to Western audiences, but nonetheless there. Peter, a South African emigré now living in Victoria, is himself personally responsive to the racial issues that today accompany a mental image of his native country, and both his novels—*Along That Coast* (1964) and *Runaway* (1969)—depict typical Jack Cope- or Nadine Gordimer-like South African 'situations'. For example, a white liberal (who still accepts remarkably defined views of racial differences) is killed by blacks who mistake him for a ruthless conservative Afrikaner; or, another white finds himself embroiled against his political inclinations in aiding a black to escape South African law. Although the ironies—the *raison d'être* of the books—do give the novels some topical force, they are effectively hidden behind the overt and less convincing stories of North Americans experiencing the South African fact for the first time. The visitors' naïveté presumably should allow Peter some objectivity towards his topic; in fact it gives him the opportunity to preach.

Along That Coast is typical. A Canadian teacher fleeing an unhappy love affair finds herself embroiled in what promises to be a fulfilling one while on her African holiday. (It is hard to know if all the Canadian women in these books are meant to represent innocence, ignorance, smugness, or objectivity. Nationality in Allen's book is artificial at best; in Peter's it has some point, but the national character being explored is unclear.) Laura Hunt meets Denton Todd at a South African resort town, observes racial inequalities around her, alternately argues about them and confesses to this older but virile male her dissatisfaction with the effete Canadian society she has left. Ultimately she comes through sex to learn love, but he, pausing introspectively before committing himself to emigrate, is mistakenly and accidently killed. His body is tossed aside "along the coast"; no one sees; and we do not observe Laura's discovery or reaction before the novel closes with much the same geographical peroration that opens it:

> Along that coast the turbulence of the tepid ocean gathers and beats, incessantly beats and goes foaming back in a sheeted recoil down the flat wet slope of the beaches, beats on the lead-coloured rocky promontories and flings up geysers of spray, then goes slopping and boiling in the gullies, sinking into eddying shallowness only to come surging up again, smashing up white again along the shuddering shoreline.

Etc. The language is consciously heightened to emphasize the urgently serious implications of the action, but the effect of the parallel verbs and the alliteration and the multiplicity of participles is one of melodrama rather than tragedy.

The wave motion that the passage evokes, however, does more than set the stage. The scenes of sexual encounter and of dying are also described by the wave image, and thus Peter relates love and death to the political framework. Uprising, conquest, and triumph loom as imminent inevitabilities, in which some will survive and some—probably the uncommitted—will be consumed. But the threat of internal political division—as in Allen's Congo—is not limited to the country in which the book is set, and Peter strives throughout to demonstrate the immediacy of the elements of the South African conflict within Canada as well. The existence of two major Western cultures in conflict with each other's religion and language—while the native population ekes out its own existence—is a problem both countries share, however different their expressions of such an attitude. And Laura's upset with South Africa counterpoints her annoyance with her home:

"I'm not in a hurry to replace faith with philosophy or superstition. Or good manners. That's what we've been doing in Canada, it seems to me. Protestant Canada, I mean. I don't know anything about Quebec. With us the only real god is propriety. Apart from money of course, that's the other one. Church is just a hallmark of respectability. We're the most respectable damn nation in the world. Even our rebels are timid. Or they're out of date. They talk as if the First World War had just come to an end."

She herself is hardly an acceptable substitute, nor is Denton a particularly likely Prince Charming, for which reasons the novel as a whole becomes rhetorical, and suffers.

In this case Allen's stereotyped vision of dark Africa does not apply—the scenes involving minor characters and the day-to-day events of their lives are quite credible—but the major characters are *literary* conventions, whose presence is staged rather than called into life. Hence their political discussions, however germane to the themes Peter wishes to convey, intrude into the humanity of their relationship and interrupt the narrative movement. A balance between idea and technique is, of course, difficult to achieve, and for a writer trying to communicate the reality of a culture other than his own, the difficulty is compounded. Paradoxically Margaret Laurence, who faces the problem more than Peter does, is more successful in meeting it; not only is her Africa alive, but her characters are too. Yet looking back at her writing and her own experience of Africa, she has commented (in *Canadian Literature* no. 41):

> *This Side Jordan* and the two other books I wrote which were set in Africa, *The Prophet's Camel Bell* and *The Tomorrow-Tamer*, were written out of the milieu of a rapidly ending colonialism and the emerging independence of African countries. They are not entirely hopeful books, nor do they, I think, ignore some of the inevitable casualties of social change, both African and European, but they do reflect the predominantly optimistic outlook of many Africans and many western liberals in the late 1950's and early 1960's. They were

written by an outsider who experienced a seven years' love affair with a continent but who in the end had to remain in precisely that relationship, for it could never become the close involvement of family.

Later in the same article she notes that *This Side Jordan* (1960) now seems "out-dated," "superficial," though "somehow retrospectively touching," because "victory for the side of the angels is all but assured." Jordan in the abstract can be, will be crossed in the minds of her characters, but in the succeeding decade, with its wars and its rebelliousness and its frequent cynicism, Africa and the world have changed.

The really good novel would survive such alteration, and if *This Side Jordan* doesn't quite make it, the reasons for its not doing so differ from those that mar the work of Peter and Allen. It is too patently a first novel; that is its problem. The labours of producing it interfered with the author's judgement of her accomplishment, and too often she indulged her style when she should have tamed it. (With the short stories of *The Tomorrow-Tamer* and a novel like *The Stone Angel* [1964] she was to demonstrate the stylistic restraint of which she was capable; only then was the talent of which the first novel promises given tangible proof.)

Like Peter's book, *This Side Jordan* concerns a Westerner in Africa, this time an arrogant Englishman named Johnny Kestoe, whose future is being threatened by Ghanaian independence and the Africanization of the company he works for. Placed beside him are Nathaniel Amegbe, a young school teacher whose idealism traps him between his traditions and his hope for the future; Victor Edusei, a militant nationalist; Miranda Kestoe, Johnny's blundering wife; and others—all of whom move through a permutation of encounters designed to show aspects of Western and Ghanaian character. If the English are well intentioned and kind, they too often express their conscience stupidly in condescending tones; the Ghanaian hospitality is thus deceived and an irritated quick cry for Free-Dom becomes both a panacea for hurt pride and a retaliation to preserve human dignity. Not Kestoe's, of course, nor even Amegbe's, but that of the people, *la nation*. They have a viable independence to shape, too, and when Johnny and Miranda at the last find each other, and when Amegbe names his long-wanted son Joshua, the trio of happy discoveries seems complete.

The fictional device being used here is completely transparent when the novel is reduced to such bones. The neatness of the quasi-allegory—each self-discovery paralleling, reflecting, and representing the others—itself demonstrates the author's inexperience with her medium, and the resolutions to which that neatness gives rise seem too pat, too *fictional*, to be acceptable. One can perhaps accept Allen's story for the one-dimensional narrative it is—just as, to begin with, one accepts the helter-skelter mythic tales of Amos Tutuola at the tale-telling level, for all his greater artistry and his stories' greater depth. But *This Side Jordan* pretends to *realism,* and the solutions Mrs. Laurence imposes, instead of continuing the 'real' world the rest of the story depicts, try to enter the prophetic spheres of the fable and romance, where issues can actually be resolved and matters do end. The Ghana that Margaret Laurence has lived in exists during most of the novel, is palpably *there*, evoked by dialect and detail, but at the end, the Africa of the popular imagination returns, impinges itself on the mind of the writer remembering the world she knew, thus momentarily allowing to exist (however insubstantially) a rather different world of challenges met and heroic success. The two do not meld, and the world of myth that Tutuola calls on so admirably remains in *This Side Jordan* unabsorbed.

In *The Tomorrow-Tamer and other stories* (1963), Mrs. Laurence returns to the severer restrictions of the short story form and to the world of observed events. The opening paragraph of the first story in the collection, "The Drummer of All the World," sets the ironic tone:

My father thought he was bringing salvation to Africa. I, on the other hand, no longer know what salvation is. I

am not sure that it lies in the future. And I know now
that it is not to be found in the past.

The English-educated narrator, Matthew, grew up in Ghana,
and he returns there later as a civil servant. As a boy he was
like a brother to his nurse's son, Kwabena; they shared confi-
dences, ambitions, and hopes, but only Matthew's appear to
have been fulfilled when they meet again as adults. Kwabena
is cordial and bitter; Matthew is ashamed. Kwabena wants to
escape the past, Matthew to find it again. Encountering such
differences, they seem unable to avoid appearing always
conscious of each other's weaknesses, and the boyhood unity
disintegrates. Memory of that unity is no help, for it reinforces the knowledge that allows the awareness of the flaws in
the first place. So they separate, and by separating pretend to
forget what in fact they cannot: that they are both human,
and that the truth and natural purity they had ironically
represented to each other as boys is something adults never
inherit.

The political sensibilities of such a story are clear enough.
The Age of Free-Dom succeeds the Age of Administration
which in turn has succeeded the Age of Missionary Salvation
—and all of them cease being ideals the moment a human
being tries to execute them. A new ideal replaces a previous
one rapidly enough, but it is only the old administration in a
new suit that stands behind it. A comic treatment of this
theme is to be found in the finest story in Mrs. Laurence's
collection, "The Perfume Sea," about a hairdresser who has
no past in Europe to return to when Free-Dom comes and
the other Europeans leave. So he must stay and (in staying)
become someone new, for the new society: a hairdresser for
African ladies. His manicurist stays, too; they discover each
other; and at the end their shadows entwine "like children
who walk through the dark." But for Godman Pira, the dwarf
in "Godman's Master," who flees bondage to a fetish priest
only to find himself in bondage to a circus troupe ("Half
god . . . Half man . . . LIVE ORACLE"), the passage from
one regime to another is pathetic. Despite this, he is able to

say " 'I fear and fear, and yet I live,' " affirming in a small voice the ability of man's *feeling* for ideals to continue to survive. Or as Mammii Ama puts it, in her song at the end of "A Gourdful of Glory":

> "Mammii Ama, she no come rich.
> Ha-ei! Be so. On'y one penny.
> She nevah be shame,
>   she no fear for nothing.
> D'time wey come now,
>   like queen she shine."

Free-Dom is coming, she knows, and with it a new age of Free Bus Rides! Interpreting independence as she does, her horizons seem narrow; but in fact, because they focus not simply upon herself but upon each man's sense of self, they are enormously wide. Whatever else Free-Dom may mean, it allows for individuals seeking their own identity some measure of self-respect.

Africa is *necessarily* Africa in these stories, then, not an accidental setting. The encounters and experiences have particular West African significance, and the sensibilities of the stories bear comparison with those of Achebe, Okigbo, and others whom Mrs. Laurence admires and has appreciated in her personal critical study of Nigerian writing, *Long Drums and Cannons* (1968). But Africa serves as a metaphor as well as a subject here. The search for a route to survival is not African alone but representative of a general search; the wry discoveries are Everyman's discoveries; and the ironic mode is the twentieth century's. What Mrs. Laurence therefore has to say in her travel book about Somaliland, *The Prophet's Camel Bell* (1963)—

> the strangest glimpses you may have of any creature in the distant lands will be those you catch of yourself

—serves as a kind of motto to her use of the African motif.

Since Mrs. Laurence first travelled to Somaliland, there have been a number of Canadians visiting and writing in Africa—David Knight in Nigeria, Audrey Callahan Thomas and Dave Godfrey in Ghana, Dorothy Livesay in Zambia, and others. Godfrey and Mrs. Thomas have both responded in the short story, and both (as experimental stylists) mark another stage in this Canadian literary exploration. On the whole Audrey Thomas's character portrayals show a more consistently good-humoured view of life, Godfrey's a more sardonic one (as in "Up in the Rainforest" or "Fulfilling Our Foray," in *Death Goes Better with Coca-Cola* [1967]). But the two African stories in Mrs. Thomas's *Ten Green Bottles* (1967)—"Xanadu" and "Omo"—are among her most ironic and penetrating studies of disillusionment. Not hers, particularly, but that of Westerners seeking paradisiacal solutions in the New Africa they go out to meet. What they find always upsets them further. In "Xanadu," for example, the narrator's servant is so adept, so honest, so humble, that her own personality starts to seem gross. Her solution—to frame the servant, planting coffee spoons in his house while he is absent on an unnecessary errand, in order that he may be 'justifiably' dismissed—is no solution at all. Like Margaret Laurence's character Kwabena, she thinks that by separating herself from a physical fact she will be able to relocate her lost equanimity, little realizing that a disturbing experience once felt is an experience known and remembered.

"Omo" states the problem even more directly:

> "This is Africa." You know, you try to look back on first impressions and of course it's impossible—you know too much later on—or you know a lot more, yet not enough. What I mean is, I'm not sure what I meant by "this is Africa."

The ambivalence carries through the whole story. The speaker is a white American peace corps volunteer, who rooms with another, an American negro. Both in Ghana to prove themselves, they encounter there a native albino named Omo, the son of a white missionary and the black woman he seduced, who takes on the kind of oracular role of Mrs. Laurence's Godman Pira. His motives are a little unclear, however, and his psychological harrying of Walter Jordan, the black American, leads to Jordan's disappearance in search of 'home' and his own death. In the process, the divisions between one person and another, black and white, Africa and America, knowledge and ignorance, certainty and doubt, fade. Involved, but not exactly participating in the conflict, the narrator observes it all—and the deceptive objectivity is important. The author's technique, combining her observations of Ghanaian culture with her inbred awareness of North America, adds another twist to the apprehensions she wants to convey. In Twi, 'omo' means 'it is not good'; but "Omo," so runs the American detergent commercial, washes "whiter than white." The persisting difference in language and implication leads to the ironic inability of people to communicate despite their common humanity, so that in the end Walter is traced to a village in the north, where he is remembered as

> a strange young African, nearly naked, who squatted in front of their fires and tried to tell them something in a language they didn't understand.

The narrator's pervading sense of sadness and lost opportunity is one we share.

Ironically, however, the story itself encounters something of the difficulty it describes, for its black men are still perceived, albeit sympathetically, from the outside. Perhaps this is all one can ever expect. Certainly it characterizes David Knight's 'public' experience of Africa, as he expresses it in one of the poems in *The Army Does not Go away* (1969):

> I and the tear-gas do not meet.
> I am a tourist on their street,
> I and my children. Still, they guess
> There must be one thing I profess
> As a professor: truth—so I
> Am smiled upon and let go by,
> A petty talisman, to find
> A smell of tear-gas in the mind
> And ghost of it upon the street . . . .

Not untouched by events and persons around him, he is not *of* them, and that makes all the difference.

Dorothy Livesay's "The Colour of God's Face" (revised and reprinted in 1967 as the "Zambia" cycle in *The Unquiet Bed*), about the land and the people and the visions of a nameless village in Zambia, approaches in effect the same question, though from a different vantage point:

> Nameless, the village
> the clay huts, the shorn grass roof
> brown to the ground
> nameless
> the woman huddled beside a pale flame
> and the child, bringing stools to sit upon
> is nameless, boy or girl.
>
> They do not love this place, or name it
> they are too much of it
> they smell of grass, of leaves
> of the pitiless dust
> they rise up with the rain
> and die with it.
>
> Between the land and themselves
> they feel no difference . . . .

But the Westerner does, as the very technique of the poem reveals. Opening with an abstraction—"nameless" (an idea repeated contrapuntally through the poem)—it continues concretely, descriptively, by *naming*: "clay huts," "shorn grass roof," "brown," etc. The details separate item from item; they set up boundaries, draw distinctions, divide the poet-observer from the village observed, so that there can never be the identification between them that exists between the land and the village people who passively accept the land. The Scientific Method and the 'realities' of Western philosophy intervene, even unconsciously, to keep the two cultures, for all their *entente*, fundamentally apart. (This does not, of course, deny the moving lyricism of the poem itself.)

This question of separation looms even larger in more recent works of fiction. Hubert Aquin's *Trou de Mémoire* (1968), for example, uses revolutionary and imaginative

parallels between Montreal and Ivory Coast scientist/revolu-
tionaries, in order to explain and urge the cultural demand
for African and Quebec independence. And David Knight, in
a less heavily symbolic book called *Farquharson's Physique
and what it did to his mind* (1971), draws upon the Biafran
rebellion in Nigeria for political metaphor; as his central
character is drawn into committed action, he paradoxically
gains and loses his independence, becoming less of a type but
less of a free agent as well. If there is a promise of fulfillment,
there is also a threat of total destruction, in other words, in
which the uncertainty of result intensifies rather than obli-
terates the need for active choice. The differences between
African and Canadian 'realities' (both empirical and metaphysical) thus serve to demonstrate the fragmentation with
which contemporary life threatens individual and cultural
identities.

In two 1970 novels set in a fictionalized Ghana, Dave
Godfrey and Audrey Thomas focus respectively on the
political and personal impact that such African realities have
upon Western residents. In so doing, they depict West Africa
closely and sympathetically, with a passionate intelligence
and with more sense of artistry than fiction in Canada has
displayed for some time. Godfrey's book, *The New Ancestors*, is the more active, the more intellectually engaged with
a world of ideas and social commitment, and it demands a
reader's participation. Audrey Thomas's avowedly apolitical
Mrs. Blood more intensely reveals the private chaos of an
individual life, yet the reader remains curiously aloof. Godfrey's book is explosive, Mrs. Thomas's implosive. But both
writers sustain impressive styles and provoke an appreciative
glimpse of their characters' lives.

Shifts in point of view are basic to the progress of both
books. In *Mrs. Blood*, where the title character identifies
herself variously as 'Mrs. Blood' and 'Mrs. Thing', the shift
signifies a tension within a single identity rather than (as
with Godfrey) a multiple perspective. But for 'Mrs. Thing',
who thinks she sees herself and her daily experiences as ob-

jects, the world is not particularly 'out there', at war with the 'in here' of 'Mrs. Blood'; rather, it is made up of what she thinks of as being the perspectives of others towards her, which is demonstrably more subjective. Names—"I am Mrs. Thing"—are an inherent part of Mrs. Thing's world; identity lies in surfaces, colour differences, colour prejudices—all intensified by her present crisis and by her constant will to organize and categorize people and events. Herself included. Carrying a child in danger of being miscarried, she at once lives the experience and—uneasily—distances it, till her 'self' becomes a vessel, counterpointed by the ship in which she has voyaged to Africa.

In such a context 'Africa' becomes a 'furthest extreme', an equatorial opposite to her northern life. It is prefigured by a Jamaican lover's appearance and by a white lover's departure for Sierra Leone. He, Richard, reaches Freetown. She, perhaps pregnant by him, then marries Jason. But years later, when she, too, approaches the African continent's direct face, she is unable to relax. Pregnant in Africa, she is not 'free', and her three loves become chaotically simultaneous in her mind. If separating them is impossible in Mrs. Thing's apparently cool perspective, it is even more difficult in the coursing, central, visceral, intensely female, subjective identity of Mrs. Blood, who is less a 'vessel' than a cyclical sense of creative flow that carries within it the knowledge of death at the same time. The tension in the book rests on this death-life opposition/duality/unity. But the loose tension between Mrs. Blood and Mrs. Thing, for all the intensity of the style and the personal experience it conveys, never electrifies the woman's dilemma into a universal experience nor engages the reader in anything more than a vicarious sense of private suffering and mental *déshabillé*. Still, that is all the book is probably meant to do. As the central volume in a proposed trilogy, it will presumably be 'placed' by the different perspective of the other volumes. If that makes it more like a segment of a work-in-progress than a whole novel in its own right, it is not to underestimate its committed artistry, however—its captivation with the passions that bind men and women brokenly together, and the coruscating way with words that reveals the author's genuine literary talent on every page.

Mrs. Thing admits at one point her awareness of the subjectivity of what she 'objectively' remarks:

> There are smells here which will always be part of Africa for me; and yet if someone asked later what Africa was like and I said "Mansion Polish," or "Dettol," or "the smell of drying blood," they wouldn't understand. And they would be right not to, for the real Africa (whatever that may mean) is none of these and my Africa is only real for me.

At first glance Dave Godfrey's *The New Ancestors* seems to run completely counter to such a private response. Intensely political, deliberately involved in the overt details of West African public life, the book seems to record a 'reality' of a different kind, recognizable outside the private consciousness and faithful to its specific geographic locale. Yet even the most superficial exploration of the book's title paradox will show that to be only partly true. Certainly the 1966 murder of a character named Gamaliel Harding (central to the book) is a political event, as are the other activities that indicate an impending coup to replace The Redeemer of Lost Coast. But behind them lie the mixed motives and responses of the various characters whose voices the novel creates in its deliberate indirectness: an ostensible thug named First Samuels; a displaced Englishman named Michael Burdener; and Harding's mother (Delicacy), sister (Ama, who is Burdener's wife), and son (Kwame Bird Lady Day); among others. People are political, but they are also individual. One epigraph (from *Religio Medici*) even affirms what Audrey Thomas's Mrs. Thing does in her own way: "We carry within us all the wonders we seek without us. There is all Africa and her prodigies in us." For Godfrey the statement becomes a declaration of ancestry as well as a description of how men perceive, which allows him to blend physics and biology with politics and psychology. Sexuality—in barren as well as uniting forms—becomes linked with political manoeuvre. Cell division creates new life, but destroys old identities in so doing. 'Africa' begins to occur both without and within, both now and in time past, in the spiritual imagination as well as in empiric reality, as a public world and as a metaphor for private identities all at once.

The recurrent references to the processes of cell division—prophase, metaphase, anaphase, telophase—recall the genealogical progress and racially mixed parentage of the Harding-Burdener family, and also contain the metaphoric meaning of Godfrey's scene and setting. Metaphase, when the split chromosomes group in the 'equatorial plane' of the cell, is followed by anaphase, when the halves of the chromosomes move to opposite sides, before the entire cell divides and new nuclei are formed. The process is ordered, the result unpredictable except on the basis of statistical probabilities—a tension which gives the book its basis for conflict (provokes Burdener in his antagonism to Gamaliel, for example) and which takes Godfrey into the principles of quantum theory and their application to political affairs. An internal quotation from Max Born is relevant at this point:

> Physics . . . is not only a factor of material progress but also an element in the spiritual evolution of man. In the final analysis, the opposition between East and West . . . is based on philosophical opinions and on ways of life which are subject to the influence of the natural sciences. Marxism teaches that the communist economy is a historical necessity. . . . This idea comes from physical determinism, which itself arises from Newton's celestial mechanics. But, in fact, physics abandoned this theory about thirty years ago. . . . American thought, for its part, is at the mercy of a superficial pragmatism which confuses truth and utility.

The equatorial African scene is thus a battleground between outmoded ideologies while of itself it gives divisive birth to its own (new, old) perspective.

The ambivalence about the age of the truly indigenous

African viewpoint stems from the paradoxical contemporane-
ity of the past in the spiritual sensitivity of Delicacy Harding
and the power of the Word as manifest (here) in Akan pro-
verb. The culture is age-old, but recreated in each generation,
passed on in didactic and indirect fable. But each generation
therefore needs the ancestor to reach it. Kwame Bird Lady
Day is confounded in his search for *"m'agya, m'agya"*—"my
father, my father"—because Gamaliel and Burdener are both
too involved in their enmities to try anything other than to
indoctrinate him in their own causes. That older generation
has abandoned its ancestors to adopt Marxism and American-
ism; names like Harding, Truman, Kayser, and Lady Bird all
tangibly indicate the African overlap with America that
Godfrey's respect for Born and for national culture protests
against.

But who are the new ancestors to serve as replacements?
Frantz Fanon's *The Wretched of the Earth* provides one kind
of commentary on the problem Godfrey raises:

> The native intellectual nevertheless sooner or later will
> realize that you do not show proof of your nation from
> its culture but that you substantiate its existence in the
> fight which the people wage against the forces of occu-
> pation . . . .
>
> Yes, the first duty of the native poet is to see clearly
> the people he has chosen as the subject of his work of
> art . . . .
>
> It is not enough to try to get back to the people in
> that past out of which they have already emerged;
> rather we must join them in that fluctuating movement
> which they are just giving a shape to . . . .
>
> [A national literature] is a literature of combat be-
> cause it assumes responsibility, and because it is the
> will to liberty expressed in terms of time and space.

The storyteller does not sterilize his observations in archaic
and inert form, that is; he emulates the function rather than
the precise pattern of his traditional model—to instruct a

generation in the ways of men and in the moral truths of the culture that is its own. In substance, as Godfrey realizes, Fanon describes Canada's tense identity as well as Africa's— both permeated by a foreign (American) culture to the point of selfconscious uncertainty. Committed to the strengthened expression of cultural independence, however, and aware of the potential interim anarchy that may bedevil (enliven?) a society that singlemindedly sacrifices its present condition to seek it, Godfrey has written a novel that powerfully seizes the imagination and scores the mind. If it ends on the words "fear and fantasy," it does not abandon itself to vagueness and hyper-emotionalism; it merely recognizes, instead, the power of dreams to draw men into action at the same time as it admits the basic weaknesses of human nature. In probing men's strengths, too, and in the complex vision of contemporary life it unravels, *The New Ancestors* introduces a novelist in command of an impressive array of resources, of which a trenchant linguistic dexterity and a disarming intelligence are not the least.

THE MIND'S
EYES (I'S) (ICE):
THE POETRY OF
MARGARET AVISON

Even with all the intelligence that hindsight allows, it is hard to see in Margaret Avison's earliest poems the poet she was later to become. "Gatineau," published in December 1939, reads this way:

> There is a rock at the river-edge
>   Girt by the chain of a boom;
> The yellow wind trickles among the sedge
>   And the air is raw with gloom.
>
> The long black river is uncoiled
>   Among the stolid hills,
> And day is like a window curtain, soiled
>   Against night's windowsills.
>
> The desolation like a churl
>   Knows only, empty-eyed,
> The bleak unconscience of a world
>   Intent on suicide.

It appears girt to the pages of the *Canadian Poetry Magazine*, another victim of the war's unkindness to poetry in Canada. Its technique is so far from that of Projective Verse that the poet's later association with the movement seems impossible to predict.

A new contributor to the *C.P.M.* at this time, Margaret Avison has never again published in the journal, but she has never been a prolific writer. To the major new magazines in Canada in the 1940's, for example—*Preview, First Statement, Northern Review*—she did not contribute. Occasional poems were scattered through *Contemporary Verse* and less specialized journals—*Canadian Forum*,[1] *Here and Now*, and the *Manitoba Arts Review*. But the small total would not alone appear to have justified her being included either in A.J.M. Smith's 1943 *Book of Canadian Poetry* or, some thirty-three poems later, in Ralph Gustafson's 1958 Penguin anthology. Her two books, *Winter Sun* and *The Dumbfounding*, with their substantial collection of new poems, did not appear until the 1960's.

Presumably Smith, aware of the growing craftsmanship which Margaret Avison's verse revealed, would also respond to its metaphysical quality.[2] That this would attach her to a catholic tradition rather than a 'proletarian' one might also explain why *First Statement*, the early *Northern Review*, Raymond Souster's *Contact*, and Louis Dudek's *Delta* did not prove attractive to her. In the 1950's, however, her work found American outlets in the prestigious *Poetry* (Chicago) and *Kenyon Review*, and (subsequently more important for her reputation, and curiously enough, related to *Contact*) in Cid Corman's new series of *Origin* in 1957 and since. It was here she found an appropriate milieu to work out her ideas of form and feeling, ideas that are expressed partly by the sound of words, by the voice projecting the poet's self onto the page, and so by the tension which the mind's response to that voice can effect. The pun in my title, for example, drawn from Margaret Avison's poems, reveals the tonally ambivalent play that can result. At once amused and afraid, the poet strives for order and finds chaos, looks for absolutes and finds moments—but then artistically presents those moments which the shifting point of view of eye and ear bring into her ken.[3]

The bookjacket of *The Dumbfounding* informs us that "As a regular contributor to Cid Corman's *Origin* in the 1950's and early 1960's, along with Zukofsky, Charles Olson, Robert Duncan, Robert Creeley, and Denise Levertov, her work has rightly been associated with theirs in the minds of American readers." Which, the dangling modifier aside, encourages us to identify her with what the *T.L.S.* in its

December 12, 1968, issue called "Black Mountaineering,"
and therefore to look for her (albeit vainly) in the pages of
Tish, the Canadian little magazine most influenced by Creeley and Duncan—edited in its heyday in the early 1960's by
George Bowering and Frank Davey. But Bowering, in a recent
poem ("Survival Course") has himself rejected the identities
to which classifications of this kind give rise:

> Duncan recruits
> a community of poets
> but communities
> are in the control
> of the merchants.
>
> I think a man
> can cook for himself
> & survive in the bush
> maybe with a wooden spoon
> & a pot full of ideas.
>
> . . . .
>
> Not that I wouldnt
> get tired
> of my own cooking
> I just need to
> reaffirm my ability
> to survive.

When from the start Margaret Avison rejects some of the
implications of William Carlos Williams's *Paterson* maxim "No
ideas but in things," it becomes difficult to put her wholly in
a category with Creeley and Co.

What Williams was saying was that ideas should come from
percepts rather than concepts, that a concept should come
only through perception and not impose itself on perception.
But then a conundrum presents itself; is the 'idea' in the
'perceived' or the 'perceiver' or the 'perception'? In "The
Mental Traveller," Blake affirms that "the eye altering alters
all," that the perceiver changes the world. Yet in a Hera-
clitean universe, *nothing* is stable, and therefore what is perceived also changes, altering the perception and so the perceiver. Such an argument provides Margaret Avison with

some of her finest poems;[4] they are cryptic, but what she experiences is 'mysterious', and easy writing is not possible.

Under the scrutiny of her intellect the world sometimes becomes austere, but the poems are never unfeeling. 'Thought' *becomes* 'feeling', and Romanticism is thus inverted—not to find its values valueless, or to praise the social world as the best of all possible, but to find another expression for a metaphysical sensibility by which 'that' world of understanding and 'this' one of perception can be brought together. The brief moment for which this may be possible is still stable, and by being, it becomes part of the future experience, or field of vision, of the poet-perceiver. Sensitivity to word and sound is not irrelevant to this pursuit, but rather the key. The very momentariness of perceptions, and the continuous shifting in point of view, are communicated to our understanding when they are rendered in sound; the multiple meanings inherent in puns immediately suggest this flux, which is the medium in which Margaret Avison looks for a self, and for both release and illumination.

So we turn back to "Gatineau," discovering at first the artificial structure imposed by the rhyme, the apparently weak unenlightening similes, the lifeless copula verbs, and the earnest but flat visual effects: "yellow wind" and "long black river." "Day" and "night" oppose each other conventionally, and, coming rather to expect the last interpretive stanza, we are forced to take stock of what's going on only by the more suggestive phrase "night's windowsills," which obviously reinforces the visual images. Its meaning, however, remains a little obscure—is night the perceiver or the medium for perception? "Empty-eyed" perhaps indicates that it makes no difference, but the inexactness here seems unplanned. In later poems, ambiguity will be more controlled. The windowsill has since become one of Miss Avison's favourite images to suggest the edge of perception, the moment when perception becomes necessary or possible. And so the environment becomes both space and time, which is what "Gatineau," for all its dubious merit, is about.

Subsequent poems during the 1940's and 1950's, were to explore the ambiguities raised by the question of perceiving, ambiguities of existence and response, inexactnesses which linguistic ambiguities could be employed to convey. So rhyme is largely cast aside, her verse becomes intentionally cryptic, and the pun becomes one of her main techniques for exploring not only the multiple meanings in the self and the world but also the ironies to which they in turn give rise. The pun inherent in the word *sense* illustrates what is going on. Images, sounds, surfaces: these are all understood both by *sense perceptions* and by the intellect—by *sense*. The linguistic ambiguity (often 'offstage' in her poems, like many of her allusions) allows the two to become one; the mind 'possesses' the body then, analysing one of its perceptions and still 'perceiving' more, postulating a series of permutations that immediately clouds the issue, making the initial perception at once justifiable and suspect. The complexity and confusion of her earlier poetry—a confusion of response, consciously understood, not of poetic organization—stems from the exploration of the mind's relationship with the world. (To see her poetry strictly as "poetry of ideas," then, as Brewster Ghiselin does in "The Architecture of Vision" [*Poetry* 1947] is a little too narrow a view.)

The intelligence does not, in other words, grasp absolutes easily. To propose one thing will immediately force a curious mind to propose alternates, and the poems' habit of shifting point of view is a logical outcome. This does not inhibit the *search* for absolutes, as the recurrence of abstract nouns in Margaret Avison's poetry clearly shows. By themselves, "New Year's Poem," "From a Provincial" (both from *Kenyon Review*, Spring 1956), and "Prelude" (*Poetry*, March 1959)—all of them collected in *Winter Sun* (1960)—contain "plainness", "largeness", "darkness", "strangeness", "coldness", "changelessness", "sadness", "stillnesses." These terms communicate some concrete quality—"darkness," for example—but convey ideas as well. The ideas have momentarily become things for the senses to perceive, or the senses in operation have discovered concepts during perception. When "Hiatus" (*Poetry*, April 1952) speaks of "Your mind's ear," or when "Prelude" declares that "the honey-combing sun / opened and sealed us in / chambers and courts / and crooked butteries, / cities of sense," the issue is restated.

"Prelude" does more than this, however. Blending several of the elements I have mentioned—the day/night opposition, the linguistic punning and play, the sensory ideas, the point-of-view shifts, and the spatial and temporal landscape—the poem, by means of a prevailing geometrical imagery, discusses the difficulty man has either locating his identity or acknowledging anyone else's in such ambivalent surroundings. If either sense or sensation expands one's perceptions, it limits them as well. Books do not help: "Tomes sag on the begrimed shelves / locking in light"—to illuminate us if we read? or to seal us in if we do read? or to remain hidden completely from view, unavailable to a reader? "Most men," the poet says, "would rather take it straight." Sensation, presumably: i.e. most men would rather understand the world by seeing it than by reading about it, but this doesn't really help either: "Sparrows in the curbs / and ditch-litter at the / service-station crossroads / alike instruct, distract." Even the term "service-station crossroads" carries multiple overtones: crossroads / wrong roads / stations of the Cross / Church service / commerce—the geometry of the image itself indicating the diametric possibilities that a choice in such conditions would allow.

The poem finely captures this complexity, but to see that it has done so is still only a partial appreciation. Other poems help to take us further. "From a Provincial," exploring various orders—Caesar's camp, Milton's candle's light—ends this way: "When day and life draw the horizons / Part of the strangeness is / Knowing the landscape." And "New Year's Poem" closes marking

> the queer delightful skull and crossbones
> Starlings and sparrows left, taking the crust,
> And the long loop of winter wind

> Smoothing its arc from dark Arcturus down
> To the bricked corner of the drifted courtyard
> And the still windowledge.
> > > > Gentle and just Pleasure
> It is, being human, to have won from space
> This unchill, habitable interior
> Which mirrors quietly the light
> Of the snow, and the new year.

So here is "night's windowsill' again, "still," reminding us of our mortality at the end of a year; the human problem, for all analysis and perception, may be insoluble. Yet in spite of that, humanity remains. Some little light is gathered inside, which will allow us to face the world and time.

"Prelude" also examines from many views such a moment of alteration. The woman with her "fixed" hair

> knows day, abruptly,
> as I, and the stone flower, abruptly,
> suffer the cryptic change.
> The turning-point of morning, and the
> unmerging child,
> like the sadness of the summer trees,
> assert their changelessness
> out of this day-change.

> Light, the discovering light, is a beginning
> where many stillnesses
> yearn, those we had long thought long dead
> or our mere selves . . .

> In each at least light finds
> one of its forms
> and is:

> even in the invisible neighbour,
> periwigged, black, in hunting pinks,
> or rinsing clouts beside the holy river,
> who does not bother glancing up to see.

All worlds and times are traversed; each moment becomes a "prelude"; even death is infused with light; and as the epigraph to the poem affirms, "The passive comes to flower, perhaps a first annunciation for the spirit launched on its seasons." Such an affirmation indicates the metaphysical path Margaret Avison was in the process of following, but before the 1960's lay a period of more disruption, of struggle and doubt, and of more dislocation of language.

The geometric imagery helps us to understand the difficulty. "Break of Day," "I Saw One Walking" and "Optional," early poems from *Canadian Forum* in 1942 and 1943, all rather wordily talk about "proportion," "four-square virtues," and "geometric stone," but their very wordiness prevents us from appreciating their word. At best they are trial runs for "Prelude." In 1943, however, in Smith's *Book of Canadian Poetry*, appeared "The Butterfly," which can fairly be said to have established Margaret Avison's reputation. It closes with the passage:

> The meaning of the moth, even the smashed moth, the
> >   meaning of the moth—
> can't we stab that one angle into the curve of space
> >   that sweeps so unrelenting, far above,
> >   towards the subhuman swamp of under-dark?

There is no answer here; the negative question in a sense precludes one. And "The Mirrored Man" (in *Winter Sun*), knowing that "We always turn our heads away / When Canaan is at hand / Knowing it mortal to enjoy / The Promise, not the Land," poses further questions:

> All of us, flung in one
> Murky parabola,
> Seek out some pivot for significance,
> Leery of comets' tails, mask-merry,
> Wondering at the centre
> Who will gain access, search the citadel
> to its last, secret door
> And what face will the violator find
> When he confronts the glass?

Again they are unanswered, and thus Identity, that will-o'-the-wisp of Canadian literature, eludes capture once again.

Winter Sun, appearing from the University of Toronto Press in 1960, was Margaret Avison's first book, a collection of most of the best poems of the previous two decades together with many new ones, almost randomly arranged. The dust-jacket announces this lack of order, which itself betrays the author's real concern for form:

> The author has arranged her poems for readers who like to skim through a book when they first take it up, since she herself approaches a new book of poetry in this way and would rather find her own groupings than have the poems already grouped for her.

So advised that groupings are possible, we can discover a number of them. "Dispersed Titles", "Chronic", "Meeting Together of Poles and Latitudes (in *Prospect*)", "Atlantis and the Department Store", "Unfinished After-Portrait (or Stages of Mourning)", and "The Artist" raise again the geometric predicament, while "Identity," "R.I.P." and "Apocalyptics" play with the question of identity; "The Swimmer's Moment", "Mordent for a Melody", "Prelude", and "September Street"—the last with its magnificently tonally ambivalent line: "Granada will not rhyme with Canada"—range over space and time, while the long final poem "The Agnes Cleves Papers," reprinted from *Origin* (1957), encompasses all these themes. Another group examines the idea of order through imagery of chalk, bones, and stones, with all their apparently rigid ("geometric") outlines: "Prelude" again, for example, and "Unbroken Lineage", "Tennis", "Butterfly Bones", "Banff", "Intra-Political"—or "Knowledge of Age," which has not been collected from *Kenyon Review* (Spring 1956), though it was reprinted in Gustafson's 1958 anthology. Any of these categorizations are, of course, somewhat spurious, for the poems defy and transcend them, but they are useful pivots from which to begin examining the parabola that Margaret Avison has herself constructed.

"Butterfly Bones; or Sonnet Against Sonnets," like "Dispersed Titles" or "Rondeau Redoublé," illustrates the complexity she experiences trying to explore these ideas in language. She knows "The cyanide jar seals life, as sonnets move / towards final stiffness," and that "Insect—or poem—waits for the fix, the frill / precision can effect, brilliant with danger," but then asks the question that demonstrates her dilemma: "Might sheened and rigid trophies strike men blind / like Adam's lexicon locked in the mind? " The sonnet is magnificently controlled, but the very control 'fixes' her thoughts—yet to deny order is to deny one of the mind's possible functions and perhaps therefore to be equally restrictive: to lock things in the mind that could be communicated. Hence even the invertebrate butterfly—that angle to stab into unrelenting space—can be structured, given bones, by the mind. And having done so, the mind immediately questions its act, wonders at the result: death or new life, rigidity or new possibilities for play?

"R.I.P." had told us that "The floor of heaven is really / Diamond congoleum. / It is a rather private place / (The Asians guessed it closest) / Where one or two / Play." And "Knowledge of Age," which "Begins in winter," reminds us of the difference between death and decay:

> Memory of last year's summer shrivels
> without nostalgia or any
> salve or sanction.
>
> Anatomist, make distinct this bone from the
> Bone of the uncorrupted dead.

So the 'uncorrupted' poem, logically, should allow structure to exist; it lives within its structure, provided that structure does not limit the multiple possibilities of the language. Hence the rondeau can be 'redoublé', the sonnet can speak against sonnets, the pun can become a virtue. First of all comes the experimentation for the poet herself, as "The Valiant Vacationist" (*Canadian Forum*, December 1944) points out:

> In the meantime anyway it might be wise
> If I made arrangements only for myself
> When I arrive. Then, if you come, we can surely
> Find accommodation without trouble.
> I haven't met any tourists since last Sunday
>   Nor anyone else in fact.

> Perhaps you'd better wait till you hear again.
> Frost burns so quickly and the sun today
> Was yellower than you are used to see it.
> Their language here you wouldn't understand.
> Myself, I find it difficult
>   and so far have been unsuccessful
>   in finding anyone
>   Even to interpret for me to myself.
> When I have mastered it, I'll let you know.

But Margaret Avison's best poems are also for others; they play with words to reveal what words can convey, working with them carefully to reveal their brilliance: their glitter and their meaning.

The puns in "Tennis," for example, pile overwhelmingly one on top of another:

> Service is joy, to see or swing. Allow
> All tumult to subside. Then tensest winds
> Buffet, brace, viol and sweeping bow.
> Courts are for love and volley. No one minds
> The cruel ellipse of service and return,
> Dancing white galliardes at tape or net
> Till point, on the wire's tip, or the long burn-
> ing arc to nethercourt marks game and set.
> Purpose apart, perched like an umpire, dozes,
> Dreams golden balls whirring through indigo.
> Clay blurs the whitewash but day still encloses
> The albinos, bonded in their flick and flow.
> Playing in musicked gravity, the pair
> Score liquid Euclids in foolscaps of air.

The tennis game turns into a Ladies' Aid meeting, a court-ship, a war, a formal five-step dance (the sonnet itself, perhaps), and a mathematical exercise. Words contain their opposites, too. Love can be happy or go sour; the ellipse can be everything or Nothing. Like the tennis game at the end of Antonioni's film *Blow-up*, the reality is once again half in the beholder's eye and half in the sensitivity of the perception.

After *Winter Sun*, few of Margaret Avison's poems have been published in periodicals, and those she has almost entirely collected in her second volume *The Dumbfounding* (New York: Norton, 1966). "Hot June," first printed in *Canadian Forum* (March 1963), is in many ways typical of the transition between books:

> People are pink-cheekt only
> long enough to
> ferret out what if we were wan and wiser we
> would let
> be.
> Give us the word and we worry
> it out of its soil and run
> off with it
>   (IN-FORM) between our teeth . . . .

The punning is reminiscent of the technique of *Winter Sun* (Richard Tillinghast ["Seven Poets," *Poetry*, 1967] attacks the word games in *The Dumbfounding*, apparently missing the relation between this book and *Winter Sun*), as is that in a few more poems from *The Dumbfounding*, like "The Absorbed," or "In Eporphyrial Harness":[5]

> Hill-hoe
> till the liberal varnish, the
> daze-sun go
> down and the pin-
>   flare-
>   finish
>   star bright
> become alltoday, furnish
> us sun (eyes) (ice).

But "Hot June" looks forward to poems like "A Sad Song," too—"June is now sealed, silent. / Form without springing makes of it / a wrong season, / makes even this perfumed rain / autumnal"—with their restrained observations of people and places around Toronto.[6] If the pun is still present it is no longer the main technique; the tone is less querying, more self-confident, and the observing mind and eye are calmer in the face of what they see.

"Hot June" takes us in yet another direction, however,

both forward and backward, to the poems about children
and their moment of change. "Prelude," for example, contains this passage, with its sense of a linguistic landscape:

> Somebody's grandpa came
> in shirt sleeves, solid
> and asymmetrical, rooting the word
> 'trunk', for the child, as right
> for man or tree.
> He stood, and gnarled
> silently, while he talked over our heads
> to some invisible neighbour
> we did not bother glancing up to see.

And in *The Dumbfounding*, in "Thaw," the poet watches
while

> A boy alone out in the court
> whacks with his hockey stick, and whacks
> in the wet, and the pigeons flutter, and rise,
> and settle back.

We can see geometric figures again in these passages, as in
others, but that is not enough. Obviously the poet is troubled
by something, looking back at childhood for freedom or
innocence and discovering only ignorance and "pink-cheekt"
naïve daring, which is in its own way a kind of limitation.
The close of "The Agnes Cleves Papers" helps us here:

> How wrong you are to think your glancing back
> Into the zones and corridors will long be tolerated
> Or, for that matter, looking will lead you back
> To the hill and the hoof-pocked dark between
> Eveningstar and mushroom.
> The wild smell is the other side
> Of the impenetrable world of stone
> And is no athlete's incense.
> After the match is called, before midnight,
> We will go dreaming into secondhand junkstores,
> Or go for a late sail out beyond the gap
> And in the morning, you will see,
> The children will be chalking hopscotch on
> The Moscow streets, on Lima's cathedral square
> Past beaky statue-shadows . . . .

Even in the "morning" children are already confined by a world in part of their own making; the chalky hopscotch squares structure them like bones, restrict their freedom even while we think of them as innocent. So, in the later "A Child: Marginalia on an Epigraph,"[7] we see that the child

> is completely absorbed
> and his heart therefore aches
> (radiant, bone-barred):
> and to long for the
> not enough out of the light yet
> to be filled,
> fullness.

In "The Absorbed," on a day when the sun "has not absorbed" the ice, is another child:

> Alone, he plays, still there. We
> struggle, our animal fires
> pitted against those
> several grape-white stars,
> their silence.

Perhaps it is inevitable that twentieth century poems about children, time, and ignorance of time should all seem to echo Hopkins' "Spring and Fall"; certainly words like "wan" in an alliterative series in "Hot June," or "leaf-stained" in "A Child" do—possibly intentionally, for Margaret Avison frequently relies on association as much as double-meaning for the effect of individual lines. The passage in "A Child"—

> Safe, at night,
> in the deeps of the night-watch kept,
> in the clean place,
> strange but trusted, as a pool among
> cedars in autumn,
> leaf-stained, gorgeous, far, deep,
> prepared for a tired
> child

—moves out to other of her own poems for its effect, too: "Branches," for example, with its explicit Christianity, or "The Absorbed," or "Ps. 19" (with its added particular Biblical analogue—"The fear of the LORD is clean, enduring for ever: the judgments of the LORD are true and righteous altogether."):

> *Clean* is the word with *fear.*
> Fear is to love high
> and know longing for clear
> sunlight . . . .
>
> Yet to love high
> is with this very fear
> to shrink *and* seek to be made plain . . . .
>
> *Enduring* is the word with *clean.*
> The fear once won
> of sunward love, it proves—not boulderstone,
> baldness, slowly in fire consuming—but green
> with life, moss, cup-rock-water, cliff riven
> for a springing pine;
> and thus, trusted to fire, drawn
> towards an enduring sun.

The sun is a paradox, then: a possible winter sun that for all the light of day will not melt ice, or a hot sealed June, or a fire that consumes and destroys, or an "enduring" fire that (trusted) will prove "Green / with life." And in exploring this image, Margaret Avison moves closer and closer to the highly personal Christianity that she feels will allow her a self, structure and metaphysical illumination.

In "Of Tyranny, in One Breath: (translated from a Hungarian poem by Gyula Illyes, 1956)," tyranny is anonymously personified:

> to your thought's faltering words, It
> adds the "or" and "but,"
> in your imagination even
> you hear It breathing:
> . . . .
> your spittle tastes of It, your skin
> oozes It, It slimes within,
> you are not you, but It—
>
> like moles we fumble in the sun,
> dark our only home,
> Sahara or a cell

would serve as well,

for where It is, all's vile,
nothing's worthwhile . . .
not this song, however true,
nothing you do.

It stands above
your waiting grave,
It tells who you have been,
your dust will serve Its ends.

Looking once again retrospectively at *Winter Sun*, we can see that these passages acquire an enormous importance, for characterized here is the kind of potential straitjacket to which intellectualism can lead, the kind that *Winter Sun* found itself in the midst of rebelling against. The intellectual response, for all its humanity and variety, continually led to alternates, unanswered questions, dead ends and dissatisfaction. Words, however useful, were ambivalent, even possibly deceitful, and 'Possible', to a mind in search of a liberating absolute, is an unhappy answer. In *The Dumbfounding*, the word becomes much more obviously the Word, a metaphysical source and end, which imbues all.

While "Intra-Political," in *Winter Sun*, explored the possibility of breaking out of boxes and discovering "a new expectant largeness," and ended "(George Herbert—and he makes it plain— / guest at this same transfiguring board / Did sit and eat)," it is not until *The Dumbfounding* that we are particularly forcibly reminded of Herbert's poetry. Norman Endicott, reviewing *Winter Sun* in *Canadian Literature*, writes that Margaret Avison does not see the world particularly "through the eyes of revealed religion," but the frame of reference is still there and *The Dumbfounding* makes it clear. Like Herbert, however, Margaret Avison does not in these later religious poems show herself in the midst of conflict; the conflict is resolved, and the poems speak in the past tense or of the fulfilled present. Several excerpts will show the direction her poetry takes:

In the mathematics of God

there are percentages beyond one hundred.

His new creation is
One, whole, and a
beginning.   ("First")

The line we drew, you crossed,
and cross out, wholly forget
at the faintest stirring of what
you know is love, is One
whose name has been, and is
and will be, the
I AM.   ("The Word")

lead through the garden to
trash, rubble, hill,
where, the outcast's outcast, you
sound dark's uttermost, strangely light-brimming, until
time be full.   ("The Dumbfounding")

GATHER my fragments towards
the radium, the
all-swallowing moment
once more.   ("Searching and Sounding")

As Lawrence M. Jones notes in *Canadian Literature* No. 38, quoting from a personal letter from Margaret Avison herself, she has come to substitute a personal Christ for the unapproachable scriptural Person:

> She then describes the single most important event in this progress of belief, the occasion of January fourth, 1963, when the "Jesus of resurrection power" revealed Himself to her when she was supposedly alone; says the poet:
>
>> I would not want to have missed what he gave then: the astounding delight of his making himself known at last, sovereign, forgiving, forceful of life.
>
> Under the influence of the refocusing caused by this experience, she looks back upon her previous life and work and notes "how grievously I cut off his way by honouring the artist" and sees her past as a "long wilful detour into darkness."

It is not an easy acceptance; behind it lies the quest for sight in a winter sun, the sense of a blind man, the myth of Plato's cave, the observation of reality in shadows, and stanza XIV of "The Earth That Falls Away":

> I knew how to live
> by hearing and touch
> and sense of place. I could pre-judge
> obstacles too: at first the couch,
> lamp, table; you have to have
> them mapped in your mind—you clutch
> notions, till you trust sense. Then I could move
> out among trees and traffic, a march
> in Nomansland to risk it, a dive
> into invisible interdependence, no crutch
> needed, for all the dread. I knew how to live.
> Please. Leave me alone.
> Bandage my eyes again.
> The dream of seeing
> I want, as it has been, open
> daybreak blue, with the sting
> of the far-off; not this urging
> of person, colour, thing.
> Unclutter Me. Relieve
> me of this visible. Give
> back my sealed-off dayshine . . . .

After this comes " . . . Person, or a Hymn on and to the Holy Ghost," with its complex involution of pronouns—or identities:

> How should I find speech . . .
>
> to you whose self-knowing
> is perfect, known to him . . . ?
>
> Let the one you show me
> ask you, for me . . .
>
> to lead *my* self, effaced
> in the known Light,
> to be in him released
> from facelessness,
>
> so that where you
>   . . . would go
> I may show him visible.

It sums up many of the problems we have been looking at, and resolves for the moment the questions of language, sight, and identity which have troubled her.

For the moment is important. "Prelude" showed us this much, with its observation of daybreak and the growth of children. But Margaret Avison's poetry takes in all places, all times. Through God, the "moment" can become "all-encompassing," as at the end of "Searching and Sounding," and for that moment, detailed by the order—the found form—of *The Dumbfounding*, more serenity is possible.

The poems in *The Dumbfounding* are arranged more or less thematically—poems of youth and age, followed by poems about God, followed by poems about seasons and places—and when we discover a few of the poems from *Winter Sun* republished, unaltered, in this new environment, we find that the new environment itself somehow alters them. Reprinted are "The Artist", "From a Provincial", "Meeting Together of Poles and Latitudes", and "The Swimmer's Moment":

> For everyone
> The swimmer's moment at the whirlpool comes,
> But many at that moment will not say,
> "This is the whirlpool, then."
> By their refusal they are saved
> From the black pit, and also from contesting
> The deadly rapids, and emerging in
> The mysterious, and more ample, further waters.
> And so their bland-blank faces turn and turn
> Pale and forever on the rim of suction
> They will not recognize.
> Of those who dare the knowledge
> Many are whirled into the ominous centre
> That, gaping vertical, seals up
> For them an eternal boon of privacy,
> So that we turn away from their defeat
> With a despair, not for their deaths, but for
> Ourselves, who cannot penetrate their secret
> Nor even guess at the anonymous breadth
> Where one or two have won:
> (The silver reaches of the estuary).

In *Winter Sun*, this coupled itself with such poems as "The Mirrored Man," where people seeking pivots wonder "at the centre" who will find ultimate secrets and what those secrets will be. And it looked back to uncollected poems like "The Iconoclasts" (*Poetry*, September 1947), or "Coward" (*Here and Now*, January 1949): "But this crude angle / Splayed through the dreamer's prairie: blackness gaped / Ugly in a charred rib cage / And he turned back to the bright company." "The Agnes Cleves Papers" shows a development beyond this position:

> Telling it in plain words
> Makes me see how I feared the wrong thing.
> The other centre, the known enigma—
> All eyes I do not own, contours
> That force familiarity where I would
> Tumult and spurn like Pan—were the mountain passes
> Pure out of thought; this iris bed
> Is scarfed in dreadful mist
> And no sun comes
> Beyond the yellow stoneway . . . .

So she accepts her moment at the whirlpool's edge and discovers the source of a more enduring illumination.

"The Swimmer's Moment" itself is too obvious a poem, too overtly declamatory to be effective, but this does not deny the importance of its message. The later "Natural/Unnatural" is far better; the controlled ambivalence suggests meaning instead of stating it, and the poem gains from its indirection. Yet "The Swimmer's Moment" with its sense of fright and the moment, helps us to see how the later poem grows out of the earlier work. "Natural/Unnatural" starts with a childish perspective, quickly shifting to an adult consciousness:

> Evening tilt makes a
> pencil-box of our
> street.
> The lake, in largeness, grapey blueness
> casts back the biscuit-coloured pencil-box, boxes, toys, the
> steeple-people, all of it, in one of those

> little mirrory shrugs.
> The north-east sky too
> grows fuselage cool.

The sense of an imminent atomic calamity disturbs even the innocent enjoyment of the beauty of a sunset. Without being actually conscious of it, naïve children are robbed of their naiveté:

> Even the west, beyond the tinged rooftops
> smells of cobalt:
>> "no—the
>> charring of the peeled stick in a bonfire
>> is the smell: newness,
>> October crackling . . . ."
> large pink children have, all the same, sniffed
> the ice in
> that quirk of sunset
> but refuse
> fear.

Refusing to fear is less human than *refusing and fearing,* however, and the poem modulates finally into a statement of personal belief:

> True, the natural night is pressure on my ribs:
> despair—to draw that in, to
> deflate the skin-pouch, crunch out the
> structure in one
> luxuriant deep-breathed zero—
> dreamed already, this is
> corruption.
> I fear *that.*
> I refuse, fearing; in hope.

Point of view is expressed by tone, and by adjectives and nouns more than pronouns. The themes remain the same as those of "Tennis" or "Prelude": childhood, change, and the ambivalence of human perceptions. But fear—of a certain kind—must now be accepted. "*Clean* is the word with *fear*," the poet affirmed in "Ps. 19," and "*Enduring* is the word with *clean*." Enduring also is the sun which is God, the Son which is in God; the linguistic play celebrates a serious moment, and so the fear becomes a religious experience and a kind of praise.

Since 1966, Margaret Avison has published no poems, but as she is a writer who labours over her work before bringing it into print—and does not revise after that—we can hope that another volume is in the making, one that will introduce us to a new group of finely wrought poems and another stage in the development that has already made her an important writer. "The Agnes Cleves Papers," at the end of *Winter Sun*, held within it much that was to be developed in *The Dumbfounding*; "The Unspeakable," at the end of *The Dumbfounding*, indicates that Margaret Avison has accepted the traditional poet's task of celebration. But of what?

> The beauty of the unused
>   (the wheatear among birds, or
>   stonechat)
> the unused in houses (as a
>   portion of low roof swept by the
>   buttery leaves of a pear tree
>   where a manx cat is
>   discovered—just now—blinking his
>   sunned Arctic sea-eyes in the
>   sun-play)
> the beauty of the
>   unused in one I know, of
>   excellent indolence
>   from season into
>   skywide wintering

There is beauty in whatever one's field of vision brings into view, then—in the almost overlooked—in the moment's discovery. This does not mean that the next moment will see the same thing or see the same way, nor does it expect the intellect to explain everything that might be known. As Robert Duncan points out, quoting Keats, he values:

"Negative Capability . . . that is, when a man is capable of being in uncertainties, mysteries, doubts, without any irritable reaching after fact and reason—Coleridge, for instance, would let go by a fine isolate verisimilitude caught from the Penetralium of mystery, from being capable of remaining content with half-knowledge."

From his own part, he adds:

> The game of tennis and the minuet both subject the Yahoo of the animal man to the manners and rules of a court and give authority to that trained horse (and house-broken, too, I hope) of the rational faculty that is a Houyhnhnm. But this Yahoo and this Houyhnhnm is one man divided against himself, fantasy of the enlightenment in his formal wig performing his ritual dance towards the riddance of Yahoos who know nothing of tennis or minuet. I think of those wigs that marked men of fashion and wit from the uneducated and impoverished mob, the conventional wig and the unconventional cap alike perched on the universally lousy scalp.

> But my point here is that the minuet, the game of tennis, the heroic couplet, the concept of form as the imposing of rules and establishing of regularities, the theories of civilization, race, and progress, the performances in sciences and arts to rationalize the universe, to secure balance and class—all these are a tribal magic against a real threat of upset and things not keeping their place.

Or a case of people fearing the wrong centre. Margaret Avison would have us praise, but continue to fear as well, knowing our place as we see it from instant to instant. *The Dumbfounding* as well as *Winter Sun* reminds us that "When day and life draw the horizons / Part of the strangeness is / knowing the landscape." In coming to know it, we discover the 'unused'—which is not formless, but should not be governed by preconception either. So, paradoxically rejoicing in a frightening prospect of swimmers' moments, we continue to perceive the world, eschewing an imposed system of geometry, and discovering form and content together. And so perhaps in discovering the various forms of the unused, lies the direction for Margaret Avison's new-found self, sight, and freedom.

1970

NOTES

1. *Canadian Forum* had, however, been an *avant-garde* journal before the war, and during the 1940's Margaret Avison shared its pages with P.K. Page, Patrick Anderson, James Wreford, and others. With Anderson she shared a sense of verbal pyrotechnics, with Page a concern for perspectives, with Wreford a feeling for tradition. (Cf. her later admiration for the poetry of Daryl Hine.) Milton Wilson remarks that "If her poems had any social implications, they certainly remained unnoticed in that company. By now she seems to have passed her contemporaries going the other way," in "The Poetry of Margaret Avison," *Canadian Literature* (1959). Like Page, she was, I suspect, distantly admired during the 1940's, and misunderstood. Like Page she has used the time between then and now to find a form for her message, her perceptions, her understandings of the world; whereas P.K. Page moved to drawing ("the same pen"), Margaret Avison has refined her sense of the word as sound.

2. See his subsequent review of *Winter Sun*: "Critical Improvisations on Margaret Avison's 'Winter Sun,' " in *Tamarack Review* (1961). In part he says that "Imagery is physical; conceit is intellectual. Here they often fuse. . . . The metaphysical conceit arises when nice distinctions in the realm of sensation are made to imply value judgements on things seen or felt, as they do when these are man-made things, not 'Nature'."

3. Cf. Charles Olson's "Human Universe," in *Selected Writings* (1966). "The difficulty of discovery (in the closed world which the human is because it is ourselves and nothing outside us, like the other) is, that definition is as much a part of the act as is sensation itself, in this sense, that life *is* preoccupation with itself, that conjecture about it is as much of it as its coming at us, its going on. In other words we are ourselves both the instrument of discovery and the instrument of definition."

Language, "in its double sense of discrimination (logos) and of shout (tongue)," is important for communicating this sense of life. "(The distinction here is between language as the act of the instant and language as the act of thought about the instant.)"

After attacking Socrates' willingness to "make a 'universe' out of discourse," Aristotle's "logic and classification," and Plato's "world of Ideas, of forms as extricable from content," Olson goes on to insist: "If there is any absolute, it is never more than this one, you, this instant, in action."

4. And with the basis for a review of Callaghan's *Collected Stories* in *Canadian Forum* (1960): "The twenties found storytellers elaborately representational, using a language that was deliberately and traditional-

ly artificial. The revolution impressionism had long since made in paint-ing had not yet had its literary counterpart, but some new way of using words was clearly needed. Two points of departure proved fruitful: how the world seems *to me*, and how I can present the world I see *in its own terms*."

5. "Eporphyrial" seems to be a concocted word. The prefix "e-" is suitably ambiguous, capable of meaning either *not* or *very* or both of these, and *porphyrial*, while carrying overtones of *rock* (i.e. rigidity), *purple* (which may not be important), and Neoplatonist philosophy (through Porphyry, a disciple of Plotinus), probably most specifically refers to *porphyria*, a disease of which the most characteristic symptom is an acute sensitivity to light.

6. James Reaney, reviewing *Winter Sun* in *Canadian Forum* (1961), has his own iminitable way of commenting on Margaret Avison's sense of locale: "Jay Macpherson talks of the marriage of Heaven and Earth; Margaret Avison tells you to look at the wedding piano stashed away in the world's most unheavenly, unwedding-like place—Toronto."

7. *Matthew 18:3:* "And said, Verily I say unto you, Except ye be converted, and become as little children, ye shall not enter into the kingdom of heaven."

Luke 9:48: "And said unto them, Whosoever shall receive this child in my name receiveth me; and whosoever shall receive me, receiveth him that sent me: for he that is least among you all, the same shall be great."

MAKER OF ORDER,
PRISONER
OF DREAMS:
THE POETRY OF
EARLE BIRNEY

Earle Birney's poetry, though it is constantly acknowledged as a central accomplishment in modern
Canadian writing, has attracted remarkably few critical
studies to explain why. Perhaps its apparent eclecticism
offers a reason for this neglect. The formal variety has proved
either baffling or an end in itself. The conventional rhymes,
the Anglo-Saxon alliterative verse, the punning squibs and the
concrete designs have been seen as either demonstrating the
range of an encompassing imagination or merely displaying
a talent for formal imitation. In actuality, the technical
development of Birney's verse inscribes an intellectual journey from anxiety to spiritual self-possession. Behind his
language lie ideas about culture and society; behind them lies
a tension between anarchic liberty and ordered constraint,
between nature and civilization, informing the poetic structures with humane optimism and ironic dismay. And in his
continuing attempt to resolve that tension, he traces the
divided character of the Canadian soul.

Two relatively early poems, "Introvert" and "Leaving the
Park," taking their metaphors respectively from St. James's
Park in London and Wyoming's Yellowstone Park, implicitly
contrast the ordered English garden and the turbulent American hot springs wilderness.

Both enclosures prove deceptive, the English one by seeming to define calm, the other by pretending to preserve the
natural wild. For the introvert, whose "mind to him is tight
as any park," hopes, fears, and dreams alike are ultimately

unpredictable and will therefore shatter him; for the Yellowstone tourist, what proves instructive is contact with the "prying prairie" outside the park. He acknowledges then that the deer were "posing" in the park and that the wild bears were given access to "viewpoints." The gamble is outside, where the moon is a "bright noose," the night rumbles, and the human wilderness exacts payment for overnight shelter. Society is thus both ordered and disordering, nature both violent and free, and individual human beings, faced with the ambivalence inherent in the option between them, must find a way to achieve liberty without self-destruction.

The two "Ellesmereland" poems give this dilemma a specifically Canadian cast. The island's wild hills are "stricken" only when men arrive to build a town, construct defence systems, introduce judicial codes, and "talk of growth." Out of the civil wilderness they make a wild civilization; the potential myth that the early explorers had left behind them is summarily destroyed. As a metaphor to describe the "civilizing progress" of Calvinist Canadian Society, it proves a devastating condemnation. Birney accepts what Malcolm Lowry averred in one of his notebooks: that the essential centre of Canada is its consciousness of wilderness, and that to Europeanize the nation's sensibility is to destroy its character. This does not mean that the nation should be structureless, but insists that any order imposed from abroad —including defining as 'disorder' that which, *within* the culture, is a genuine 'reordering'—inhibits progress and so wounds the spirit.

Just as this affirmation of the evolving wilderness can be seen as part of an aesthetic credo explaining Birney's formal variations, so it affects his view of history, broaching problems of tradition and memory ("no servant / But a stubborn master"). At one level the halter on progress is material; at others it is emotional and institutional. The desire for security, for recognition, for respectability, all spur people into action, but often this seems vain, like mere movement, all the more hurried because it leads to nothing beyond itself. To admit such aimlessness in one's life would take individuals and cultures alike into despair, so they perpetuate known social and mental structures in order to guard against the "night's abyss." Daring to face the chaos, however, may be the only way to prevent sterility from enclosing them. As the description of a cross-country airplane flight puts it, in "North Star West":

> Billboards and baggage checks master us
> headlines open old wounds
> we bruise in a cabfull of cares to the city
>
> Yet for a space we held in our morning's hand
> the welling and wildness of Canada . . .
>
> We . . .
> return to our ferment of earth with a memory of sky

If soaring into the night takes the poet above the land and westward, it also takes him momentarily beyond "tight" St. James's, beyond transplanted European rational and social conventions, to intuit his urge to transcend the land's realities while accepting his need to live among them.

Put another way, he must live in a world of time while striving to stay conscious of a timelessness that is neither escapist nor coercive. While to acknowledge personal and cultural mortality without some sense of direction would again be to invoke despair, to refuse at all to participate in temporal reality would be inconsistent with his social conscience and sensory perceptions. He must therefore reconcile the two stances without compromising his integrity. The ironic stance taken in so many of the poems, distancing the speaker from the absurdities of the temporal-material society, provides one kind of answer, but no resolution. The options enunciated by the chauvinist truck driver in "Billboards Build Freedom of Choice," for example—

> yegotta choose fella yegotta
> choose between
> AMERICA and UN-

—utter a false dichotomy, which the poet cannot accept as

the *basic* tension informing modern life. To observe them in the witty way he does makes their absurdity apparent, but it does not provide an explicit solution to his dilemma. Nor does the praise of art in such poems as "El Greco: *Espolio*", "Cartagena de Indias", "For George Lamming", or "Tavern by the Hellespont", for Birney remains conscious in all of them of the social responsibility of art. Each artist, isolated from his society to the extent that his artistic identity differs from his nationality, nonetheless participates in social ferments and causes.

Birney clarifies the pressures of his own poetic tasks, when in several other poems he tries to disentangle the Canadian ties to Europe. English literary traditions and the affirmative belief in humanity he finds in Langland and Chaucer continually attract him, for example, but they can, if merely transplanted, distort the experience of his native land. Langland does not speak the true voice of Vancouver in *Damnation of Vancouver*, therefore, for he sees the society's institutions but not its dreams. The dreams are Mrs. Anyone's even if she does have difficulty articulating them. And when in "North of Superior," Birney criticizes Canadian literary artifacts, he draws on European comparisons that at once he is aware do not apply:

> See where the unexorcized dragon   Fire
> has breathed unwieldy lances from the wilds
> for wars already waged   and planted one
> charred pine to fly a pennant still   a husk
> of golden needles—yet no mute or glorious
> Milton finds Azazel here   no Roland
> comes to blow defiance by this serpent stream

The wild spirits of Canada require a different voice to summon them, not the ballads of the mind but a paradoxical "soundless fugue." The technical challenge is obvious: in Canada, European rational traditions somehow lead to impasse, and Canadian poets require instead a sensibility embracing both Western and Eastern styles of thought.

What finally emerges from the poems on aging, history,

tradition, and time is a vision not just of an individual facing twentieth-century change but also of a society confounded by its sense of its mortality, or of what Mircea Eliade, in *Myths, Dreams and Mysteries*, calls a Western "awareness of historicity", which "discloses the anxiety of confronting Death and Non-being."

Eliade avers that the discovery of historicity prompts Indians, for example, to try to deliver themselves "from its illusions, whilst . . . Europeans seem to be content with the discovery, and to put up a nihilistic and pessimistic vision of the world." If a European insists that he cannot give up his being in History in order to live an "inauthentic experience," an Indian would reply that the state of temporality is not absurd, but a "divine creation, a cosmic *play*, of which the end and aim is human experience, as well as deliverance from that experience." To become conscious of it is not to surrender to Nothingness, but to find that the "state of ignorance and illusion is not that of *living* in History, but of *believing in* its ontological reality." "Our human condition," therefore, "ought not to be regarded as an end in itself."

Obviously any society (like that in "Billboards") which insists that its roads, its structures, are the "TRUWAY", confines its breadth of vision, inhibiting its own growth by inhibiting its sensitivity to other cultures. The same holds true even when the structures are less concrete. The simultaneous attraction-repulsion that affects Canada's artistic ties with England, that is, takes another form in Birney's war poems of the 1940's, which probe directly this 'dubiety' of Eliade's modern European man.

The "primal ink" "welling from Europe's bog", for example, which "beleaguers" "Vancouver Lights" at the far edge of the continent, is the same disordering abyss Birney elsewhere plumbs. But this time any commitment to return eastward in order to re-establish order for the sake of humanity carries with it a much more potent threat of enslavement. The choice is his own: "No one bound Prometheus / Himself he chained". Or as "Conference of Heads" puts it: "There is no fog but in the will / the iceberg is elective." Yet to revisit Europe combines an entry into present cultural chaos with a return to a past civilization. Either way the action makes the poet conscious of history and therefore of eschatology. Peace becomes a kind of Golden Age that preceded and will follow the chaos, but to reach it involves death, for it means the end of time. "Space is now and now is time", he insists in "Lines for a Peace." More despairing, "Mappemounde" goes on to explore that space and find it limited:

That sea is hight Time   it hems all hearts' landtrace. . . .
Adread in that mere   we drift to map's end

Fixed in the present moment, he can dream no acceptable future, and no myth.

That constrained sensibility affects most of the poems Birney wrote on Canada in the 1940's and 1950's. The Western movement of "North Star West" and "Transcontinental", from "Atlantic Door" to "Pacific Door", and the dying illusions of "David" and "The Ebb begins from Dream" all reiterate the pursuit of myth and the failure to find it. "Pacific Door" speaks directly

the problem that is ours and yours
that there is no clear Strait of Anian
to lead us easy back to Europe

A later poem, "Way to the West," acknowledges that part of the problem lay in the inability of modern man to distinguish the passage of imagination from the movement of commercial transport; it is therefore only after the night-jet passes that "we begin to realize / we'd been hearing the river too." That reaffirmation of imaginative power could only come after recognizing Canada's geographical/mental relationship with Asia as well as with Europe. If "dying Bering lost in fog / turned north to mark us off from Asia still," it remains for Asia, that Oriental West, to be reunited with the Pacific Coast. "Looking from Oregon" acknowledges the need:

There's no good my searching the horizon
I'm one of those another poet saw

> sitting beside our other ocean
> I can't look farther out or in

> Yet up here in the wild parsnips and the wind
> I know the earth is not holding
> tumbles in body-lengths
> towards thunderheads and unimaginable Asia

To reach the *idea* of Asia, however, Birney had to be able to reconcile history and historylessness, and his fascination with indigenous American myths provided him with a route.

An early attempt to bring 'natural' ritual and contemporary society face to face can be found in the speeches of the Salish chief in *Damnation of Vancouver*, but more successful are the poems of the late 1950's set in the Caribbean and Latin America. The "timeless cliffs" of the "State of Sonora" emphasize that what he finds there is as much a state of mind as a physical geography. "Transistor," making him conscious of the simultaneous Jamaican "fear of Mamba hope of Jesus," allows him emotionally to "exchange pasts" with an old woman singing folk songs. The sight of "Machu Picchu" lets him grow "suddenly back into . . . legend." And most important of all, "Letter to a Cuzco Priest" and "Six-Sided Square: Actopan" show him how ritual can interpenetrate current events without conflict. In answer to the lady tourist who thinks Mexico forgets her history, that is, the Actopan guide can answer:

> Madam, I suspect
> that patterns more complex must have precedence:
> she yearns to croon in Harlem dialect
> while still her priest to Xipe prays for intercedence

The commitment to present action within society does not mean, in other words, that one surrenders to a *pessimistic* apocryphal vision; it sees the anguish of historicity, instead, as an indispensable and redemptive rite of passage that leads to spiritual birth.

"The Bear on the Delhi Road," which is probably Birney's finest poem to date, holds within it just such a revelation. A great Himalayan bear, "Unreal tall as a myth," is brought to two "spindly" men from "fabulous hills" to a populated plain in order to dance with them by the roadside and survive life. But despite the physical pressures it exerts, that mortal world, in which all three move "galvanically," is no more 'real' than the dreams of the mountain meadows or of divine and limitless possibility. As the world of the fable takes imaginative precedence over the temporal one, moreover, it is the temporal world that becomes illusionary. Birney writes:

> It is not easy to free
> myth from reality
> or rear this fellow up
> to lurch   lurch with them
> in the tranced dancing of men

The equably paced phrasing and the finely controlled vowel harmonies help establish the poem's central intellectual tension between timelessness and time. The Asian experience described lets Birney also discover his ability to reconcile history and myth and to face the idea of "Nothing" with equanimity.

Finding "nada" within "Canada" can therefore become for him on return a kind of cosmic joke. And when in "Can. Lit." he writes that "it's only by our lack of ghosts we're haunted," he is denigrating only the compulsion to define by imitation, to lock oneself in one time and perspective and thereby fail to recognize the voices and silences that do animate the land. Silence and absence become curiously positive virtues. Furthermore, in "November Walk Near False Creek Mouth"—the title redolent with images of European despair: the dying year-end, the explorers' failure to find the Strait of Anian eastward—the poet can reject a wholesale importation of European mythologies, approach an articulation of truly native ones, and look musingly westwards into the unknown once again:

> And I on the path at the high-tide edge
> wandering under the leafless maples
> between the lost salt home

and the asphalt ledge where carhorns call
call in the clotting air by a shore
where shamans never again will sound
with moon-snail conch the ritual plea
to brother salmon or vanished seal
and none ever heard
the horn of Triton or merman. . . .

The tree-barbed tip of Point Grey's lance
has failed again to impale the gone sun
Clouds and islands float together . . .

washed by the curve of timeless returnings
lies the unreached unreachable nothing
whose winds wash down to the human shores . . . .

The tone is not the Classical fatalism of a poem like Daryl
Hine's "Point Grey," musing "A beauty of sorts is nearly
always within reach." In uttering the midway Canadian position between Occident and Orient, Birney accepts the elusive
identity of land and sky—adumbrated so often by his mountain and flight metaphors—and the ambivalent nature of illusion. As Eliade puts it, in part quoting Heinrich Zimmer:

to rediscover the initiatory meanings and the spiritual
values of anxiety, meanings and values well known to
certain European mystical and metaphysical traditions
. . . is as much to say that a dialogue with the *true*
Asiatic, African or Oceanian world helps us to rediscover spiritual positions that one is justified in regarding
as universally valid . . . .

"it is only after a pious journey in a distant region, in a
new land, that the meaning of that inner voice guiding
us on our search can make itself understood by us."

For the literary artist there is a further side to Eliade's
theory, which demands a reconciliation between the method
and function of literary creation:

poetic creation . . . implies the abolition of time—of
the history concentrated in language—and tends towards
the recovery of the paradisiac, primordial situation; of
the days when one could *create spontaneously,* when
the *past* did not exist because there was no consciousness of time, no memory of temporal duration.

The paradoxical overlap of spontaneity and what Birney calls "the art of indefinitely delayed communication" takes him into the ambivalences of formal arrangement—most recently illustrated by typographically enfranchised concrete verses—which allow him to convey his sense of coexistent mythic and empirical realities. Words by themselves, that is, ultimately seem untrustworthy, to be merely part of the physical world. In "A Walk in Kyoto," for example, he asks:

> Where in these alleys jammed with competing waves
> of signs in two tongues and three scripts
> can the simple song of a man be heard?

Implicitly the answer lies in visual symbol, in the *sight* of a small boy's golden kite rising "into the endless winds of the world." In "The Mammoth Corridors," moreover, he makes explicit the contrast between the false Eden fabricated by words—the "angler's paradise" spoken of in a British Columbia guidebook, for example—and the true myth, unreachable and therefore largely unutterable, that engenders a people's spiritual life. The two-column structure of the poem visually contrasts these opposing ways to knowledge, but at the end poet and landscape are identified, while silence and time are accepted and affirmed:

> Hoarding her cold passion she lies   the Greenland lodger
> and the land's long face   no more than mine can forget
> is graved with her monstrous rutting
> Her time is our secret clock   She waits for all to slow
> Then to lust back   wider than Europe and Pacific deep
> bringing her love   the rounded silence
> a long hard peace.

The last line of the revised "Alaska Passage" condenses into a successful concrete verse this journey of the mind from temporal confinement to freedom:

> age alaska passage alaska passage alaska passage alaska pass

In the progress of its dreams the Canadian culture finds its true identity, and its geographical landscape is transformed.

In exploring the transformation Birney becomes a kind of

spiritual geographer, perceiving the interpenetration of history and myth and trying to utter a language of vision as much as a language of time. The poetry that has resulted from such endeavour to join disparate perspectives into an integral view links the generation of Scott and Pratt formally and intellectually with that of bp nichol and Margaret Atwood. It also captures something of the essential progress of the Canadian imagination, explaining why Birney continues to reach Canadian audiences so immediately. For all its variety his work speaks in a single and distinctive voice, in which a national culture, a modern anxiety, a universal spiritual sensitivity, and a flair for image-making all blend.

index